Introduction to Countertra in Therapeutic Practice

While transference has been fully described in the literature, countertransference has been viewed as its ugly sibling, and hence there are still not as many reflective accounts or as much guidance for trainees about how to handle difficult emotions, such as shame and envy and conflict in the consulting room. As a counterpoint, this book provides an integrative guide for therapists on the concept of countertransference, and takes a critical stance on the phenomenon, and theorising, about the "so-called" countertransference, viewing it as a framework to explore the transformative potential in managing strong emotions and difficult transactions.

With an explicit focus on teaching, this book informs therapeutic practice by mixing theories and case studies from the authors' own clinical and teaching experiences, which involves the reader in case studies, reflection and action points. Countertransference is explored in a wide range of clinical settings, including in reflective practice and in research in the field of therapy, as well as in art therapy and in the school setting. It also considers countertransference in dream interpretation, in the supervision and teaching environment and in work with groups and organisations.

Introduction to Countertransference in Therapeutic Practice offers psychotherapists and counsellors, both practicing and in training, a comprehensive overview of this important concept, from its roots in Freud's work to its place today in a global, transcultural society.

Paola Valerio is a BPC/UKCP reg. psychotherapist and senior lecturer at Roehampton University, where she convenes the psychodynamic theory and practice module on the Psych. D. She has been a visiting lecturer and supervisor in psychotherapy at Regents' College, Surrey and Kent Universities and at the Tavistock and East London University.

"As psychological therapists, what do you do with your thoughts and feelings that arise in the consulting room? Are you more 'person centred', only occasionally telling the client how they make you feel? Are you 'relational', thinking it would be wrong not to share something of yourself? Are you a 'Freudian', assuming it is important to maintain that blank screen? Are you a 'Lacanian', who thinks it would be persecutory to interpret the therapeutic relationship? Are you 'existential', valuing phenomenology's bracketing/ the epoché? Are you more 'behavioural', and consider your experiences of the client relatively unimportant? Or, are you none of these? If you ever wondered about any of them – this is the book to find answers!"

Del Loewenthal, Professor of Psychotherapy and Counselling,
University of Roehampton, UK

"A diverse and stimulating collection of essays on countertransference and the therapeutic process. Illustrated throughout with case study vignettes, this book should be a helpful resource for those wishing to deepen their understanding of the client-therapist relationship."

Mick Cooper, Professor of Counselling Psychology,
University of Roehampton, UK

Introduction to Countertransference in Therapeutic Practice

A Myriad of Mirrors

Edited by
Paola Valerio

Routledge
Taylor & Francis Group

LONDON AND NEW YORK

First published 2018
by Routledge
2 Park Square, Milton Park, Abingdon, Oxon OX14 4RN

and by Routledge
711 Third Avenue, New York, NY 10017

Routledge is an imprint of the Taylor & Francis Group, an informa business

British Library Cataloguing in Publication Data
A catalogue record for this book is available from the British Library

Library of Congress Cataloging in Publication Data
Names: Valerio, Paola.
Title: Introduction of countertransference in therapeutic practice :
    a myriad of mirrors / edited by Paola Valerio.
Description: Milton Park, Abingdon, Oxon ; New York, NY : Routledge,
    2018. | Includes index.
Identifiers: LCCN 2017025470| ISBN 9781138690103 (hbk) |
    ISBN 9781138690110 (pbk) | ISBN 9781315462097 (ebk)
Subjects: LCSH: Countertransference (Psychology) | Psychotherapist
    and patient.
Classification: LCC RC489.C68 I58 2018 | DDC 616.89/14—dc23
LC record available at https://lccn.loc.gov/2017025470

ISBN: 978-1-138-69010-3 (hbk)
ISBN: 978-1-138-69011-0 (pbk)
ISBN: 978-1-315-46209-7 (ebk)

Typeset in Garamond
by Swales & Willis Ltd, Exeter, Devon, UK

For Alex, and in memory of Tia and Rob

Contents

Contributors

Russel Ayling, Ph.D., is a clinical psychologist, psychoanalytic psycho-therapist and trainer in counselling psychology. He is currently Course Leader of the Doctorate in Counselling Psychology programme at Regent's University, London, a member of the Site for Contemporary Psychoanalysis, and, with colleagues, runs an independent academic consultancy practice, London Counselling Psychologists, alongside his own therapy practice. He is interested in 'between positions' – the development from psychologist to analyst; the interface between relational and poststructural psychoanalysis; and the intersection of teaching, supervision and therapy.

Onel Brooks, Ph.D., completed a doctorate in philosophy before training as a social worker and then as a psychoanalytic psychotherapist. He is a senior lecturer in Psychotherapy, Counselling and Counselling Psychology at the University of Roehampton, London, where he contributes to the Research Centre for Therapeutic Education, Psychology Department. He has held a number of posts as a senior counsellor and was a senior social worker and psychotherapist at the Tavistock Clinic for a number of years. He is in inde-pendent practice as a psychotherapist and supervisor, and is a member of the Philadelphia Association. He is interested in the details of our theoretical models and claims, and the details of what we say and do with clients. He often finds that he is provoked into thinking by psychoanalysis, as well as philosophy and literature, and particularly Nietzsche and Wittgenstein.

Sofie Bager-Charleson, Ph.D., is a psychotherapist, supervisor and writer. She draws from psychoanalytic and existential theory, with an interest in relation-ships and in postmodern influences on therapy. She holds a PhD from Lund University in Sweden, where she specialised in education and attachment pat-terns within families. She is the Director of Studies for the new MPhil/PhD programme for psychotherapists at Metanoia. She also works as an academic supervisor for psychotherapists on 'the Psych. D.' with Metanoia/Middlesex University. She has published widely in the field of reflective practice and research reflexivity, including the textbook *Practice-based Research in Therapy:*

A Reflexive Approach (2014) and acting as guest editor in the UKCP journal *The Psychotherapist* (2016) about creative use of self in research. She studies research training for psychotherapists; her latest project is titled *Therapists' Use of Self in Research: Embodied Situatedness and Emotional Entanglement during Data-analysis* (Bager-Charleson & Du Plock, 2017, in preparation).

Angela Devon, Ph.D., is a consultant clinical psychologist and Director of Therapies in an NHS Foundation Trust. Angela trained in clinical psychology and worked using a psychodynamic approach, but was also trained in behavioural approaches and CBT. As NICE developed and CBT became recognised as the evidence-based approach in the NHS, Angela trained more in CBT. She became the Clinical Lead for IAPT. Angela has maintained her love of psychodynamic approaches, and recently completed the Leicester Conference, looking at the functions of role and authority in ourselves and in organisations. Much of her current work in the NHS is addressing group relations and organisational and systemic issues. Angela also has a private practice and consultancy firm. She works in leadership and management development, runs training courses and works as an executive coach.

Nicola Diamond, Ph.D., is a senior lecturer at the University of East London in Psychosocial Studies and teaches at the Tavistock Clinic. She is also a psychoanalytic psychotherapist BPC reg. in private practice. She is a former psychotherapist at The Women's Therapy Centre and at the Helen Bamber Foundation, London, and is one of the founders of THR The International Attachment Network. Her specialist interest is in attachment and the body. Her book publications are *Between Skins: The Body in Psychoanalysis, Contemporary Developments* (Wiley, 2013), *Attachment and Intersubjectivity* (2003) with Mario Marrone, and numerous article publications in peer-reviewed journals and book chapters.

Janek Dubowski is an academic working for the Department of Psychology at the University of Roehampton, London. He has trained as an art therapist, counsellor and psychotherapist and has been involved in training therapists for over 30 years. He has been instrumental in establishing courses in Art Psychotherapy internationally, including Singapore, Republic of Ireland and Finland and has an international reputation in respect to master-classes in the discipline including the USA, Japan and Lithuania.

Anastasios Gaitanidis, Ph.D., is a senior lecturer in counselling psychology, counselling and psychotherapy and member of the Research Centre for Therapeutic Education (RCTE) at the University of Roehampton, London. He is also a psychoanalytic psychotherapist in private practice and a member of The Site for Contemporary Psychoanalysis. He has published several articles on psychoanalysis and psychotherapy in peer-reviewed journals, and he is the editor of two books: *Narcissism: A Critical Reader* (2007) and *The Male in Analysis: Psychoanalytic and Cultural Perspectives* (2011).

Mario Marrone, Ph.D., trained in group analysis at the Institute of Group Analysis (London) and in psychoanalysis at the Institute of Psycho-Analysis (London). He has had clinical supervision with a number of senior psychoanalysts, including Martin Miller, Patrick Casement, Pearl King and John Bowlby. He studied attachment theory with John Bowlby over a period of 10 years. He was a full-time hospital psychiatrist and psychotherapist in the National Health Service (United Kingdom) between 1977 and 1991. He is a founding member and Chairman of the International Attachment Network and cofounder of *The Journal of Attachment and Human Development*. He has published many papers and books, including *Attachment and Interaction* (1998, 2014), *Attachment Theory and the Psychoanalytic Process* (with Mauricio Cortina, 2003) and *Attachment and Intersubjectivity* (coauthored with Nicola Diamond, 2003). He has also published books in Italian and Spanish and lectures internationally.

Egle Meistaite is a final-year-trainee counselling psychologist at the University of Roehampton, London. Originally from Lithuania, Egle moved to England following a career shift during which time she received several grants from the Arts Council England. Her recent interests include an application of critical pluralistic framework and non-psychology theories and observations, such as nonlinear dynamic systems, to counselling psychology. Egle enjoys exploring the creative connections between arts–sciences blend, therapy and systems thinking. She codeveloped a number of photography and multimedia exhibitions and biofeedback chamber music projects/tours. The most recent project aims to explore the co-creation of the intersubjective field using the intersection of biofeedback, performing arts and kinetics.

Cynthia Rogers is a training group analyst, teacher and supervisor for the Institute of Group Analysis, and has lectured for over 20 years. Her paper on projective processes in groups is a standard text. She has worked in the voluntary sector with young adults, in the NHS and also in independent practice. Her current academic interests are researching the psychotherapy profession, thinking about the needs of GPs and writing about larger groups. The early results of her research, which focused on the difficulties therapists experienced in their work, were published by Wiley as *Psychotherapy and Counselling a Professional Business* in 2004. Cynthia is interested in how group analytic thinking can enable psychotherapists to use their countertransference reactions to enhance the therapy.

Andrew Samuels was chair of the United Kingdom Council for Psychotherapy and the joint founder of Psychotherapists and Counsellors for Social Responsibility. Trained as a Jungian analyst, he served as a founder Board Member of the

International Association for Relational Psychoanalysis and Psychotherapy. He is Professor of Analytical Psychology at the University of Essex and holds visiting professorship at New York, Roehampton, Macau and Goldsmiths, University of London. His books include *Jung and the Post-Jungians* (1985), *The Father* (1986), *A Critical Dictionary of Jungian Analysis* (1986), *Psychopathology* (1989), *The Plural Psyche* (1989), *The Political Psyche* (1993), *Politics on the Couch* (2001), *A New Therapy for Politics* (2015). Co-edited volumes include *Relational Psychotherapy, Psychoanalysis and Counselling* (2014) and *Analysis and Activism* (2016). www.andrewsamuels.com

Paola Valerio, Ph.D., is a Jungian analyst in private practice in London. She has 20 years clinical experience in the NHS, running services and supervising psychotherapists and psychologists and in leadership roles. She facilitates reflective practice groups for clinical and management teams in NHS, charity and business settings. She has represented a large mental health trust in serious case reviews and domestic homicide panels. She is a part-time senior lecturer at the University of Roehampton, London, where she convenes the Psychoanalytic/Jungian analytic module on 'the Psych. D.' and is a member of The Centre for Research in Social and Psychological Transformation (CREST) and the Research Centre for Therapeutic Education (RCTE). She has been a visiting lecturer and supervisor in psychotherapy at Regents College, Surrey and Kent Universities and at the Tavistock/East London University, Metanoia and numerous professional trainings. She has published several journal papers and chapters in analytic books and taught and presented widely in the NHS and at conferences.

Linda Verbeek, Ph.D., is a chartered counselling psychologist and integrative psychotherapist working in private practice in Southwest London. She recently completed her doctorate in Counselling Psychology and Psychotherapy at Metanoia. She also has specialist training as a Master Practitioner in Eating Disorders and Obesity with the National Centre for Eating Disorders, and her professional interests include working with eating disorders, body image problems, trauma and relational difficulties.

Suzanne Weeks is a leadership development consultant and coach, currently based in Switzerland. She has master's degrees in Management (Oxford) and Consulting and Coaching for Change (INSEAD). She has developed and delivered leadership development and team programmes for multicultural teams across three continents. She is on the board of directors for Group Relations International and a member of the British Psychological Association, the Maclean Institute of Coaching and the International Coaching Federation. She has published in academic management journals.

Foreword

Andrew Samuels

Aren't the purposes of a foreword to praise appropriately, to challenge tactfully, and to mediate between the book and the world? If so, then does that make the writer of a foreword equivalent to being a therapist of the book? And if that is so, then does he or she inevitably have a *countertransference* to the book? Or, as some of the contributors herein suggest, would it be better to refer simply to having a *therapeutic relationship* with the book? But couldn't the same definition of a foreword also support the argument that says the writer of a foreword is also the client of the book, without which she or he would have no existence as a writer, and is thereby likely to have a transference to the work? This confusion – transference or countertransference or the relationship between – is, like most confusions in the therapy project, of considerable utility. I don't think anyone believes that merely constructing a term like *transference–counter-transference* gets round the difficulty of not knowing, of not always needing to know, whose 'stuff' it is.

The first stage of what I called 'the countertransference revolution' in psychotherapy (Samuels, 1989) developed the position that the 'stuff' was the client's or patient's despite the appearance of belonging to the therapist. So the therapist's depression was really a projection of the client's depression, or the manifestation in the person of the therapist of the client's depressive mother. The second stage of the countertransference revolution allowed for the fact that the therapist might actually be depressed or have had a depressed mother, and I wrote about this in 1993. The third stage seems to be evolving a more complex formula in which either the depression belongs both to client and to therapist, as well as to their relationship itself – or that we really don't know, and it is all huge conundrum with which it is valuable to struggle (Samuels, 2014b).

The scope of this unique book is vast – yet detailed and specific – which makes it both an incredibly useful introduction to the topic, and also something likely to educate and influence more experienced practitioners. Just using the briefest of tags to indicate the content, these are the manifold themes covered: trauma, 'race', disassociation, imagery and nonverbal communication, CBT, training and supervision, groups, organisations, reflective practice, research, eating disorders, dreams and the therapeutic encounter itself. I can't recall previously reading anything quite as comprehensive as this before. The editor's introduction offers very useful synopses of the chapters, as well as an educated and educational overview of the subject. This has greatly simplified the task of writing the foreword. She ends her introduction with the conclusion that in spite of the therapist's best attempts to create a coherent, linear, 'knowing' narrative of the process, there will always be aspects of the therapeutic encounter that will remain mysterious, private and incommunicable/ineffable.

On a few occasions in the book, the phrase 'real person' is used, and this seems to involve the wounds of the therapist. Many discussions of countertransference these days boil down to the therapist's wounds (held to be central in enactments), and this highlights her or his motivation for taking up the work of psychotherapy, analysis and counselling. This focus on therapists' wounds is both implicit as well as explicit in the majority of the chapters and the fascinating research question of therapists' motivations for taking up their profession – that which they 'profess' – is a matter for further study.

What we see in several of the chapters is a foregrounding of the role of the client, and this, it seems to me, is the next frontier in clinical writing and theorising. Summarising a mass of research findings, Norcross (2011) has forced us to consider whether it truly is the therapy relationship that is the decisive factor. Is the private and highly personal therapy relationship, including transference–countertransference, the main thing that makes therapy work? Norcross (and others) say: Not really. Incredibly, they suggest that unexplained and extratherapeutic factors amount to some 40% of efficacy variance; the client accounts for 30%; the therapy relationship, 12%; the actual therapist, 8% and the school or tradition or modality of the therapist, 7%. Of course, Norcross would be the first to admit that therapy is a mélange of all of these, and I would add that the findings do not do more than force us to consider our ideas about our clients.

Now, using Norcross as a springboard and with the intention of issuing a gentle challenge, I will take the opening offered to me by the role of forewordwriter to make a few suggestions concerning the centrality of the therapy relationship in our clinical thinking. When I was chair of the United Kingdom Council for Psychotherapy, we actually considered mounting a campaign for 'real psychotherapy' (as opposed to what the Government was offering in its Improving Access to Psychological Therapies scheme [IAPT]). Our proposed slogan was: 'It's the relationship, stupid!' This was a take-off from Bill Clinton's admonition, posted on the wall of his campaign headquarters, to remind the staff that 'It's the economy, stupid!' We didn't go ahead with this slogan, but it had mileage because nearly all therapists are, these days, what we call 'relational'. All are therefore interested in what is sometimes summarised as 'the therapist's use of self', which is a useful contemporary definition of countertransference. And there are arguments – which this book manages to avoid, thank goodness – over which school was relational first, or does the relational thing best, and so on and so forth (Samuels, 2014a).

First, there are social critiques of the proposition that the therapy relationship is ineluctably central to practice. Isn't therapy an induced relationship, not a natural one? Isn't the therapy relationship imbued with the history, power dynamics and authority structures of therapy itself? If so, then the emergence of countertransference is not of special significance; it is just a sporadic field effect. In several of the chapters to this book contributors take up this point.

Next, there are systemic critiques of the therapy relationship mania that has afflicted the therapy world. Doesn't a focus on the therapy relationship miss out on the presence and impact of the wider human systems in which client and therapist are embedded: families, friends, other people at work, society and so on? Just to give a simple example, it has been illuminating to listen to the answers when I ask a potential new client what his or her partner or family thinks about having therapy. Paradoxically, nothing is more potent in this regard than to be told that the client has not told anyone.

Third, we may construct ecological and political critiques. Emphasis on the interpersonal/intersubjective therapy relationship makes it even more difficult for the client to express the impact on him- or herself of planetary/environmental crisis or any other collective field of emotional distress.

Lastly, we can consider ethical and epistemological critiques. Without intending it, proponents of the centrality of the therapy relationship are buying into a particular view of human relationships. In this view, people are regarded as atomised, isolated beings who have to struggle into relationship, and when they achieve relationship with a therapist, the two people in the relationship 'own' it. This fits in well with neo-liberal conceptions of society and culture. But this is not the only narrative of relationality. What about those narratives in which people are always already in connection and relationship? They do not meet each other via the hurling of projections (from the Latin *proicere*, to throw a spear) across empty space. For there does not exist any empty space between people, even though it may look that way. What if we conceive of a socially derived rhizome, or nutrient tube, buried out of sight, which throws up separate stalks that are, nevertheless, already connected? What if we understand the two people 'in the room' as linked by their citizenship, their membership of the *polis*, no matter how different that experience might be for them? Or perhaps we should understand the members of the therapy pair as linked via their experiencing, and perhaps exploring, the manifold bodily, physical phenomena present in the therapy room? In the book, there is a divide – an understandable one – between those writers who stay closer to the idea of transference and countertransference taking place via projection and introjection – and those who take more of an 'already connected' line (Samuels, 2014b).

Coming to the end of the foreword, I hope that I have done justice to the tripartite aims of it mentioned in the opening paragraph: to praise appropriately, to challenge tactfully and to mediate between the book and the world. This volume is an outstanding contribution to the clinical literature, and I earnestly hope I have done justice to it and its editor who kindly invited me to contribute the foreword.

London, May 2017

Bibliography

Norcross, J. (2011). Psychotherapy relationships that work. Oxford, UK: Oxford University Press.

Samuels, A. (1989). The plural psyche: Personality, morality and the father. New York, NY: Routledge.

Samuels, A. (1993). *The political psyche*. New York, NY: Routledge.

Samuels, A. (2014a). Shadows of the therapy relationship. In D. Loewenthal & A. Samuels (Eds.), Relational psychotherapy, psychoanalysis and counselling: Appraisals and reappraisals (pp. 184–192). New York, NY: Routledge.

Samuels, A. (2014b). Everything you always wanted to know about therapy (but were afraid to ask): Social, political, economic and clinical fragments of a critical psychotherapy. *European Journal of Psychotherapy and Counselling, 16*(4), 315–330.

Acknowledgements

For all that I have learned about countertransference, I am grateful to my patients, supervisees and students, past and present. I very much wish to thank Sofia for sharing her dreams and artwork. I am truly indebted to my fellow contributors for all their hard work and support and inspiring writing. I still recall a one-line mail from one: 'Bloody hell Paola – this doesn't bring out the best in you!' – but to be fair only after receiving further last minute edits. They were all most tolerant and supportive. I would also like to thank Professor Andrew Samuels for agreeing to write the foreword to this book and for remaining true to his inspiring and thought-provoking spirit.

I would especially like to thank Nicola Diamond, Russel Ayling, Jaqueline Hayes and Anastasios Gaitanidis for reading and commenting on the introduction to this book, and my colleagues Mark Donati, Rosie Rizq and Onel Brooks for reviewing Chapter 6. Further, but not by any means in order, I would like to thank all my colleagues on the Psych D. at the University of Roehampton; Professor Mick Cooper and fellow colleagues of The Centre for Research in Social and Psychological Transformation (CREST); and Professor Del Loewenthal and other members of The Research Centre for Therapeutic Education (RCTE) for much lively inspiration, support and debate. Thanks also go to my ex-students and now good friends, Deborah and Mog and colleagues and friends, Angela, Howard and Ansgar for endless cups of Earl Grey, stirred with inspiration and countless texts during this project.

I would also very much like to thank Joanne Forshaw, Charlotte Taylor and colleagues at Routledge for their support.

Paola Valerio

Introduction

Paola Valerio

> The meeting of two personalities is like the contact of two chemical substances: if there is any reaction, both are transformed.
>
> (Jung, *Modern Man in Search of a Soul*, 1933, p. 49)

One of the most difficult aspects of learning how to be a psychologist, counsellor or therapist is how to make use of the so called 'real' person of the therapist in our professional work. This is especially true in relation to a key skill the trainee must acquire: learning how to work with the countertransference. Of course, this also takes us into 'wounded healer' territory, in terms of the wish to cure others and the question of what drove us to become therapists or counsellors in the first place; for in what other profession does one have, or perhaps hope, to give over so much of one's self, of one's very being, in the service of our clients?

This book is about countertransference, about which much has been written, yet as a lecturer and supervisor in psychotherapy and psychology trainings, I am struck by how much working with the countertransference still confounds trainees. If so much has been written about countertransference, why do trainees still seem to struggle with this and the attendant revealing of themselves to their clients? I wonder what this is about? In this introduction, I have chosen to highlight some of the main theorists that are taught in such courses; it is a selective overview in which I suggest that the stereotypical idea of the neutral or anonymous therapist still seems to preoccupy or even haunt us, despite developments in theories highlighting the essentially interactional nature of the transference–countertransference matrix. Yet, even these more relational approaches which encourage us to be authentic can seem technically difficult for all but the most experienced therapists, perhaps generating an anxiety about how to be 'good enough authentic therapists' as much as 'good enough anonymous' therapists. In many respects, the idea for this book, then, was instilled in me by my students' concerns about this, but is equally born of my own experiences as a trainee.

When I began my analytic training, I was enthusiastic about how to learn 'proper' technique. There was an emphasis on learning from experience, through one's own intensive analysis and supervision, a period that stretches over 5 and for some up to 10 years of training or indeed more. I suppose I naively imagined that this lengthy analysis would cure us all of our neurosis, enable us to rein in our unconscious complexes, and assist our patients and clients[1] with theirs, hopefully free from contamination from ours. Fortunately, this stereotypical view bears very little relation to how many contemporary analysts think today.

In university doctoral-level psychology and psychotherapy trainings, there is more of an emphasis on academic learning, and less intensive personal psychotherapy is required of students. However, as in most professional trainings, there is also an emphasis on 'learning on the job' and acknowledgement that we cannot learn about transference and countertransference without at least some experience of psychodynamic therapy.

We are now fairly aware that many of our patients or clients struggle with the 'all too detached' or conversely, 'ever-compassionate' therapist, and they end up feeling pretty frustrated with our 'all too measured' responses. Jungian analysts Guggenbühl-Craig (1971/2015) and Groesbeck (1975) advised us that as analysts we too often identify with the 'healer' archetype, leaving our patients as the only 'wounded' party. Guggenbühl-Craig (1971/2015) cautioned against colluding with the idea of rescuing the patient, reminding us that we need to access our own wounds in order to free the patient from our need to remain in the role of helper.

Some patients affect us more deeply than others. We may dislike, or be bored by or envious of our patients. We may be flattered by or sexually attracted to them, among many other reactions. I have written elsewhere about patients whom I disliked and how acknowledging this sometimes became transformative. We are caught up in strange enactments with our patients, and sometimes these may even react synchronistically with the external world. With one male analysand, for example, I was feeling guilty about my active dislike of him, and for thinking that he was somehow a dishonest character, when several policemen burst into my consulting room. It seemed that my neighbours, having had similar thoughts, upon seeing him loitering outside my house, pre-session, mistook him for a burglar and called the police (Valerio, 2004, 2005)!

We are all familiar with and have probably experienced our own and our analyst's countertransference in unhelpful ways. Falling asleep, boredom, preoccupation and dislike are all common enough countertransference experiences. There are also situations when therapists unconsciously rely on clients to comfort them, or may expect their clients to meet their needs for intimacy, or mothering, or indeed may well need their clients to make them feel special. Some clients become dependent on their therapists, or stay too long in therapy, colluding with the therapist's avoidance of loneliness or loss. Therapists may unconsciously be too curious about intimate experiences, encouraging erotic feelings in their clients or make penetrating interpretations, too often and/or too soon, along with inappropriate self-disclosures (Gabbard, 1994;

Marroda, 2004). Joy Schaverien's (2006) book is especially helpful in thinking about our erotic countertransference and acknowledging desire in the consulting room, rather than retreating into infantilising our patient's sexuality in order to lessen its impact (Valerio, 1997).

In a recent book, Hirsch (2010) discussed ways in which the therapist 'coasts in the countertransference', acting more from self-interest than client welfare. Perhaps self-interest is the first place we should look in unpacking the countertransference. Certainly, the reality is not so much that we can avoid such self-interest, but that we need to attempt to uncover these sometimes-subtle countertransference responses, and to highlight behaviours which may have provoked strong reactions by the client in others too, possibly (although not always) contributing to keeping the client or ourselves unwittingly isolated, dependent, feeling rejected or misunderstood.

Key concepts and theories continually undergo transformation within psychotherapy over time, and countertransference is an example of this. While transference has been fully described in the literature, countertransference has been viewed as its ugly sibling, and hence there are still not as many reflective accounts or sources for guidance for trainees about how to handle difficult emotions, such as shame, envy and conflict, in the consulting room. In its narrow sense, countertransference was classically seen as muddying the analytic frame, as something to be overcome by the therapist, but in more contemporary notions of countertransference, it has had a fairly radical makeover and is seen as something intersubjective and co-created, a product between but not exclusively belonging to either party.

Freud (1912a) initially recommended that the analyst remain anonymous so as not to contaminate the transference – he 'should be opaque to his patients and like a mirror, should show them nothing but what is shown him' (p. 118). Freud (1910) spoke of countertransference as something to be mastered and thoroughly scrutinised:

> We have become aware of the 'countertransference', which arises . . . as a result of the patients' influence on his [the physician's] unconscious feelings. . . . [T]he analyst must begin his activity with a self-analysis and continually carry it deeper while he is making his observations on his patients.
>
> (Freud, 1910, pp. 144–145)

Freud's views on countertransference were very much influenced by his encounter with Jung, who had sought his advice following his affair with Sabine Spielerien, as documented in the Freud–Jung letters. Freud, presumably concerned for Jung's welfare, advised him to 'dominate his counter transference' (McGuire, 1974).

In 1912, Freud advised that the analyst make use of his unconscious as a receiver in order to attune to the patient's unconscious free from countertransference contamination:

> The analyst . . . must turn his own unconscious like a receptive organ towards the transmitting unconscious of the patient . . . in order to reconstruct [the patient's] unconscious.
>
> (Freud, 1912b, pp. 115–116)

Later, in his collaboration with Ferenczi, Freud, at least for a brief period, became interested in telepathy. In part VI of *The Unconscious*, 'Communication Between the Two Systems', he wrote:

> It is a very remarkable thing that the unconscious of one human being can react upon that of another, without passing through the conscious. This deserves closer investigation, especially with a view to finding out whether preconscious activity can be excluded as playing a part in it; but, descriptively speaking, the fact is incontestable.
>
> (Freud, 1915, p. 394)

Whilst Freud did not pursue these ideas, Ferenczi did continue, rather radically for his time, to speak openly about the issue of countertransference, not as something to be mastered but rather its value in understanding the patient. In 1919, he spoke of the fact that patients have an intuitive understanding of the therapist's emotional responses advocating disclosure of certain of the therapist's subjective experiences. Following Ferenczi, we find countertransference feelings in the analyst or therapist being viewed as providing crucial data about the patient, and, by association, the analyst also.

Paula Heimann was one of the first to recognise the concept of countertransference as more than a hindrance to the relationship, but rather as a totality, including all the attitudes and feelings the therapist experienced toward his or her clients, conscious as well as unconscious. In her seminal paper 'On Countertransference' (1950), Heimann widened the concept to include all the analyst's subjective experiences resulting from the patient's projections, recommending that analysts use their hovering attention to also gauge their own emotional responses in order to elicit valuable data about the patient. Such data were not to be shared with the patient, but would provide important insight into the patient's conflicts and defences. And, as the analyst has had the benefit of a training analysis, he or she could subordinate any feelings that were stirred up in service of the analytic task.

The Argentinian analyst Henry Racker (1957) was a pioneer in thinking about countertransference and in viewing the analyst as a real person whose unconscious could influence the patient in the same way that a lens might colour the encounter in different ways with different analysts. 'The first distortion of truth . . . in the myth of the analytic situations is that analysis is an interaction between a sick person and a healthy one' (1957, p. 307). Racker (1968) suggested that therapists and clients not only project and introject but also identify with parts or aspects of the other. Projective identification is now seen as being less of a fantasy or defence, as Melanie Klein conceived of it (1946), and more of an interactional process in which the therapist will receive these unwanted parts that have been split off, and will feel a pressure to identify with these, provoking powerful emotions in him or her, including persecutory or violent feelings. The analyst may then engage in counter-projective responses toward the patient. Thus, while projective identification is the basis of empathy, in its healthy aspects, the ability to imagine and empathise with the other's plight, in its more disturbing mechanisms, is linked to countertransference.

Racker also distinguished between 'concordant' countertransference (1957), which seems to be a direct or an emphatic response to the patient, and 'complementary' countertransference wherein the analyst responds emotionally to the patient's projections. In *complementary* countertransference, the analyst's identification may include figures in the patient's internal world who evoke memories and fantasies, including supervisors, teachers or other influential figures of his or her own. Once the analyst acquires insight, through self-analysis, in theory he or she may be able to tease out why this particular transference–countertransference constellation is being enacted with this particular patient in order to make an interpretation. However, Racker was cautious about direct communication of the countertransference other than to formulate an intervention, although his work was a significant bridge to the more relational approaches described below.

Several seminal thinkers shared and deepened this wider view of countertransference. In 1949, Donald Winnicott had already published his well-known paper, 'Hate in the Countertransference', illuminating the important role negative transferences play in working with more disturbed patients, and stating that the evocation of these feelings is an essential ingredient in successful treatment. Margaret Little, writing in 1951 and 1957 about work with 'severely disturbed patients', noted that 'we often hear of the mirror which the analyst holds up to the patient, but the patient holds one up to the analyst too' (Little, 1951, p. 37). The patient's fantasies are often based on glimpses of the real feelings of the therapist. Little suggests the need for sensitive disclosure, if in a selected manner.

Bion (1940) and Winnicott (1958) are among many analysts who were influenced in the post-war period by their own and their patients' traumatic experiences. Bion (1962a, 1967) was concerned with a theory of thinking, and psychotic processes in particular. He suggested the notion of *beta elements*, presymbolic material that can be viewed as unmentalised contents, which, through the analyst's *alpha function* and *reverie*, can be transformed into symbolised *alpha elements* – from the unknown, psychotic thinking into something that can be digested and contained. Bion focused on working with more psychotic or borderline presentations, highlighting a capacity in such individuals, to really 'get inside and affect' or 'infect' the analyst, through projective processes. In this sense, Bion viewed the countertransference as part of the therapist's containing role – much as the mother contains her baby's primitive anxieties – and assists the patient to 'metabolise' difficult emotions.

This idea of the therapist as container has been popularised and linked to both Winnicott and Bion, despite their theoretical differences. Bion (1962b) cautioned that in order to overcome our omnipotence we had to abandon our a priori theories approaching each session without memory or desire, which is both radical, and, for many of us, rather difficult to operationalise, especially when in the grip of strong countertransference feelings. This is also suggestive of the need to remove the effects of projective identification, as the analyst must once again become a neutral presence, perhaps returning to Freud's ideal of anonymity.

Writers from different schools may be said to constellate loosely around this wider view of countertransference, penetrated by the idea of projective identification, perhaps despite their theoretical differences in other respects. Joseph (1985) and Steiner (1993) are rooted in the post-Kleinian view of countertransference in which the analyst's subjective experiences are primarily, but not exclusively, the product of projective identifications; hence, the impact of the patient's projected paranoid-schizoid states of mind concern the analyst as the most useful aspect of countertransference. Kernberg (1965, 1976), Kohut (1959, 1971), Odgen (1979) and Searles (1955 and 1955) focus more on the fertile ground within the analyst that may enable him or her to process the projections. Searles' (1959) writings about his work with borderline patients, for example, pose the interesting question of not why we have loving or hateful feelings towards our patients, but given our yearnings and need for intimacy in the encounter, why indeed we don't!

However, even from within this perspective, the focus is still primarily on the analyst's role in interpreting or containing his or her patient's unconscious conflicts through using his or her countertransference, although the analyst's neurosis or perverse structures, for example, when in the grip of projective identifications, may provide a hook or a certain valence for the patient's projections. In Stolorow (1991, 1993, 1997) and Kohut (1971, 1982), we find a development of the more relational approach to countertransference, which is viewed as an interpersonal process in which the exchange takes place in the space in-between. Henceforth, countertransference is no longer viewed through a single lens; the mirror becomes more reflective, moving more toward a myriad, suggestive of infinite reflections in both directions. Thus, countertransference becomes less 'counter', since client and therapist as subjects influence each other in mutually reciprocal ways.

Studies from a variety of disciplines point in different ways to the historical and cultural specificity of our modern/Western individualistic conception of the self. As suggested by Nicola Diamond (2003), intersubjectivity is a fundamental challenge to an intrapsychic approach and a one-person psychology. There is no primacy of the individual – there is always an overlap between me and you and the world of others. Even in the heart of the self, there is an interdependence with the other, both significant others with whom we are in permanent conversation and others that we encounter throughout the life cycle (Diamond & Marrone, 2003).

This relational turn, which is supported by contemporary research in neuroscience and infant development, moves away from the idea of a dynamic unconscious, which consists of what was once known and has then been repressed, toward a notion that the mind and the brain have been shaped and sculpted by patterns of interaction in our earliest relational matrix. Benjamin (in Mitchel, 1993) equates the development of the mind with the experience of the self as a subject in relation to the subjectivities of others. From this inter-subjective perspective, it is assumed that a 'shared reality' is established by means of a subtle intertwining of both intrapsychic and interpersonal process.

The relational community, located mainly in New York and Boston, has built upon the work of key analysts, including Ferenczi, Winnicott and Fairbairn, among many other authors, as well as from a range of disciplines, but it also moves away from these writers in key ways. Fairbairn's focus in particular on the patient's actual experience in the external world, particularly early traumas, greatly influenced Bowlby's theory (1969).[2] An overview can be found in Stephen Mitchell (1997). Here we focus on Stern's work and the work of the rest of the Boston Change Process Group (BCPG, 2010). As Bromberg noted, what holds this community together is its belief that

> the process of expanding a patient's self-experience in based not on enduring truths, (which as an objective reality is deemed not to exist in one or other alone), but its actuality of two human beings co-creating what they do together with increasing spontaneity.
>
> (2009, p. 348)

Marrone (2014) helpfully linked Daniel Stern's (1985) research in neuroscience with attachment theory. Stern saw internal working models as dynamic structures that define the child's subjective experiences and are organised as 'schemas or ways of being with'. Stern paid particular attention to the episodes during which internal working models form. These episodes have a rhythm, a sequence and an interpersonal choreography. According to Stern, there is intentionality in these early interactions manifested in ways that follow a sequence, have a beginning, a middle, an end and moments of affect regulation that occur in which both participants (usually mother and baby) tend to meet their needs, which he called *proto-narrative*. Stern observed that infants have expectations of what they anticipate their exchange with their attachment figures will be, which are confirmed at a presymbolic level of interaction which in time establishes a regulatory process that is later stored at the level of *procedural memory*, or what Stern calls *implicit relational knowledge*. Stern suggested (1985) that therapeutic change has its central axis in these moments of meetings, but importantly these moments in therapy occur not through verbal interpretation, but by the therapist making use of his or her real personality through experiencing the uniqueness of each moment in each session and through promoting this mutual reciprocity (rather as the mother had ideally done with her baby).

Stern and the BCPG studied these noninterpretative mechanisms in psychotherapy. From this perspective, change is not based on verbal interpretations or the containing role of the therapist alone, although this is a factor, but *something else*. This 'something else' is related to implicit procedural knowing and the opportunity to create intersubjective regulation though significant *moments of meeting*. The process of making implicit knowing conscious is not the same as accessing repressed material. What is significant is that these 'moments of meeting' are new and that something is created intersubjectively that alters the analytic atmosphere, not by employing the familiar methods of verbal communication or interpretation but indeed through a 'sloppiness' in which reality is always a co-creation in the therapeutic space

Indeed, from this perspective we may learn as much from our patients' understanding of us as our attempt to analyse them. As Mitchel stated,

> Unless the analyst affectively enters into the patient's relational matrix or, rather, discovers himself within – unless the analyst is in some sense charmed by the patient's entreaties, shaped by the patient's projections, antagonised and frustrated by the patient's defences – the treatment is never fully engaged, and a certain depth within the analytic experience is lost.
>
> (1988, p. 293)

Jung's theory (1966a, 1966b) in many respects preempted this contemporary developmental framework in emphasising the mutual influence between analysand and analyst and the deep involvement of the analyst that of necessity occurs in this encounter. In analytical psychology, 'wounded' and 'healer' are seen as a duality, not a dichotomy. It is the activation of the wounded–healer continuum for both the patient and the therapist that empathically informs the healing process, but this is as Sedgwick (1994) noted because the analysand's identification is based on real components of the analyst's personality. In the 'Psychology of the Transference' (1969), Jung understood transference as both intrapsychic and interpersonal. He described a multidimensional encounter not only of the patient's and the analyst's relationships with their own unconscious but also of the effect they have on one another. Through his concepts of the *transcendent function* and the *conuinctio*, he suggested a relational field in which countertransference reactions have no sense of history; past and present are jumbled, patient and analyst are in the alchemical bath together and generate data, which is in fact suggestive of a co-created third position.

Jungian analyst Andrew Samuels (1989) wrote about the embodied style of countertransference wherein we may embody an aspect of the patient's inner world, for example, a depressed parent as an incarnation, often in a preverbal sense, and in a bodily form. The analyst may share his or her images or experiences, of course, but this process opens us to the interconnectedness or shared realm of the *'mundus imaginalis'* or in-between area. As Samuels stated,

My suggestion is that there is a two-person or shared *mundus imaginalis* that is constellated in analysis . . . in which the analyst's body becomes a subtle body, . . . the analyst's body is not entirely in fact his or her own. . . . Images pertaining to one person crop up in the experience of another person because on the imaginal level of reality, all images pertain to both parties.

(Samuels, 1989, pp. 164–171)

The relevance of projective identification is that its main occurrence is at a time in early development before psyche and soma have truly differentiated (Gordon 1965, p. 119, as quoted in Samuels, 1997, p. 170). Jung's notion of an a priori connectedness in the analytic couple, moments of meeting which are new and created intersubjectively, now seems surprisingly modern.

These meetings significantly alter the analytic atmosphere. It is misleading to refer to this as a two-person psychology, as the two persons do not remain separate and intact throughout this process, but interact in such a way as to change both parties.

In many of the contributions in this book we discover the emotional and personal struggles that contributors have engaged in, discussing the 'real' person of the analyst in effecting change. A technically correct, well-timed interpretation, it is suggested, will be far less potent than one in which the therapist as a person is present in communications that reveal an authentic personal aspect of the self that has been evoked in an affective response to the patient.

In this volume, contributors in this process also share the difficult, perhaps impossible, task of when, and, importantly, perhaps even when not, to turn the therapist's own emotional responses into 'data' about the client – exploring, for instance, the 'timing' of interpretations, disclosure at times, the need for supervision and peer support or indeed the therapist's need for further personal therapy. Using one's countertransference with a client can be a long journey, rather like a chess game; there are many moves and possibilities leading up to an intervention. These may include clarification, empathy, supporting or containing our patients but always with attention to the present moment and the bodily and nonverbal aspects of the encounter. Which way we go depends on our intuition about how the patient or client is responding to us and us to them, and for that our barometer is very much our countertransference feelings. Yet, this is often about processing the inevitable enactments that occur after our errors or blunders in retrospect with clients. Sometimes we remain in our own dark unknown places that cannot be helped. It is worth emphasising that not all enactments are relational or in the sense of a rather irresponsibly 'free for all, or anything goes' kind of way, but that there is now an acceptance that two subjects or unconscious minds collide as well as communicate. Hence, as Benjamin advises, not only must the analyst survive the patient, but the patient must survive the analyst. In other words, we aim to facilitate the survival of the relationships, or third, as a safe environment in which such struggles and resolutions can occur.

(Benjamin, 2010, p. 117)

This book also focuses on countertransference research. As Kachele (2015) noted, countertransference is an integral part of psychoanalytic interaction; it expands to dreams, and between sessions and activities, and shapes the microstructure of the psychoanalytic dialogue (2015). Nor can countertransference be divorced from the political psyche (Samuels, 1997). We need not only more research about what lies behind but also on the surface of the various feeling states, ruptures or wounds that impact on the researcher and the data. We also need to move toward more intersubjective approaches about how data is co-created in a research setting in an intersubjective third position (Holmes, 2014; Saffron & Kraus, 2014; BCPG, 2010).

While illuminating work has been done, much of this research in countertransference transfers a one-person perspective from the clinical setting into the research setting. Kachele et al. (2015) in their research review posed the seemingly contradictory question: Is countertransference an object of empirical research? They alluded to an interesting piece of research by Anssi Peraklya (2011a) suggesting that the analyst's countertransference response 'was most often indirect and intuitive . . . coming from a resonating alignment' (p. 105). The study is an attempt to demonstrate how analysts resonate with patients in search of the 'something more than' which captures some of the 'sloppiness' of Stern et al.'s (1998) position and Jessica Benjamin's 'moral third' (2004).

The final section of this book includes chapters which are cowritten with patients in long-term analytic therapy, in contrast to the traditional case study approach wherein only the analyst's voice is heard. Writing about 'cases', let alone with patients, is enormously complicated. Kantrowitz (2006) studied analysts of diverse orientations and demonstrated that relational analysts were more likely to involve their patients in the write-up and publication of case reports. She also emphasised that there are responsibilities, risks and ramifications that go with professional publication of case reports. But, as Aron argued (in Loewenthal & Samuels, 2017), 'the analyst's . . . is not a privileged or superior view, but that their own perspective [the patient's] may have a great deal to teach us'. Think of the benefit to psychoanalysis if each of our famous case histories had an addendum with the patient's view of their treatment. Might we have benefited if Breuer had asked Anna O. to write her own narrative of their talking cure or if Freud had asked Dora to tell her own story of her analysis?

This book also focuses on countertransference outside and not exclusively inside psychodynamic therapy, for example, from within an integrative perspective in humanistic therapy and practice or in using the countertransference in cognitive behaviour therapy (CBT), a model which is often seen as being in opposition to or even in competition with psychodynamic approaches, particularly in an NHS setting where there is the need to demonstrate therapeutic effectiveness. The idea of transferring concepts from one seemingly incompatible model to another may not appeal to those of us who are analytically trained. Yet, empirical research demonstrates that the most effective therapists are those that recognise transference and utilise it therapeutically, regardless of what types of therapy they are practicing, including CBT models (Albon & Jones, 1998; Jones & Pulos, 1993, quoted in Shelder, 2010, 2006a). And, since most people accept that transference is not ubiquitous to formal therapeutic relationships, perhaps we can now think of countertransference in a similar fashion.

In our focus on reflective practice and research, we also introduce the idea of 'cultural countertransference' (Alvesson & Skolderberg, 2000), a stance which encourages the therapist to attempt to defamiliarise him- or herself with one's cultural bias and adopt an 'attitude of not knowing' in his or her work with clients. In this approach, we are perhaps reminded of Bion's (1967) advice to approach each session 'without memory or desire'. Yet we acknowledge how difficult this is, since, as psychotherapists, we are already embedded in dominant systems and culture, and we will always be influenced by areas of lack of awareness in ourselves.

This book captures this increasingly broad use of countertransference as a framework to explore the transformative potential for both client and therapist in managing these collisions and difficult transactions. What is not important here is the idea that countertransference is useful. That is established. One important thing about the book, which I hope will also be of use to the reader, is the placement of countertransference in a wide range of 'settings', including in reflective practice and in research settings. Additionally important is concluding with a chapter which takes a critical stance on the phenomenon, and theorises about the 'so-called countertransference' since its inception in 1910 (Freud, 1910).

My impression is that each chapter in this book can be read in isolation; whilst there are some similarities, there are also some contradictions. Perhaps this diversity is inevitable in attempting to describe such personal and emotional journeys with such depth, and in so many settings wherein so many different histories are constellated, and, hopefully, contaminated, by the other.

The first part of this book – Chapters 1 to 5 – focuses on the countertransference in work with individual clients. Section 2 – Chapters 6 to 8 – focuses on countertransference in the wider context of supervision and teaching, group therapy and in organisations. The final section of this book – Chapters 9 to 13 – is reserved for reflections on reflective practice and research in countertransference, including research that is published for the first time and case studies which are cowritten with analysands.

In many of the chapters we are introduced to the 'real' person of the 'professional helper' and his or her journey, these deeply honest and, at times, brave examples of their countertransference dilemmas. I am thankful to my coauthors for the opportunity this affords the reader who may share these struggles.

Chapter 1: Between bodies: Working in the liminal zone with traumatised clients, by Nicola Diamond and Paola Valerio

In this chapter, Nicola Diamond and Paola Valerio explore, through the use of several clinical examples, how the body can be the means of communication when no words are possible or when words are not enough. Nicola and Paola address this in the context of working with abused and traumatised clients, and show how it is largely through enactments that such clients bring their experience. In psychoanalysis, 'acting out' used to be seen as simply repeating repetitive patterns and a move away from thinking and insight, however we consider this behaviour as an 'acting in', and argue that enactment in the consulting room involving both therapist and client is necessary for psychic change to take place. We suggest it is only by mobilising bodily based memories that these traumatic levels of experience can be shifted and reconnected to reflective processing. Drawing on the work of the Boston Change Process Group, we understand the process of change in therapy as involving perhaps a 'sloppy' encounter or 'moment of meeting' which results in change for both parties in the encounter.

Chapter 2: A therapist goes back to school: Therapeutic experience with three black boys at risk of exclusion, by Onel Brooks

In Onel Brooks' chapter, the political and personal is movingly illustrated through his countertransference in individual sessions with three very different black boys, all of whom have been excluded from school. In his unique but gentle way, he forces the reader to think about how race and culture, a sense of things being unfair, as well as poverty and class are at work in his three accounts. Onel encourages the reader to think of how our views influence things and how these might be related to our own 'partiality'. In a sense, this chapter is about a therapist returning to school, working as a school counsellor, and in the sense of reflecting on what he is doing, what he has been taught that he is supposed to do, and how this is sometimes out of step with what the situation seems to call for. Onel does not focus on relatively comfortable themes in psychoanalysis or psychotherapy, at the risk of excluding what is often regarded as political. Although this theme is not developed, there is some acknowledgement that psychotherapeutic practitioners struggle with schools and schooling – with fitting in, with belonging, with being excluded – and some of the most important figures in psychoanalysis, for example, are the ones who left or were excluded from the school they began in.

Chapter 3: A case of missing identity: Working with disassociation and 'multiple selves' in the countertransference, by Mario Marrone and Nicola Diamond

Mario Marrone and Nicola Diamond begin this chapter with an amusing anecdote, but as the story develops about individual sessions with a patient, who has a history of severe sexual and emotional abuse, we find their description poignant and moving. Yet, how do you work with a patient who has not only left the room (dissociated), but later forgotten that she came in the first place, and indeed with the intent to kill her analyst! In this chapter, the authors explore working with an extreme state of disassociation in the transference–countertransference relationship. They address, through a theoretical and clinical journey, how they work individually with patients with 'multiple disassociations' which are rooted in severely traumatised attachment histories, as well as exploring the multiplicity of the self in more secure attachment patterns. Mario and Nicola's moving exploration foregrounds the importance of bodily based procedural memory though clinical examples and a discussion about working with enactments and multiple selves.

Chapter 4: Countertransference, art psychotherapy and the prediscursive abject, by Janek Dubowski

The *weltaschauung* of the talking cure has left us with less experience or training and hence expertise in nonverbal communications. Art psychotherapy involves the therapeutic relationship being mediated through images, and these images may express embodied aspects which are difficult to arrive at merely through talking. It is understood that the transference can also be mediated in this way and that countertransference can be elicited when the therapist views the client's image. Yet, as Janek Dubowski argues in this chapter, less attention has been placed on the performative elements of the art-making process itself. Janek presents the client's images and explores their creation in his session with her as a form of 'enactment transference' which allows for the exploration of art-making as narrative. He suggests that witnessing and welcoming the client's projections through the creative process involves the therapist as participant observer, and when this takes place, the performative narrative might be considered as a form of ritual or ceremony. Through the use of a single image and account of their mutual process, Janek exemplifies art psychotherapy practice. Further, he demonstrates the manner in which – the art-making, in this case – the psychotherapy resulted in the expression of something that is nonsymbolic and an incidence of what Julia Kristen terms the *abject*. The crucial role of the therapist's gaze and witnessing the enactment as a form of countertransference is discussed.

Chapter 5: CBT versus the unconscious: Ignore countertransference at your peril, by Angela Devon

Traditionally CBT and psychodynamic approaches were seen as very different species. In this chapter, Angela Devon suggests that these models are using different language to describe similar processes. Angela considers developments in first-, second- and third-wave CBT suggesting that there has been an increased integration of models, particularly around the need to assess the efficacy of therapy. She argues that professionals need to be aware of the influence of their attachment style and countertransference enactments equally in CBT as in psychodynamic approaches. Angela describes her individual sessions with several clients, sharing her countertransference responses and enactments to further illustrate this argument. She argues that CBT therapists need to have some training in psychodynamic approaches and ideally personal therapy to further understanding of countertransference and the interactional aspects of their work. Illustrations and suggestions of how to use an integrative approach in clinical work are also given.

Chapter 6: "Impossible to do, but possible to say": Using countertransference in the trainer-trainee relationship, by Russel Ayling, Egle Meistaite and Paola Valerio

This chapter is set in the context of a counselling psychology doctoral programme. It is co-written by a trainer and trainee who talked about their countertransferential experiences together to try to make sense of a 'perverse' dynamic that was emerging in several ways, of perhaps getting into the alchemical bath together and then having to surface. There is a common expectation that trainees should talk about their countertransference in the service of learning about themselves and their patients, but there is much silence and fear about trainers doing the same. Russel Ayling and Egle Meistaite present the background events and thinking that resulted in the trainer presenting his countertransference about the trainee, to her. It does not take the view that this was the 'right' thing to do, rather just that this is what happened, and the authors reflect on whether it was useful for them, but more importantly, whether it was useful for the analytic work, which is perhaps the more important consideration. Finally, they invite the reader to engage in similar reflection to consider their own position on this complex use of countertransference.

Chapter 7: 'Just don't get involved': Countertransference and the group – Engaging with the projective processes in groups, by Cynthia Rogers

Cynthia Rogers writes about countertransference and projective processes in groups, adopting a helpful teaching style and advising us provokingly – Just don't get involved! This chapter is based on Cynthia's 20 years of teaching about countertransference and projective identification in groups, for the Institute of Group Analysis. It describes how therapists use their countertransference to alert them to the hidden dynamics in a group and attends to the split off feelings that play out in a group through projective processes. What is being denied, where it becomes located and how it can be reintegrated. Cynthia provides a clear theoretical exposition of splitting both as a healthy defence and its more toxic elements. It includes practical examples of how the resultant feelings can be detected and responded to. The reader is encouraged to monitor their countertransference response to the individuals in the group, subgroups and the group as a whole. A particular focus is avoiding scapegoating through attention to delicate countertransference reactions.

Chapter 8: Can organizations use countertransference to reflect? by Suzanne Weeks

Suzanne Weeks highlights the importance of the consultant's awareness of her countertransference in work with organisations, drawing upon four case studies and 20 years' experience of work within organisations. Recognition of the unconscious dimension of organisation is discussed along with the participant observer's subjective emotional response. The final piece is the exploration leading up to the interpretation: what happens to the consultant within the organisation, who becomes part of the culture yet needs to maintain an ability to think and reflect upon organisational dynamics as well as the life of individuals, subgroups, and other groups within that organisation. Suzanne makes use of Hinchelwood and Skogstad's framework to review these four case studies, bringing in the concepts of person in role, different levels of analysis but ultimately through using her own countertransference, including identification with her clients, in order to access the unconscious of the organisation. The reader is asked to think about how they might respond in similar situations.

Chapter 9: Countertransference in reflective practice: An integrative approach to monitor self-awareness in clinical practice, by Sofie Bager-Charleson

Sofie Bager-Charleson argues that post-modernism and post-structuralism have given voice to feminist-, sociocultural- and LGBT-related interests both within and outside of the field of psychotherapy. Illustrating her thesis with rich clinical material, she suggests that the shift from essentialism and individualism to a constructionist and relational perspective on therapy impacts the way we define our role as a therapist. Sofie reviews early definitions of countertransference in the context of what Schön (1983) refers to in terms of 'single-loop learning', where the practitioner is presumed to know, and must claim to do so, regardless of his or her own uncertainties. She suggests abandoning Freud's deterministic, realist perspective on how therapy changes our epistemological positioning towards a collaborative, ever-changing understanding of knowledge. Schön's (1983) idea of 'double-loop learning' conveys an emancipatory angle. Sofie expands the analytical frame beyond 'the obvious' with the therapist's underlying cultural, personal and theoretical assumptions in mind. Sofie invites the therapist to consider countertransference in terms of conscious and unconscious responses across modalities and with an interest in self-awareness on a personal, cross-cultural and meta-theoretical level.

Chapter 10: Countertransference in research: An intersubjective reflexive approach, by Sofie Bager-Charleson

There is relatively little written about the therapists' relational, embodied and emotional attunement in research. Through illustrative case studies, Sofie Bager-Charleson uses her countertransference and emotions as part of the data in her research/case studies. Finlay and Cough's (2003) way of highlighting different reflexive 'variants' provides a framework for her exploration with an interest in how researchers may engage reflexively and relationally in their research, with parallels to ways in which therapists think about knowledge in their practice. The 'free association' interview and the 'infant observation' model are used as examples of reflexive approaches where transference and counter transference are becoming significant means to generate 'data' and new 'knowledge' in research. Sofie illustrates through recent work how we may draw from countertransference in research. She encourages us to think about how to identify and communicate the researcher's personal, emotional responses during the different stages of the research.

Chapter 11: 'The recovered therapist': Working with body image disturbance and eating disorders – Researching the countertransference, by Linda Verbeek

In this chapter Linda Verbeek presents her research with female therapists who have a history of eating disorders or body image difficulties, suggesting that they are often drawn to working in the field of eating disorders, body image and body dysmorphic disorder. She suggests that as 'wounded healers', recovered therapists have a lot to offer their clients, however it is common for this client group to evoke various embodied and emotional countertransference reactions in the therapist. Linda explores therapists' own experience and management of countertransference reactions with their clients who were struggling with eating disorders and/or body image disturbance. She describes their struggles and their personal and professional strategies for self-care and self-support.

Chapter 12: Countertransference and the chance to dream, by Paola Valerio

This chapter is about dreaming, or mostly countertransference and dreaming, and about how the therapist's countertransference might influence the dream interpretations. It is also about valuing our dreams and their place in therapy. This first part of this chapter is written with Paola Valerio's tutee/supervisee, an experienced psychotherapist, about her patient's dream and how this resonated with the student's journey and how it was then explored in a dream workshop. The second part is co-written with Paola's analysand, Sofia. It is co-written in a certain sense, but also written 'alongside'. We all had our own journeys, and sometimes, we intermingled. Sometimes we lost each other. The importance here seemed to be in the finding each other again.

Chapter 13: The so-called 'countertransference' and the mystery of the therapeutic encounter, by Anastasios Gaitanidis

In this final chapter, Anastasios Gaitanidis engages us in a brave and moving account of his mutual journey with his patient. He begins by deconstructing the notion of 'countertransference' through the use of a case presentation written together with his patient. Anastasios argues that the co-creative, unpredictable and mysterious nature of the therapeutic encounter does not allow the therapist to have privileged access to the internal world of the patient through a reflective examination and interpretation of his or her countertransference. In spite of the therapist's best attempts to create a coherent, linear, 'knowing' narrative of the process, there will always be aspects of the therapeutic encounter that will remain mysterious, private and incommunicable/ineffable.

Conclusion

Many of the chapters in this volume highlight the shift from an approach which considers verbal interpretation as the gold standard, or as 'proper' technique, toward an interest in the stories or other activities leading up to an interpretation. From this frame of reference there is not so much a focus on the countertransference effect that can spoil or contaminate the therapy by an 'improper' disclosure or technical error; our unconscious complexes, rather than needing to be 'reined in', important as that may be sometimes, also contribute to the bones of the work with clients, and may even become more conscious to both therapist and client in the encounter. And of course, there will always be our tendency to locate our shadow – our most unknown, unbearable or most painful aspects of ourselves in others.

This book also encourages a stance where transparency and engagement in research play a significant role in the practice. For instance, how can strong emotions within the therapeutic relationship be conceptualised though countertransference? And how can we conceptualise countertransference in the twenty-first century, which typically includes online relationships and focus on marginalised groups within psychotherapy? The book aims to encourage us as practitioners to consider how our personal conflicts may create bias within us in various respects.

Aron (1990) suggested we replace the terms *transference* and *countertransference* with *intersubjective* as an overall, less pathologising, bidirectional term. The analyst, as Racker (1957) first suggested, cannot be without his or her own desires, or self-interest, but has to harness or use his or her awareness of countertransference. Finally, then, countertransference is seen not so much as the ugly sibling in relation to transference, but rather exists in twinship, with recognition that the patient is equally aware of the analyst's wounds and his or her unconscious.

Yet, whether we wish to hold on to the notion of '*counter*'transference, or feel that it is no longer justified from an intersubjective perspective, our responses to our inevitable enactments in the presence of the other are viewed not as technical errors, but as an opportunity afforded to us and our patients, clients or tutees who observe us working with our own struggles and curiosities – an opportunity to view *us* and not just our therapist *personas*, in not so much a 'talking' cure as a 'being with the other' cure, and not so much making an interpretation as looking for the poetry in the gaps.

Notes

1 In this book, the terms *analysand*, *client* and *patient* are all used interchangeably in order to reflect the multiplicity of professional trainings in which psychoanalytic and Jungian theories are located, and consequently result in different usage. Similarly, *psychoanalytic* and *psychodynamic* are both used to refer to therapy, although the latter term, generally speaking, refers to therapies that are less intensive, perhaps weekly or twice weekly sessions, in contrast to psychoanalysis, which is usually seen as a minimum of four to five times a week.
2 For an excellent and contemporary discussion of attachment theory and the relational school of thought, see M. Marrone's *Attachment and Interaction* (2nd ed.), 2014, Jessica Kingsley Publishers.

Bibliography

Alvesson, M., & Skoldeberg, K. (2000). *Reflexive methodology*. London, UK: Sage.

Aron, L. (1990). One person and two person psychologies and the method of psychoanalysis. In L. Aron (Ed.), *A meeting of minds: Mutuality in psychoanalysis*. Hillsdale, NJ: The Analytic Press.

Aron, L. (2003). The paradoxical place of enactment in psychoanalysis: Introduction. *Psychoanalytic Dialogues*, *13*, 623–631.

Aron, L. (2005). Acceptance, compassion, and an affirmative analytic attitude in both intersubjectivity and compromise formation theory. *Psychoanalytic Dialogues*, *15*(3), 433–446.

Benjamin, J. (1995). *Like subjects, love objects: Essays on recognition and sexual difference*. New Haven, CT: Yale University Press.

Benjamin, J. (2004). Beyond doer and done to: An intersubjective view of thirdness. *Psychoanalytic Quarterly*, LXXIII.

Benjamin, J. (2010). Where's the gap and what's the difference?: The relational view of intersubjectivity, multiple selves and enactments. *Contemporary Psychoanalysis*, *46*(1), 112–119.

Bion, W. R. (1940). The war of nerves. In E. Miller & H. Crichton Miller (Eds.), *The neuroses in war* (pp. 180–200). London, UK: Macmillan.

Bion, W. R. (1962a). A theory of thinking. In *Second thoughts: Selected papers on psychoanalysis* (pp. 110–119). London, UK: Heinemann.

Bion, W. R. (1962b). *Learning from experience*. London, UK: Heinemann.

Boston Change Process Study Group. (2010). *Change in psychotherapy: A unifying paradigm*. New York, NY: Norton.

Bowlby, J. (1969/1999). *Attachment: Attachment and loss* (Vol. 1) (2nd ed.). New York, NY: Basic Books.

Britton, R., & Steiner, J. (1994). Interpretation: Selected fact or overvalued idea? *International Journal of Psychoanalysis*, *75*, 1069–1078.

Bromberg, P. M. (1996). Standing in the spaces: The multiplicity of self and the psychoanalytic relationship. *Contemporary Psychoanalysis*, *32*, 509–535.

Bromberg, P. M. (2009). Truth: Human relatedness and the analytic process. *International Journal of Psychoanalysis*, *90*, 347–361.

Diamond, N., & Marrone, M. (2003). *Attachment and intersubjectivity*. London, UK: Whurr.

Fairbairn, W. R. D. (1952). *Psychoanalytic studies of the personality*. London, UK: Routledge & Kegan Paul.

Freud, S. (1910). The future prospects of psycho-analytic therapy. *S.E. 11*, 139–152.

Freud, S. (1912a). Recommendations to physicians practicing psycho-analysis. In J. Strachey (Ed. and trans.), *The standard edition of the complete psychological works of Sigmund Freud* (pp. 109–120). London, UK: Hogarth.

Freud, S. (1912b). The dynamics of transference. In J. Strachey (Ed. and trans.), *The standard edition of the complete psychological works of Sigmund Freud* (pp. 97–108). London, UK: Hogarth.

Freud, S. (1914). Observations on transference-love. *S.E. 12*, 157–171.

Freud, S. (1915). Instincts and their vicissitudes. *S.E. XTV*, 109–140.

Freud, S., & Ferenczi, S. (1992). Letters 72–75, August 11–October 11, 1909; Letters 84–86, November 19–21, 1909. In E. Brabant, E. Falzeder, & P. Giamper (Eds.), *The correspondence of Sigmund Freud and Sandor Ferenczi, Vol. 1*. Cambridge, MA: Belknap Press.

Gabbard, G. (1994). Sexual excitement and countertransference love in the analyst. *Journal of the American Psychoanalytic Association*, *42*, 1083–1106.

Groesbeck, C. J. (1975). The archetypal image of the wounded healer. *Journal of Analytical Psychology*, *20*(2), 122–145.

Grotstein, J. S. (1994). Projective identification and countertransference: A brief commentary on their relationship. *Contemporary Psychoanalysis*, *30*, 578–592.

Guggenbul-Craig, A. (1971/2015). *Power in the helping professions*. New York, NY: Spring.

Hayes, J. A. (2004). The inner world of the psychotherapist: A program of research on countertransference. *Psychotherapy Research*, *14*(1), 21–36. doi:10.1093/ptr/kph002

Hayes, J. A., Gelso, C. J., & Hummel, A. M. (2011). Managing countertransference. *Psychotherapy*, *48*(1), 88–97. doi:10.1037/a0022182

Heimann, P. (1950). On counter-transference. *The International Journal of Psychoanalysis*, *3*, 181–184.

Hirsch, I. (2011). *Coasting in the countertransference: Conflicts of self interest between analyst and patient*. New York, NY: The Analytic Press.

Hoffman, I. (1983). The patient as interpreter of the analyst's experience. *Contemporary Psychoanalysis*, *19*, 389–422.

Holmes, J. (2014). Countertransference in qualitative research: A critical appraisal. *Qualitative Research*, *14*(2), 166–183.

Joseph, B. (1985). Transference: The total situation. *International Journal of Psychoanalysis*, *66*, 447–454.

Jung, C. G. (1951/1966a). The fundamental questions of psychotherapy. In H. Read, M. Fordham, G. Adler, & W. McGuire (Eds.), *The collected works of C. G. Jung (Vol. 16)* (pp. 116–125). Princeton, NJ: Princeton University Press.

Jung, C. G. (1946/1966b). The psychology of the transference. In H. Read, M. Fordham, G. Adler, & W. McGuire (Eds.), *The collected works of C.G. Jung (Vol. 16)* (pp. 163–201). Princeton, NJ: Princeton University Press.

Kächele, H., Erhardt, I., Seybert, C., & Buchholz, M. B. (2015). Countertransference as object of empirical research? *International Forum of Psychoanalysis*, 24(2), 96–108.

Kantrowitz, J. L. (2006). *Writing about patients*. New York, NY: The Other Press.

Kernberg, O. (1965). Notes on countertransference. *Journal of the American Psychoanalytic Association*, 13(1), 38–56.

Kieffer, C. C. (2007). Emergence and the analytic third: Working at the edge of chaos. *Psychoanalytic Dialogues*, 17(5), 683–703.

Klein, M. (1946). Notes on some schizoid mechanisms. *The International Journal of Psychoanalysis*, 27, 99–110.

Kohut, H. (1959). Introspection, empathy, and psychoanalysis—An examination of the relationship between mode of observation and theory. *Journal of the American Psychoanalytic Association*, 7, 459–483.

Kohut, H. (1971). *The analysis of the self*. New York, NY: International Universities Press.

Little, M. (1951). Countertransference and the patient's response to it. *International Journal of Psychoanalysis*, 32, 32–34.

Little, M. (1957). The analyst's response to his patient's needs. *International Journal of Psychoanalysis*, 38, 240–254.

Loewenthal, D., & Samuels, A. (2017). *Relational psychotherapy*. New York, NY: Routledge.

Maroda, K. (2004). *The power of countertransference* (2nd ed.). Northvale, NJ: Jason Aronson.

Marrone, M. (2014). *Attachment and interaction* (2nd ed.). London, UK: Jessica Kingsley.

McGuire, W. (Ed.) (1974). Letter from Sigmund Freud to C. G. Jung, June 7, 1909. In *The Freud/Jung Letters: The correspondence between Sigmund Freud and C. G. Jung*. Princeton, NJ: Princeton University Press.

Mitchell, S. A. (1988). *Relational concepts in psychoanalysis: An integration*. Cambridge, MA: Harvard University Press.

Mitchell, S. A. (1997). *The analyst's intentions: Influence and autonomy in psychoanalysis*. Hillsdale, NJ: The Analytic Press.

Mitchell, S. A., & Black, M. (1995). *Freud and beyond: A history of modern psychoanalytic thought*. New York, NY: Basic Books.

Modell, A. H. (2005). Emotional memory, metaphor, and meaning. *Psychoanalytic Inquiry*, 25(4), 555–568.

Norcross, J. C. (2002). *Psychotherapy relationships that work: Therapist contributions and responsiveness to patients*. New York, NY: New York University Press.

Oelsner, R. (2013). *Transference and countertransference today*. London, UK: Routledge.

Ogden, T. H. (1979). On projective identification. *International Journal of Psychoanalysis*, 60(3), 357–373.

Ogden, T. H. (2004). The analytic third: Implications for psychoanalytic theory and technique. *Psychoanalytic Quarterly*, 73(1), 167–195.

Racker, H. (1957). The meanings and uses of countertransference. *Psychoanalytic Quarterly*, 26, 303–357.

Racker, H. (1968). *Transference and countertransference*. New York, NY: International Universities Press.

Reich, A. (1951). On counter-transference. *The International Journal of Psychoanalysis*, 32, 25–31.

Renik, O. (1993). Analytic interaction: Conceptualizing technique in light of the analyst's irreducible subjectivity. *The Psychoanalytic Quarterly*, 62(4), 553–571.

Renik, O. (1993). Countertransference enactment and the psychoanalytic process. In M. J. Horowitz, O. F. Kornberg, & E. M. Weinshel (Eds.), *Psychic structure and psychic change* (pp. 13–158). Madison, CT: International Universities Press.

Rosenberger, E. A., & Hayes J. A. (2002). Therapist as subject: A review of the empirical countertransference literature. *Journal of Counseling and Development*, 80(3), 264.

Saffron, J. D., & Kraus, J. (2014). Alliance ruptures, impasses and enactments: A relational perspective. *Psychotherapy*, 51(3), 381–387.

Samuels, A. (1989). *The plural psyche*. London, UK: Routledge.

Samuels, A. (1993). *The political psyche*. London, UK: Routledge.

Sander, D.L., Nahum, J., Harrison, A., Lyons-Ruth K., Morgan, A., Bruschweilerstern, N., & Tronick, E. (1998). Non-interpretive mechanisms in psychoanalytic therapy: The 'something more' than interpretation. *International Journal of Psychoanalysis*, 79, 903–992.

Schaverien, J. (Ed.) (2006). *Gender, countertransference, and the erotic transference: Perspectives from analytical psychology and psychoanalysis*. London, UK: Routledge.

Searles, H. F. (Ed.) (1955). The schizophrenics vulnerability to the therapist's unconscious process. In *Collected papers on schizophrenia* (pp. 192–215). Hogarth Press Ltd.

Searles, H. F. (1959). Oedipal love in the countertransference. In H. F. Searles (Ed.), *Collected papers on schizophrenia and related subjects*. New York, NY: International Universities Press.

Searles, H. F. (1979). The patient as therapist to his analyst. In H. F. Searles (Ed.), *Countertransference and related subjects: Selected papers* (pp. 380–459). New York, NY: International Universities Press.

Sedgwick, D. (1994). *The wounded healer: Countertransference from a Jungian perspective*. New York, NY: Routledge, Taylor & Francis Group.

Shedler, J. (2006). *That was then, this is now: Psychoanalytic psycho-therapy for the rest of us*. Retrieved from http://psychsystems.net/shedler.html

Shedler, J. (2010). The efficacy of psychodynamic psychotherapy. *American Psychologist*, 65(2), 98–109.

Smith, H. F. (2000). Countertransference, conflictual listening, and the analytic object relationship. *Journal of the American Psychoanalytic Association*, 48(1), 95–128.

Solms, M., & Turnbull, O. (2002). *The brain and the inner world: An introduction to the neuroscience of subjective experience*. New York, NY: Other Press.

Steiner, J. (1993). *Psychic retreats*. London, UK: Brunner-Routledge.

Stern, D. (1985). *The interpersonal world of the infant: A view from psychoanalysis and developmental psychology*. New York, NY: Basic Books.

Stern, D. (2003). *The interpersonal world of the infant: A view from psychoanalysis and developmental psychology*. London, UK: Karnac Books.

Stern. D. (2004). *The present moment in psychotherapy and everyday life*. New York, NY: W. W. Norton.

Stern, D. N., Sander, L. W., Nahum, J. P., Harrison, A. M., Lyons-Ruth, K., Morgan, A. C., Bruschweilerstern, N., & Tronick, Z. (1998). Non-interpretive mechanisms in psychoanalytic therapy: The 'something more' than interpretation. *International Journal of Psychoanalysis*, 79(5), 903–921.

Stolorow, R. D. (1991). The intersubjective context of intrapsychic experience: A decade of psychoanalytic inquiry. *Psychoanalytic Inquiry*, 11, 17.

Stolorow, R. D. (1993). An intersubjective view of the therapeutic process. *Bulletin of the Menninger Clinic*, 57(4), 450.

Stolorow, R., & Atwood, G. (1997). Deconstructing the myth of the neutral analyst. *Psychoanalytic Quarterly*, 66, 431–450.

Valerio, P. F. (2005). Broken boundaries: Perverting the therapeutic frame. In M. Luca (Ed.), *The therapeutic frame* (pp. 116–127). London, UK: Taylor & Francis.

Valerio, P. F. (2006). Love and hate – a fusion of opposites: A window to the soul. In D. Mann (Ed.), *Love and hate in the transference* (pp. 253–266). London, UK: Routledge.

Valerio Smith, P. F. (1997). Secret friends: Borderline personality and post traumatic stress disorder in a case of reported sexual abuse. *British Journal of Psychotherapy*, 14(1), 18–32.

Winnicott, D. W. (1949). Hate in the counter-transference. *International Journal of Psychoanalysis*, 30, 69–74.

Winnicott, D. W. (1958). *Collected papers: Through paediatrics to psychoanalysis*. London, UK: Tavistock.

Part I

Countertransference in work with individuals

Chapter 1

Between bodies

Working in the liminal zone with traumatised clients

Nicola Diamond and Paola Valerio

> A skin surface . . . exists in its most radical state as a liminal zone, a threshold that is potentially shifting . . . on the borders of an inside-outside. It is precisely a border zone.
>
> (Diamond, 2013, p. 160)

This chapter is based on a workshop that we facilitated at a Social Justice and Body Conference at Roehampton University in 2016 about countertransference and the liminal zone, or in-between space, in therapeutic work. In this chapter, we explore the countertransference as taking place in an interpersonal space where the clear borders between 'I' and 'you' seem to breakdown, and it is not easy in these moments to decipher if the affective state (often somatic in nature), derives from the analyst or the analysand.

Liminal derives from the Latin *limens* and means 'threshold'; it refers to an ambiguous space. In anthropology, it is a term used when participants 'stand at the threshold' between the previous way of structuring identity and the transition to another emerging mode of being. A liminal space is undecidable, anticipatory and unknown, a transitional temporal dimension. It could be said to be a moment of creativity, where self becomes other in a communal activity. A liminal space in many ways encapsulates our thinking about the transference–countertransference relation, where the boundary of self and other organised around the ego breaks down, and there is a more intimate exchange between analyst and analysand. This liminal communication in the analytic encounter we will link to intersubjective and intercorporeal ways of being and we shall also root the transformation that brings about psychic change to this liminal 'moment of meeting'.

Our focus is on working with trauma, as this kind of therapeutic work readily shows the limitations of conventional analytic approaches, which traditionally define the transference–countertransference experience as dominated by reflective processes and speech. In work with traumatised clients, the clinician is faced, often starkly, with the direct nature of the traumatic experience, which renders verbal transference interpretation unhelpful, involving the analyst in sensitising to these embodied and enacted styles of communications.

In psychoanalytic therapy, there is a process of 'working through' in the transference relationship to the therapist. This can be difficult with severely traumatised patients, since telling the story is not always available to the traumatised patient, and interpretations can be too penetrative, abusive or simply too frightening in dissociative states when the attachment system is activated. Studies in memory research suggest that it may not be possible to tell the story or recover memories of abuse. This can be because the trauma was so overwhelming that it cannot be processed and the impact remains as an unprocessed affective state, or there is a form of amnesia, as in a number of cases of childhood abuse. We have noticed in our work that narration of experience is arrested when the patient has been neglected in childhood and there has been no validation of self so that the autobiographical fails to be elaborated and reflected on (Diamond, 2013; Valerio, 2011). This problem of accessing a verbal narration of experience renders affective communication as more direct and immediate in the room, via experiences that remain nonverbal and communicated in bodily form.

The therapeutic relationship, which involves expressing one's vulnerability to a perceived more powerful other, leads to the activation of the attachment system, often of an abusive, disorganised pattern from childhood. Understandably less has been written about the impact on therapists and counsellors as witnesses and coauthors in the transference of such traumatic events which are conveyed in bodily form. This raises the question of whether present external reality may remain a continuing trauma – for both parties, and hence unmetabolised by the analyst who may also dissociate (Valerio, 2011).

Feeling bored or cut off from patient is very common in work with abused patients. We have come to see this in our practice often when working with clients who have been sexually abused or traumatised. We see this as a form of counterdissociation, for example, when clients are painting a very rosy picture of events or of people who have abused them. It is as if the analyst's body mirrors theirs in cutting off from feelings which exist in the patient, yet without narrative and verbal recall of events. The thing about embodied countertransference reactions is that the therapist will also have periods of unawareness. The hope is to have enough active engagement with one's own unconscious process to rapidly bring this into greater awareness so it can be worked with in the consulting room.

When it is impossible for traumatic events to be comprehended in their time, they cannot be restored to the generational history, and therefore cannot become history to the patient. Such events remain like 'foreign bodies'; they are conveyed in their unmetabolised form as unprocessed affects which are passed down through the generations, who receive them in their unconscious minds and, more pertinently, bodies. Fraiberg, Adelson and Shapiro (1976) noted that there are negative patterns of attachment–reenactment that haunt us like 'ghosts in the nursery', and will repeat themselves in the mother's way of treating her child. What Fraiberg is talking about is reenactment based on intergenerational transmission; the 'ghosts' relate to the associated affective experiences that are not remembered, the terror, the helplessness and humiliation that have undergone repression. Repression is not quite correct here, and dissociation, we would argue, is more accurate in terms of the mechanism of transmission; what gets inherited is not only the tendency to abuse but also the tendency to dissociate (Valerio, 2011).

Arguably there has been a paradigmatic shift in psychotherapy; no longer is it 'all in the mind', but 'in the body'. Both in theory and in practice, the focus is on the body, whether it is neuroscience, the importance of bodily memory or the way in which therapist and client communicate through the body. Countertransference communications are experienced affectively, by the therapist, feeling states or mood alteration, but often as a bodily reaction. Increasingly therapists are writing about this (Stone, 2006; Lemma, 2014; Orbach, 1999, 2010) and we now believe that an authentic 'talking cure' is not possible without some 'interacting cure', since enactment is often the communication wherein bodily memory is what is primarily accessed, and repetition and reworking is required in this nonverbal mode to facilitate the emergence of fertile thought and psychic transformation.

Current interdisciplinary thinking in psychoanalysis, developmental psychology and neuroscience is recognising the importance of the nonverbal level of communication and experience in depicting unconscious processes. Peter Fonagy argued (1999) that bodily memories cannot in fact be retrieved in psychoanalytic psychotherapy because these memories are largely preverbal and therefore cannot be accessed verbally. However, they can be accessed directly through action, as in the example of the sexually abused infant who acts out the memory through showing. The infant's experience is enacted, in the way he or she plays with the dolls (Mollon, 2002; Valerio, 2011). In the same way, the client who persistently arrives late lets the therapist know through action what it's like to be kept waiting by a neglectful parent (putting the therapist in her shoes), before words are found for the painful experience.

It used to be thought that the therapist observes the client's subjective states; now there is recognition of a much more interactive process, which is interpersonal, and the therapist and client's subjectivity is mutually involved. This is viewed as an *intersubjective experience*. Whereas interpretation had been seen as key, putting feelings into thought for the client, 'the talking cure', recent developments place greater emphasis on unconscious nonverbal bodily communications, interpretation being a more secondary process, tapping into this bodily mode of relating is seen as necessary if deep psychic change is to take place.

Intersubjectivity is now viewed as also intercorporeal (Diamond, 2013). Instead of contemplative thought, the emphasis is placed on enactment, what we do before we reflect, as a way of 'knowing', and this has changed the meaning of 'acting out'. Hence 'acting out' is no longer simply viewed as a bad thing, as a way of evading thinking, but rather it is now seen as a required form of 'acting in', in order to find a way to reorganise past experience. Procedural body based memory as a nonverbal mode of relating has to be in play for more reflective and processed symbolic modes of thought to develop in the work. Embodied enactment is how the transference–countertransference interaction is expressed.

One of us was working with a male patient whose father had committed suicide when he was 4 years old. He was talking about this in a very matter of fact way when the therapist's eyes started to well up with tears. My own history is that I lost my father when I was not yet 2 years old. I felt embarrassed and relieved that my blurry eyes did not lead to actual tears. I sensed my patient had observed my disposition, and was watching carefully. I said something about his reluctance to acknowledge his loss, based on what we had been speaking about in previous sessions, that somehow keeping his father alive meant that he had not really been abandoned by him, and that he would not have to get in touch with his anger in relation to his father's abandonment. But actually, I felt that it was only in our mutual and shared recognition, wherein he had witnessed my wound in the room, that he could now metabolise this verbal interpretation. I did not have control of my bodily response and could not have orchestrated this, what Stern et al. of the Boston School (1998) may refer to as a spontaneous 'moment of meeting', where my own experience was simultaneously a direct acknowledgement of his, an empathic joining.

I also wondered if the experience had been more healing for me, yet I felt almost sure that a similar comment at any other time would not have had an effect upon my patient. I say this because it is important to own what is mine, and yet the experience benefited the patient. There is a fine line between a productive 'moment of meeting' and one where there is an unhelpful breaching of boundaries where either the therapist's identification with their own pain supersedes their response to the patient's needs or/and the analyst's narcissism prevails (Valerio, 2005).

The therapist cannot be reflectively aware at every moment, and is also unconsciously engaged in the relational process, and this can involve a 'more messy exchange' where it is not always so easy to disentangle what is mine and what is yours, and this fuzzing of boundaries can be considered part of the communication.

As noted, contemporary understanding identifies intersubjective and intercorporeal relating as the basis of an embodied transference–countertransference communication. Intersubjectivity brings a new paradigm to traditional psychoanalytic understanding. Freud described the phenomena of transference and countertransference, but it remained difficult to explain how feelings and affective-body states could be passed so readily from one person to another. If we think of two discrete persons in the consulting room, how is it that feeling-body states jump across such an unbridgeable gulf? Indeed, as Freud (1915) observed, it is rather like a form of telepathy:

[I]t is a very remarkable thing that the unconscious of one human being can react upon that of another, without passing through the act of consciousness. . . . This deserves closer investigation, especially with a view to finding out whether preconscious activity can be excluded as playing a part in it; but, descriptively speaking, the fact is incontestable.

(p. 194)

Intersubjectivity is a paradigm derived from phenomenological philosophy and introduced through developmental psychology, notably by Colwyn Trevarthen (1978, 1979) to psychotherapy and related understanding, and this answers the question of how to overcome the unbridgeable gulf (Diamond & Marrone, 2003). This paradigm involves a number of philosophical thinkers, not only Habermas, whom Trevarthen refers to, but also Husserl, Heidegger and Merleau-Ponty, to name a few.

There is a much more intimate connection between self and other than had been traditionally assumed. Heidegger noted that the idea of the two discrete individuals with a measurable distance between them is based on a Euclidean geometric notion of space, and whereas human beings are not pure objects, we affect one another; Heidegger refers to this as 'dwelling in one another'. Someone can walk into a room and immediately we can pick up their mood state and are affected by it; this can be keenly felt, 'in the gut' so to speak, and groups can be 'contagious' in the way they can spread 'felt states'. This we know does not just happen in the consulting room, and intensifies when we are attached to someone and build a more intimate relationship. The client–therapist relationship is a special type of relationship of this sort, in which there is intense involvement and a deep attachment is formed.

There is so much evidence now, from neuroscience, developmental psychology, attachment studies, philosophy and relational psychoanalysis, that my bodily self is intertwined with the other from the first and throughout the life cycle. From attachment neuroscience literature (Schore, 1994, 2003, 2010), we know that the baby and mother are in an interaction, where they directly affect each other, and that biological processes are simultaneously altered in this process. The positive or negative interaction in the attachment relation can alter the production of brain cells, hormones and the nervous system, and the regulation and deregulation of these systems. This is not one-way traffic, since the mother is likewise affected by her baby; she is less vulnerable, but still affectively and physically affected. We also know from developmental psychology (Trevarthen, 1978, 1979) that the baby and caretaker are interacting in an interpersonal space. This is an interpersonal bodily exchange dominated by nonverbal bodily communication, referred to as intercorporeal in nature. From the first, the baby derives the sense of embodied self via the other's mirroring and tactile interactions. This interpersonal bodily experience is something that carries on throughout our lives, and is happening all the time on less conscious levels in human interaction whatever age we are.

We commonly think of the skin acting as a literal border, indeed a protective barrier that separates my body from others. Freud refers to 'the ego [as] first and foremost a bodily ego; it is not merely a surface entity, but is itself a projection of a surface' (1923, p. 16), making it clear the skin surface is endemic to this embodied ego/self. If we take into account what Heidegger says about two senses of space, one Euclidean, where the skin is in a physical concrete space separating my body from yours, and another equally valid sense of space, where sentient beings affect one another; in the latter case, the skin as a surface is open to being affectively sensitive, and in a similar way to when someone walks into a room and we pick up their mood state, the affective state is felt, often visceral and tangible, indeed – 'contagious'. The skin becomes no longer the sealed off protective barrier, but instead is experienced as porous and, similar to osmosis, the affective state directly permeates.

The skin as a surface is open to the other from the start; it is touched and mirrored by others and is indeed a projected surface in the sense of being derived from others, as it is construed through how others mirror and touch us – it is constantly negotiating this experience. The skin surface is both literally and affectively touched by the other, and this is further understood within the context of what we know about the intercorporeal exchange, whereby the other affects us biologically as well. This is described by people like Schore, in baby–parent interactions, in an affective-biological exchange that continues to happen throughout the life cycle. From this we can say that the countertransference, which is a form of affective intimate relation, occurs between skins, a porous liminal space, where my body opens to yours, in a more intercorporeal and affective way (Diamond, 2013).

Thus, as noted, the countertransference takes place in an interpersonal space where the clear borders between I and you seem to break down and in these moments it is not easy to decipher if the affective state (often somatic in nature) derives from the analyst or the analysand. The countertransference quite literally occurs between skins, where the skin, instead as acting as a protective barrier, becomes permeable and opens up to the other's projections.

For psychic change to take place in the analytic encounter, unconscious bodily states and nonverbal processes need to be accessed, transformed and integrated. Schore (2003) noted that shifts have to take place in bodily states themselves that then integrate with reflective insights. Schore would say this double process has to happen for psychological depth-change to take place in therapy. In contrast, a person can go through years of psychotherapy and end up with a pseudoanalysis. Clients may have a capacity for conscious reflection and insight, but deep down feel stuck, and may reveal this to us in actions and/or behaviours in their private life that may frustrate us, suggesting they have not in fact shifted one bit! We are all familiar with the depressing scenario, often after years of analytic processing, of clients who return to an abusive partner or family or who abuse their own children (Valerio & Lepper, 2009, 2010).

There is now greater awareness of the nonverbal exchanges which occur in the consulting room and of possible limits to the 'talking cure'. The articulation of feelings into thoughts and speech is not enough; bodily affective states have to be transformed in the process for a profound alteration in 'state of being'. Bion (1967) referred to transforming 'beta into alpha elements'; this we would stress involves a processing and refinement of somatic experience in connecting bodily states and reflective alpha function, an integration and not an actual shift away from the soma to a higher, more cortical order of functioning, although cortical functioning can be refined and enhanced in this developmental process (Diamond, 2013).

Change does not involve simply contemplative thought. It implies action – for a real shift in experience, thought and action need to be altered together. This increasing focus on the power of enactment causes us to reevaluate our terminology. Do we term this bad and/or good acting, or acting out and acting in? Sometimes it is only by *doing* that we can find out what is bothering us, what we might need to reflect upon and change. It has been easier in psychotherapy to refer to the client 'acting something out' in relation to the therapist; it is more uncomfortable to admit that the therapist can get caught up in some kind of enactment as part of the therapeutic process as well, and only after this learn what the problem is and hopefully then facilitate the reflective process with his or her client.

Peter, a client, was furious when I opened the door to greet him (Diamond, 2005). I was a couple of minutes late, but this evoked such fury in Peter that it was clear that he was in a transference reaction, because his response was so excessive. He shouted at me, saying, How I can keep him waiting like this? I asked him how he was feeling; furious, he said. I was feeling outraged as well, which surprised me, and I wanted to snap back and indeed I almost did. I asked myself, Why this palpable rage? I was thinking that he was entitled and how dare he, which did not really make sense to me at that moment. Then he said, 'It reminds me how my parents kept me waiting for my handicapped brother, and did not give a damn about me'.

Instead of my response being empathic towards Peter, I felt like I literally wanted to hit back. Still, my thoughts stayed with me that somehow he was being entitled, yet why? Then I realised I was feeling like his parents perhaps felt, like he was a 'whippersnapper', he did not have the right. In my thinking, now he was able-bodied son, and hence all the attention was going towards the handicapped brother. So we, Peter and I, reenacted a scene together; by acting it out in bodily felt ways we were really sensing it all, which gave us the opportunity to change a lived state. It is only by actually *feeling* something that the experience is alive in the present; one has to be in touch with the experience in order to alter it.

By adopting the parents' response, I understood something that I had not understood about Peter before – Peter's experience had been dismissed. He had not been heard, and had no rights as the able-bodied son. Now, learning from this experience, I could be appropriately empathic in the way Peter really needed as I interpreted what had happened between us. From that moment on, communication was easier between us, but it was not so much the interpretation as the fact that something about his hurt had been really embodied by me, got inside of me, and was hence understood. An empathic response was possible; this spontaneous validation promoted a psychic shift.

Another client, Janet, came to therapy (Diamond 2003). She was a prim-looking woman, formally dressed, mid-40s, a kind and thoughtful woman, who was living alone and wanted to find a partner. I saw her twice weekly over a 4-year period. In the second year of therapy, I noticed a very strong reaction in me when, in-session with her, I struggled to stay awake. I wondered if this was a countertransference reaction, as I was not so disinterested with other clients whom I worked with. What was overwhelmingly evident was 'I felt bored', I was so bored I could not stay awake, 'I had lost all interest in her'. On the surface, this was terrible, as I knew what this client needed most was someone to take an interest in her, but my bodily response was to do the complete opposite. This was an incredibly powerful somatic response to this patient in the room with me, and I took this as a countertransference communication. I was feeling like the entirely disinterested parent who neglected her. Janet felt deep down she had nothing to offer, that she was nothing to everyone and this lack of self-value was transmitted powerfully to me. It was such a core belief, that she was experienced that way by me too.

Jane's parents had owned a shop, and when Jane was born they were so busy with the shop she was left for the first 6 months of life upstairs and on her own. She suffered hours of neglect and, importantly, significant lack of stimulation, which retrospectively had a profound impact on Jane's sense of aliveness. How can you feel alive for yourself if you have not been alive for another? And how can you invest objects in the environment with a sense of value, purpose and meaning if you have not established an alive, connected experience with others?

Apparently, she was fed but stimulation and attention were minimal, not so far off the feral-child experience of neglect, and, indeed, Jane's speech and social skills related to right-brain and body development suffered severe delay, slowness in development and significant impairment in imaginative skills, such that still haunted Jane as an adult. At 6 months, when she could sit up, she was brought downstairs to sit perched on the counter; then she got some interactional stimulation from the hustle and bustle of the activity in the shop, but lacked one-to-one attentive play with key attachment figures, as her parents were fully engrossed in serving customers and running the shop. Passers-by would attend momentarily, but without the more substantial investment of love through interaction, Jane readily merged into feeling part of the background with animate beings and inanimate objects in the shop. Hence, any feeling of specialness, for someone who so desperately needed it, was stunted in development.

I think this 6-month period in which Jane lacked stimulation resulted in what we call a *privation*, which implies never having, as opposed to a *deprivation*, when a provision is given, however imperfect, and then withdrawn. With deprivation, there is some bringing to life and then an experience of less than, whereas with privation, something has not been brought into being in the first place. This 'non-mattering', a lack of any self-value, was so fundamental to Jane's primary constitution as a subject, that the deadening effect was all the more powerful in the experience of the countertransference, not even feeling like a neglectful parent, but in becoming a dormant one, I became for that period of the work a therapist/parent who was entirely indifferent to Jane's being.

As noted, we think there is some truth in the belief that you need to have gone through an experience to know what it feels like and to access some real understanding of what it must have been like for the other person. Of course, we never experience in an identical way to another, as we have different histories and pathways of development, but nevertheless, having access to some elements of the experience that we can use to develop some understanding of the other's state of being is essential. The level of embodied-affective experience has to be touched somehow in the room, otherwise the process of therapy becomes too intellectual and overcognitive, and depth-change is not possible.

I had a patient (Valerio, 2011) who, for the first 9 months, would lie on my couch four times a week in stony silence. In my countertransference response, I wanted to end her therapy; I felt repelled by her and found her loathsome and contemptuous. At the end of a session she would often leave me with some nebulous critical comment, such as 'That was a waste of time'. I felt my hatred of her in the belly region and in my bones. Actually, I really hoped she would leave, but yet also wanted her to stay, and I felt a desperate need to engage her. My failure to engage her continued until in a moment of drift or dissociation in one session, my body gave way to a painful memory and image from my own childhood, and suddenly embodied feelings of grief from which I had become split off and had disassociated. After my father's death when I was just a toddler, and with an even younger sibling, I had tried to rouse my mother, who suddenly came to mind, sitting at the kitchen table, head in hands, crying, and according to me, neglecting her usual chores. I became the child who parented, feeling a weight and responsibility to keep my mother on task in order to care for my younger sibling, and to preserve a relationship with a mother, who, in her grief for my father, felt the burden of having me around, a feeling I then reenacted with my patient.

My enactment came from my own deep wound and my feelings of utter helplessness, shared at least on an implicit relational level. After this moment of mutual meeting occurred, and exactly after 9 months of therapy, she seemed to become more alive and engaged, or at least seemed to acknowledge therapy was a two-person relationship. In particular, she spoke about her mother and her seething hatred for her, of how her mother had told her that she had prayed for a miscarriage as her religion and husband denied her an abortion.

As Davies argued (2004):

> I believe that we must be able to fully occupy the countertransfer-
> ence as it is constructed in the enactment with any given patient. My
> point has been to emphasize that particularly toxic impasses can occur
> when something in the patient's history of extruded self-states engages
> with something in the analyst's history of extruded self-states. In such
> instances, the boundary between self and other collapses in the mutual
> spit-fire projections and counter projections that ensue. The analyst's
> space for self-reflective processes becomes compromised and potentially
> shuts down when overwhelming shame contributes to his or her rejection
> of a patient's unconscious communication.
>
> (p. 179)

Retrieving a living strand of my history and the realisation of my involvement was significant in creating an inner shift, which allowed the opportunity
and 'freedom' (Symington, 1983) to understand the transference–countertransference dynamics and relational configurations being (re)enacted. We
were enabled, therefore, to shift from a stuck and polarised position of impasse
(Ehrenberg, 2000). This resonated with me I realised that I had also felt forced
to carry my patient. It was a dull ache in my belly or womb, and I had to
experience her mother's hatred in my own body along with my own memories
within my consulting room, now experienced rather like a birthing chamber.
Interestingly, but only after the 9-month gestation period, I noticed that my
patient was a truly striking woman and it was indeed curious that I had not *seen*
that as I had been consumed in the countertransference by a blinding cohatred.

Group exercise

Reflecting on some of the patients described above, can you think of
similar bodily experiences or difficult emotions with particular clients?

What do you think about the timing of interpretations? Discuss some
examples when you got the timing wrong and how you managed this
with your client.

Was supervision helpful?

The increasing awareness of enactment as a primary unconscious means of communication has placed importance on procedural-action body-based memory.
In development, the earliest experience of bodily self is nonverbal, derived from

when baby and mother interact and preverbal modes of communication develop and build. This communication alters and influences bio-affective processes in interaction between baby and other, as well as embodied modes of communicating via the senses. Early bodily memories begin to be laid down in this process, and intermingle with linguistic processes that come properly on line a little later. We never escape the profundity of this procedural action mode of communication; it returns in love making and falling in love, and when we are with our children and form attachments with them and close friends and/or community. It is the basis of our current understanding of Bowlby's 'internal working model', of a sense of embodied self in relation to the other(s) as key attachment figure(s). This relational embodied 'know how' is linked to autobiographical memory in the right brain. A sequence of embodied action-based behaviour based on the attachment history gets reenacted, and this forms the prereflexive 'know how' that you come to do without consciously thinking about, but it can be problematic if the attachment history has been disturbed and the person is still in 'the throws of' the experience and has not been able to process it adequately (Diamond, 2013).

There is a form of procedural 'know-how', patterns of behaviour and bodily expression which we form throughout our attachment years. Experiences are revisited through forms of reenactment in the therapy room via transference–countertransference communications. We can all find ourselves at some point in our life repeating, despite ourselves, a way of acting, which goes against our best intentions. Somehow our procedural 'body know-how' leads us back to a place time and time again. Of course, patterns of this sort can be grosser or subtler, for example, panic attacks that occur as a way of expressing performance anxiety due to low self-esteem, or the effects of a critical undermining parenting style which led a patient to repeat life-threatening harmful situations and/or abusive relationships. Freud (1920) referred to the 'compulsion to repeat'. At first, he noted that a compulsion to reenact an experience relates to the desire to master an experience that had been difficult in the past, but then he noted that when someone gets into the grip of trauma, and the experience becomes too overwhelming, then the compulsion does not turn into an experience of mastery but a repetition of suffering.

The basis of the procedural action body memory, formed out of historical interactions with others, underlies the linguistic and more conscious ego-self. We use our bodies to understand our clients, and work hard to monitor and bring actively into reflection what is going on in our own bodies and how we can possibly use this to make sense of our own and our client's experience. We would suggest that it is precisely when boundaries between therapist and analysand become 'sloppy' (Stern et al., 1998) that the most is learned experientially about our client's state of being.

Daniel Stern and colleagues (1998) suggested that this procedural mode of relational knowing, which is also referred to as implicit 'know-how', is about tapping into this form of prereflexive embodied memory-based experience. Stern and colleagues (1998) challenged the idea that interpretation is the way to bring about psychic change.

We are all familiar with a failed kind of interpretation; where words are used, they might well be quite clever, but the interpretation does not 'hit the spot' for the client. It is only in conjunction with reenactment, and restaging an experience in the therapeutic rapport, through a mutually relived moment, that effects change. This 'moment' is not planned, is often unexpected and occurs through enactments, as we have tried to illustrate in our examples. The idea of implicit relational know-how is the intersubjective prereflective understanding that can occur between therapist and client; it is sloppy because there is no perfectly attuned know-how, and any connection or 'moment of meeting' is unpredictable.

John was a successful psychiatrist, good looking, charming and accomplished, but as I got to know him better I realised he felt the opposite about himself. He was profoundly insecure and lacked confidence. I worked with him face to face, and I got a sense that this was the right thing to do, but I was not quite sure why. I sensed a lack of mirroring in early childhood, and I got some feeling about the importance of being *seen* as well as being heard. His defence against any vulnerability, feelings of impotence and helplessness, seemed to be to sexualise his feelings. He seemed to be preoccupied by omnipotent fantasies of his prowess in bed. He used internet sex and he was preoccupied by how exhilarated he felt when online. I became aware that the sense I had of his needing to be *seen* could have an exhibitionist element, but somehow it felt different in the room, his confident fantasies most obviously existing in a virtual world. With me, he seemed to keep his sexuality at bay; I felt genuinely I was not being defended when I tuned in more to the little boy feelings underlying the bravado of the man. Then in one session a moment occurred; he went red, buried his head in his hands and looked downward. I felt as if I had attacked him, as one who had shamed him in public.

It has been observed (Lemma, 2006, 2014) that a return to a more symbiotic type of communication is activated in bodily countertransference communication between therapist and client. We might also say that therapists who have blurred boundary issues may be more likely to pick up bodily communications through their own bodies. However, it is also the case that traumatised clients who have difficulties in processing experiences are likely to communicate in this fashion.

However, diagnostic personality disorder labelling of clients with a history of sexual abuse has been questioned by many writers, including, among others, van der Kolk (1998), Herman (1992) and Valerio (1997, 2011). They have pointed out that so-called 'borderline features' parallel complex posttraumatic stress disorder symptoms, and indeed, such labelling only exacerbates an abused child's sense of being at fault or 'damaged goods'.

Working in a specialist NHS mental health children's service and later in setting up services for adults who were referred with truly heart-wrenching and disturbing histories of sexual abuse, I was often at a loss for words when witnessing their stories. I sometimes still reflect with horror and shame upon some of my earlier unprocessed and inexperienced interventions. I remember one astounding young woman, who eventually entered a long-term therapy programme, and who against all the odds had achieved some semblance of a life and relationships. She had been referred to me by her psychiatrist, and I saw her for an initial assessment. I had been warned she was prone to dissociating at times, but I was not prepared for this to happen moments after her arrival in the initial session! I had just had a sandwich in my office followed by an orange. Oranges are indeed the only fruit she could not bear. After her abuse in a sadistic paedophile group, she had been offered a segment of orange to share with her attackers. The smell of oranges in my office drew us both back 27 years to that shivering cold, dark room, where a 7-year-old girl lay naked, endlessly, upon the cold marble table. There are no words for that experience; if you listen you can still hear the silent screams.

In conclusion, we recognise that part of the curriculum for trainee psychotherapists and psychologists must include not only learning intellectually from the fields of neuroscience and infant research – important knowledge as this is – but also how to fine-tune our affective and subjective experiences in relation to our patients and clients when no words are possible, or when experiences are not remembered in words. In this chapter, we have explored the importance of working on the embodied liminal zone, the in-between, overlapping space where mutual enactment happens. However, this means we need to find a way to process and talk more openly with colleagues and peers about the inevitable restaging of experience that we will inevitably be drawn into and undergo with our patients. We are suggesting that these interactions are not to be seen as blunders to be overcome but as the 'sloppy' (Stern et al., 1998) or chaotic moments when we are also forced to resonate with the primitive; the banal; the senses, smells and colours; and the frightening or unknown in ourselves.

Bibliography

Bion, W. (1967). *Second Thoughts* (Maresfield Library Series). London, UK: Karnac Books.

Davies, J. M. (2004). Whose bad objects are we anyway? Repetition and our elusive love affair with evil. *Psychoanalytic Dialogues*, *14*(6), 711–732.

Diamond, N. (2002). Attachment and the body: A case of sexual abuse. In M. Cortina & M. Marrone (Eds.), *Attachment and the Psychoanalytic Process*. London, UK: Whurr.

Diamond, N. (2005). When thought is not enough. In J. Ryan (Ed.), *How Does Therapy Work?* London, UK: Karnac Books.

Diamond, N. (2013). *Between Skins: The Body in Psychoanalysis – Contemporary Developments*. Hoboken, NJ: John Wiley & Sons.

Diamond, N., & Marrone, M. (2003). *Attachment and Intersubjectivity*. London, UK: Whurr.

Fonagy, P. (1999). Guest editorial: Memory and therapeutic action. *International Journal of Psychoanalysis*, *80*, 215–221.

Fraiberg, S., Adelson, E., & Shapiro, V. (1976). Ghosts in the nursery. *Journal of the American Academy of Child and Adolescent Psychiatry*, *14*(3), 387–421.

Freud, S. (1910). The future prospects of psycho-analytic therapy. *S.E.*, *11*, 139–152.

Freud, S. (1920). Beyond the pleasure principle. *S.E.*

Freud, S. (1923). The ego and the id. *S.E.*

Heidegger, M. (1978). *Being and Time*. (J. Macquarrie & E. Robinson, Trans.) Oxford, UK: Blackwell Books.

Herman, J. (1992). *Trauma and Recovery*. New York, NY: Basic Books.

Lemma, A. (2006). *Introduction to Psychopathology*. New York, NY: Sage.

Lemma, A. (2014). *Minding the Body: The Body in Psychoanalysis and Beyond*. London, UK: Routledge.

Mollon, P. (2002). *Remembering Trauma: A Psychotherapist's Guide*. Hoboken, NJ: John Wiley & Sons.

Nahum, J. P. (2005). The 'something more' than interpretation revisited: Sloppiness and co-creativity in the psychoanalytic encounter. *Journal of the American Psychoanalytic Association*, *53*(3), 693–729.

Orbach, S. (1999). *The Impossibility of Sex*. New York, NY: Scribner.

Orbach, S. (2010). *Bodies*. Hampshire, UK: Picador.

Schore, A. (1994). *Dysregulation and Disorders of the Self*. New York, NY: John Wiley & Sons.

Schore, A. (2003). *Affect Regulation and Repair of the Self*. New York, NY: W. W. Norton.

Schore, A. (2010). *The Science of the Art of Psychotherapy*. New York, NY: W. W. Norton.

Smith, P. F. V. (1997). Secret friends: Borderline symptomology and post-traumatic stress disorder in a case of reported sexual abuse. *British Journal of Psychotherapy*, *14*(1), 1–135.

Stern, D. N., Sander, L. W., Nahum, J. P., Harrison, A. M., Lyons-Ruth, K., Morgan, A. C., Bruschweilerstern, N., & Tronick, Z. (1998). Non-interpretive mechanisms in psychoanalytic therapy: The 'something more' than interpretation. *International Journal of Psychoanalysis*, *79*(5), 903–921.

Stone, M. (2006). The analyst's body as tuning fork: Embodied resonance in counter-transference. *Journal of Analytical Psychology*, *51*(1), 109–124.

Symington, N. (1983). The analyst's act of Freedom as an agent of therapeutic change. *International Review of Psycho-Analysis*, *10*, 283–291.

Trevarthan, C. (1978). Secondary intersubjectivity: Confidence, confiding, and acts of meaning in the first year. In A. Lock (Ed.), *Action, Gesture and Symbol: The Emergence of Language*. Cambridge, MA: Academic Press.

Trevarthan, C. (1979). Communication and co-operation in early infancy: A description of primary intersubjectivity. In M. Bullara (Ed.), *Before Speech: The Beginning of Human Communication*. Cambridge, UK: Cambridge University Press.

Valerio, P. F. (2002). Love and hate: A fusion of opposites – A window to the soul. In D. Mann (Ed.), *Love and Hate: Psychoanalytic Perspectives* (pp. 253–266). London, UK: Routledge.

Valerio, P. F. (2005). Broken boundaries: Perverting the analytic frame. In M. Luca (Ed.), *The Therapeutic Frame* (pp. 116–127). London, UK: Taylor & Francis.

Valerio, P. F. (2006). Love and hate – a fusion of opposites: A window to the soul. In D. Mann (Ed.), *Love and Hate in the Transference* (pp. 253–266). London, UK: Routledge.

Valerio, P. & Lepper, G. (2009). Sorrow, shame, and self-esteem: Perception of self and others in groups for women survivors of child sexual abuse. *Psychoanalytic Psychotherapy*, 23(2), 136–153.

Valerio, P. & Lepper, G. (2010). Change and process in short- and long-term groups for survivors of sexual abuse. *Group Analysis*, 43(1), 21–49.

van der Kolk, B. A., McFarlane, A. C., & Weisaeth, L. (Eds.) (1999). *Trauma Stress: The Effects on Mind, Body, and Society*. New York, NY: Guildford Press.

Chapter 2

A therapist goes back to school

Therapeutic experience with three black boys at risk of exclusion

Onel Brooks

Introduction

This chapter consists of three accounts of my work in schools and how I am implicated in what unfolds in the consulting room. I begin, though, outside the room.

On a beautiful summer's day, I arrive at Brighton beach with a group of psychiatric patients. People and colour are everywhere, in the lovely light breeze, blowing, cooling and calming, providing invisible support to the birds hovering and frolicking above. Suddenly, Mary shouts, 'Look! Those black boys are beating up that white boy! You've got to do something!'

Casually and wordlessly I had seen the three boys referred to by Mary as 'black' grab the lad designated 'white'; it looked like a fight. I say, though, 'Ah, they're just a group of lads messing around!' 'No', she responded, 'they are hurting him. You've got to do something!'

The 'fight' continues: I am untroubled. 'Look!' Mary exclaims again, as two other running young men appear. 'Those two are joining in. You've got to do something!'

Mary is relentless. My confidence in my judgment is beginning to wane. The lads continue their fight; Mary continues her pressure on me. I begin to feel anxious and stupid for misjudging the situation. Suddenly, the lads stop 'fighting' and are clearly hugging. We can see that six young men are meeting up for a day at the seaside. It used to be called 'messing around', 'high spirits', and so on, and is not, as far as I know, illegal, or an official sign of psychopathology. Well, not yet anyway. Mary cannot believe it: 'I was sure that they were fighting!' she states.

Past experiences mean that Mary and I stand in different places on the beach, or maybe we are not even on the same beach. Our different histories of violence, experiences of groups of young men and of interactions between people regarded as being from different 'races' play their part in what we see. I grew up with black, Indian and white people; Mary seemed to have spent little time around people who are not white. I see from the perspective of having been a boy involved in 'play fighting' and competitive sports; sometimes tempers boil over and someone is hurt, but this is not what usually happens, and it is often both subtle and clear when things are getting or have gotten out of hand. These sorts of things are not learned formally in the classroom: You pick them up, get a feel for them. It is not easy to say how you know when to be worried, when something needs to be done, and when things are on the edge. I do not immediately assume that if a group of black and Indian or Pakistani lads rush up to a white lad, they clearly mean him harm. My experience is that 'mates' manhandle each other sometimes and no one gets hurt. A possibility that I am more open to than Mary is that they could be mates or friends. Mary experiences from a history of having been a girl in a home where there was serious violence, where things often got out of hand, and nobody did anything to stop it. She was not sporty, hardly went to school, so does not have experiences of teammates, competitiveness, high spirits, displays of aggression that do not lead to anyone being attacked and hurt.

This incident prompted me to reflect on a number of issues: First, the subtle or gross and always fallible distinctions most of us make much of the time, based on and part of our very quickly seeing something in one way rather than another, highlighting some aspects but backgrounding others; second, how much our seeing in a certain way and not another is related to our membership of particular groups and our history; and third, my beginning to doubt and argue with myself under pressure from Mary. These three issues are at least part of what I mean by *partiality*: First, our 'partiality' in the sense of our biases, prejudices, tendencies and histories on which our seeing in a particular way rest; second, our being partial in the sense of being a part of some groups of people who have shaped how we see and judge our not seeing for 'mankind', and third, our being partial in the sense that we are not whole, but divided or divisible, able to disagree with and disapprove of ourself, able to be divided against ourself (Saito, 2009).

'Observation' and the pure clinical gaze are sometimes emphasised in psychotherapy, and claims are made that a version of psychoanalysis is derived 'as directly as possible from clinical experience rather than abstract speculation' (Gomez, 1997, p. 46). Freud tells us that psychoanalysis is 'a science based on observation' (Freud, 1924, p. 37). Peter Gay (1995) tells us that Freud 1920 'must be read not as an exercise in autobiography, but as a turning point in theory' (p. 594). Here is a common rhetorical device, a recurring theme in psychotherapy too, a declaration of respectability or chastity, a denial that anything to do with pleasure or familiarity has gone on with the flesh-and-blood human being who writes or uses the theory. I am suspicious of such statements of epistemological purity, and those that 'doth protest too much'. Furthermore, does psychoanalysis not teach us to be suspicious of repeated claims to purity, sharp distinctions between autobiography and pure theory, and of being told that something must not be read in a certain way?

My experiences in secondary schools are bound up with and help to form my partiality. As a black man who has been a black boy in schools in London, and as someone who has worked with what used to be referred to as 'disadvantaged' people – working class and unemployed-class white adults and children, as well as black adults and children – I cannot present myself as someone who is impartial in this kind of work, as someone who practices pure observation and makes unbiased use of pure theory, uncontaminated by any biographical element. As someone who has perhaps overvalued formal education, I cannot present myself as unbothered by my awareness that being a working-class white boy, a black boy, or someone with special educational needs means that you are more likely to do badly in terms of educational attainment, to be excluded from school and left to fall into an underworld existence of poverty, unmet needs, gangs, crime, prison.

These three accounts of subtle, gross and always fallible distinctions, assumptions and actions in my therapeutic encounters reveal my partiality. Prior to our meeting, each boy was described as 'black', in danger of being excluded from school and I was asked to see each boy at his school.

Alan

Alan was a small 11-year-old. Violent and disruptive behaviour put him at risk of exclusion. My sense of being with a small boy increased when, at the beginning of the session, he produced two of his toys and began to play a game that I saw as the big toy chasing the small toy. I wondered about its significance. Alan said he did not know why he had been sent to see me, but told me, when asked about school, that he often got into fights with other boys at school and had conflicts with his teachers.

He sits in front of me, not speaking but noisily playing. I want to ask about his game but worry about inhibiting his play by doing this. It occurred to me too that I am a man, he is a small boy, and that my asking him a lot of questions could be seen and experienced as my chasing him around the room. However, what if he is trying to show me something that he cannot quite tell me right away, and I do not respond to it? In this way, I silently debated with myself as if I were two rather than one.

As he seems happy to play in this way, speaking sometimes about school, black hairstyles and culture, perhaps testing me, I decide to allow things to unfold. He soon voices interest in my hair, and reveals that he is growing his hair, but is not sure whether to grown an afro, to have it plaited in neat little rows or to let it grown wild like mine. (Black boys, and white ones too, have been excluded from schools in Britain for their hairstyle [Paton, 2013]. In some schools at various times, to have your hair plaited in neat little rows may lead to your being excluded, even though many Caribbean boys and men wear their hair in this way. Our conversation is not without significance.) He follows this by asking me where in the Caribbean I am from. I respond playfully, as I sometimes do with children: How do you know I am from the Caribbean? I could be from Africa. 'No', he replies confidently, 'I don't think you are from Africa. You might be, but I think you are from the Caribbean.

Am I right?' It seems to be important to tell him. He tells me immediately that his father is from the same Caribbean island. I suggest that this might be important. He agrees and continues playing his game with his two figures, saying no more about the similarities between his father and me or about hair and the Caribbean. I debate with myself, and decide not to pursue him on this but to wait to see what will develop.

Toward the end of the session I ask, looking at his toys, 'So what are they doing?' 'I don't know', he replies. So, giving myself permission to play with what his play could be, I suggest that it could be a big dinosaur chasing someone. His immediate response is, 'Oh, I never thought of that. It could be, but it is a monster chasing someone'. He goes on to tell me that the little one is afraid but is faster. He continues to play this game, but with a 'running commentary' now, as well as allowing the soundtrack of the playing to be more clearly heard, with its screeches, crashes and explosions. It seems obvious that the small figure could be him. Who is the monster? Dad? I decided to wait for him to indicate this. The monster keeps on chasing; the little one keeps on running. I do not chase or abandon by saying nothing at all.

At the beginning of our third session, no longer playing the monster chasing the little one, he looked directly at me, suddenly an older boy, and asked if I knew that his father used to beat him up. I asked him to tell me about this. He told me that his parents had separated, Dad wanted him and his little sister to live with him, and they were too afraid to say no, because Dad can get very angry when you try to say no to him. So they lived with Dad who used to beat Alan up, but not his sister. One day, however, he started to beat Alan's sister. Alan phoned the police. The police came, took Dad away, charged him and took him to court. Alan fell silent after telling me all this.

I said it sounded as if he had quite an awful time living with his father, that it must have taken quite a lot for him to phone the police, but it is really important that he did this. I said too, with some feeling to the small boy in front of me, that it is terrible for a grown man to beat up a child. He listened to my response looking at the floor. I added that he had done something brave and I wondered whether he might be afraid that his father may still be angry with him about this and may want to beat him up for it.

Alan denied this immediately, and claimed he was not afraid of his father, then he looked at the floor again and admitted that he was afraid that his father would get him. The only contact he had with Dad since then was a telephone conversation. Dad said that he was sorry for what he had done, and that Alan had done the right thing by calling the police. Alan said he was pleased that Dad said this to him, but that he still did not trust his father: Dad could be just saying that, but he could really be angry and want revenge. He had in fact seen his father on the street about three times, he revealed, but he made sure that his father did not see him, although he had watched his father. (The smaller figure is faster, I thought.)

As I thought I saw that his becoming more violent at school clearly coincided with his living with and being regularly beaten by his father, I said that I thought that if you have to get ready for and cope with violence at home, when you get to school you are more likely to be ready for violence and to try to protect yourself; and also, if someone is beating you up, you might find that you want to beat someone else up. Alan agreed to all of this and confirmed that his becoming more aggressive at school began when he went to live with his dad and his dad started to beat him up.

In one of the next sessions, Alan came in wearing a very distinctive cap, and although he had a lot to say about school, I found that I could not take my eyes off his cap. I wanted to ask him where he got it, as I had never seen one quite like it. Damn, I wanted one too! I rebuked myself severely. You call yourself an experienced professional? What are you doing? Why are you 'distracted' by his cap, attending to shallow sartorial matters rather than what this lad is saying to you?! Yet, in spite of my efforts to stay with what he was saying to me, and behaving as I had been taught to behave in my schools for psychotherapists, I heard someone say, 'That's a really nice cap. I have never seen one like that before'. As I heard the words and realised that that someone was me, I felt that I had done something rather stupid.

To my surprise, Alan beamed and the session was suddenly very alive. 'You can't buy them in this country', he pronounced proudly. 'You can only get them in the States'. Stirred up now by something I simply do not understand and do not feel in control of, I felt myself about to ask him when he was on holiday in the States, but another question came out as a statement. 'It's a present, isn't it?' (I felt that I just 'knew' this and the answer to my next question.) 'Yes!', he said in the same proud manner. 'Who gave it to you?' Everything changed about him, he looked at the floor and seemed quite puzzled and confused and said very quietly, 'My dad'. He was silent and remained looking at the floor. During this time I thought of a number of things I might ask about his thoughts and feelings to do with his father, but I thought he had already shown me that he was puzzled, confused and struggling with his feelings about his father. I had some sense too that I had somehow been caught up in something with him, being attracted by what I thought I should not be attracted by, feeling puzzled, confused and as if I had let myself down. Incidentally, once the cap had been spoken about, I lost all interest in it, which led me, eventually, to the thought that it would have been a mistake not to have commented on it, and brought into our conversation the distinctive object he sported like a flag during our session.

After a while I said rather quietly and slowly that it is very difficult when people who do bad things do nice things as well, and when people who do nice things do bad things. Alan agreed and was quiet for a while, then said that he had been thinking that he would like to see his father again, but he did not know if his father would beat him up again, he did not know whether he should trust him. I said that I understood that he might want to see his dad again and agreed that it is difficult to know if Dad should be trusted.

In the next session, he surprised me by announcing at the beginning of the session that he had seen his dad again. No, not just on the street. He had gone to his dad's house and knocked on the door. Dad, surprised and pleased to see him, welcomed him in, apologised repeatedly for how he had treated Alan and his sister, and claimed that he, Dad, was at fault, not Alan. Alan said it was good to see him again and that they had arranged to meet again the following weekend.

I was now worried about his not having told his mother. Suppose Dad hurts him, or worse? There would be many voices telling me that I am stupid and irresponsible, that I clearly do not know what I am doing, that it is a safeguarding matter that should have been reported. In this worry about what others may say or think about my actions, perhaps I was stepping back to look at myself as if I were one of the others. I was dramatising my concern. Rather than panic and try to persuade him to tell his mother and social services, or decide to do this myself because of the risk, I listened very carefully, worried silently and kept talking to him about how things were going with Dad, how Dad seemed, what it was like to be with him. Fortunately, later in supervision my supervisor kept calm.

After that session in which he told me, he told his sister. She too wanted to see Dad, so they went to see him together. So now I knew that two young children were meeting with a father who had been violent to both of them, and charged for this, but neither their mother nor social services had been informed. From what Alan said to me, though, there was no indication that they were in danger from their father. They eventually told their mother, who was surprised but not angry with them, as they feared she would be. Social services and the school were told. This caused a ripple in social services and the school. Someone from the school phoned me to make sure that I knew that Alan and his sister were going to see their father; I thanked her for letting me know. Nobody panicked or tried to stop them. I could breathe out now.

Slowly, I began to get the impression that Alan was looking after his father as well as his mother, that he was partly going to check if his father was alright, and that I was working with a neglected, unsupervised and underfed child, very poor, with parents who had been struggling for years. I heard what he had to say about 'unfairness' and 'racism' at school against this background, but tried to take each of his comments about racism as doorways into what he experienced, felt and thought, without thinking that the point was to try to know for sure whether it was or was not really about racism. Subtle hands and time are needed to get hold of the play of race and poverty and his sense of unfairness in all of this.

The school's family worker contacted me and told me that Alan's mother was 'white' and had a long-term drug problem; Alan's father had 'a mental health problem'. The parents were and continued to be at war with each other, unable to negotiate with each other or to come to any decisions about the care of their children. Alan, she told me, had been for years the most reliable and capable member of the family.

In the 2 years we worked together, he was in less trouble at school. His teachers were surprised and pleased that he was managing himself and situations much better. Alan began to talk to me about how angry he was with his parents, because, as he said, they cannot stop behaving like children and start being parents. They kept on trying to get him to choose between them, when he did not want to do this.

I was moved from that school: a kind of exclusion for me, subject as I am to management decisions. Through the professional involved with the family, I kept track of him. Although his parents collapsed and both had a period of being 'ill', he continued to keep himself and them going, as well as look after his little sister. He was excluded permanently at 15.

Bill

Bill was 13; a chatterbox, arguing with other pupils and his teachers, and fighting with other boys. The school suspected that he was being physically abused by his father. I met a lively boy, cheeky, quick witted, inquisitive and, he claimed, easily and often bored in class, who often finished his work long before anyone else in the class, and would eventually start a conversation with someone next to him. Bill said that he and his engineer father got on very well. They spent a lot of time together, tinkering with electronic equipment, making computers. Bill liked to take things apart to see how they work, then put them back together. He liked to fix things and wanted to be an engineer like his father. Bill said that on two occasions, after the school had been in contact with his father about Bill's behaviour, his father had lost his temper and slapped him once on the backside, whilst shouting at him about not hitting others.

Two occasions of being slapped once by an exasperated father who is present, attentive, supportive, engaged and otherwise loving did not seem to me to be a major cause for worry, and I found myself wary of the school's suspicion about his father, as if they might be encouraging me to focus my attention on his home life rather than school.

I asked him why he thought he was often in trouble at school. Bill said he thought that some of his problems came from the fact that he has always had a lot to say for himself (since he was a baby, he talked back); that he picks things up quickly, gets impatient and wants to go faster than his class is going, but sometimes it is school. You have to stand your ground, he said. He explained that if other boys 'cuss' you, you 'cuss' them back; if they hit you, you hit them back. This often escalated, leaving him in trouble. Sometimes, though, the teachers caused problems. The example he gave me was of his being called a Caribbean name by some of the boys in the class. He responded by calling them names. Perhaps what he related to me was not unlike the situation Mary and I faced on the beach: something that seemed like a fight but turned out to be playing at fighting, but might well have been something that looked like play fighting but turned out to be a real fight. Misjudging the subtle clues in front of her and trying to join in what might have seemed to be good-humoured banter, not understanding that she was witnessing a joust in which at any time participants may abandon the lance of the taunt for hacking each other to death in the mud, a young teacher then called him the name the other boys were calling him. He became very angry with the teacher, who did not understand why he would react like this to her but not to the other boys. He found himself in trouble for his reaction, although he insisted that she should not have called him names, especially as she did not know what the term meant. Although it seemed as if his rage had been disproportionate, displacing what belonged to the other boys on to this young and new teacher, and she might have been repeating the term to him because she did not know what it meant, I thought he made a good case to the effect that he should not have been in so much trouble and the situation should have been handled differently.

Did his constant talking and need to be active in fact hide worry, sadness, something more depressed? Maybe. Of course I worried about this. But he seemed to be a young man who enjoyed and was interested in a lot of things, and had a lot to say. As I sat with him, I did not feel that I was with a depressed boy who was hiding this by constantly getting into trouble and doing. Did his need to challenge, talk back, stand his ground and protest about being treated unfairly indicate that he was 'touchy' or 'a bit paranoid'? I did not think so: He was direct, and often he did not really think about the consequences of what he was saying and doing. As we met each week, I heard from him and from the school that there were fewer incidents and less serious ones. Mindful of the fact that I did not have very long with him, I spoke to him about how he might further improve things at school. One of my suggestions was that he took the book he happened to be reading – he was a relentless reader who was always keen to discuss books – to school with him, and when he finished his work, he could read that rather than talk to anyone. He liked this simple and practical idea, did it, and stopped talking in class. I was accused by some of the teachers of being a magician.

In our final session, he asked, looking incredulous, 'Is this what you do then? I mean is this your job? Do you get paid for talking to people about their problems?' I said, 'Yes; and do you think that I shouldn't be paid for it?' His response was that he did not know. Then he said, 'I could do this! It's not like a real job!' exhibiting his typically challenging and provocative responses. I imagine that this sort of exchange often landed him in trouble. However, I thought hearing it as just 'cheek' might be a way of missing something; I heard something else also. 'What's a "real job?"', I asked. 'When you make or fix something', he came back at me. 'Something like what your father does?' 'Yes!' I paused for a while and said that it was hard to see what is 'made' or 'fixed' here, but maybe there is something. Responding to his claim that he could do this job, I said 'You could!' and asked 'Do you think you might like to?'

His response was to say that he thinks he might like to be a counsellor too. Before he had always thought that he would be an engineer, like his father, but he could be a counsellor. I said that he could do what his dad does, he could do what I do, and actually he could do something else.

Has his brief therapeutic relationship with another black man opened up a number of possibilities for him? How important is race here, or is it gender, or just the relationship? Was he trying to pay me a compliment in what sounded as if he was rubbishing what I was doing? Perhaps too there was something about saying goodbye and missing me. Perhaps to feel able to do what I do is a way of keeping hold of something that he had come to value, even though he could not take it apart to see clearly how it works.

Collin

Collin, a strong athletic 15-year-old, was said by his referrer to be 'a character'. I met a quiet, thoughtful, self-confident adolescent, who I could not help being immediately fond of, but I could not see what the problem was.

He said he likes arguments, hopes to study law or philosophy at university, reads much more than the set texts and often found himself arguing about how ideas are being spoken about. Nearly all the arguments with teachers were about ideas, concepts or explanations. Most of the teachers liked this and found it useful to have an interested, prepared and engaged pupil in class, behaving more like a keen undergraduate than a reluctant pupil in a tough school in a rough part of town. The problem, he claimed, was the racism of one teacher.

I was unable to understand why Collin would be at risk of exclusion or demotion from the top set. The teacher Collin called racist claimed that Collin had an aggressive attitude and behavioural difficulties. I saw no signs of this and began to worry about my own judgment. Am I too identified with him?

As soon as I arrived in school the following week, a teacher came to talk to me about an incident with one of the boys at the school, and after that he mentioned Collin. He had witnessed a disturbing exchange between Collin and the teacher that Collin has so much trouble with. This teacher, T, screamed aggressively at Collin, charged up to Collin, so they were nose to nose, then repeated the order he had given the boy. The teacher speaking to me was clear that his colleague had been the aggressive one in this situation. Collin had been remarkable: he had not returned the aggression, by shouting or posturing, but had calmly and confidently explained why he could not take part in the after-school event, as he was being ordered to, when something like this should have been his choice. The teacher speaking to me said he left the situation because he was late for something, but wanted to speak to his colleague. A little later he entered the staff room to find teacher T giving the other teachers a version of his encounter with Collin in which it was Collin who was angry and threatening. The teacher speaking to me said he did not know what to do, as this bore no resemblance to what he had witnessed. He later learned that T had phoned Collin's mother to pass on the false version of the incident and was talking, again, about having the boy excluded from the school. The teacher speaking to me said he did not know what to do, as T is a very powerful teacher in the school, and it is not wise to cross him.

When I saw Collin an hour later, he was furious and gave me the same story. He had not allowed himself to be provoked or bullied by this teacher, but became furious when he realised that the teacher had phoned his mother and lied about what had happened. Now his mother was upset, more worried about his education and not sure if her son lies to her. It was his word against the teacher's. Everyone knows that in this situation, the teacher wins. Collin was so angry that he wanted to go and thump the teacher. Pleased that he came to his session with me to tell me this, and was not wandering around the school looking for the teacher, I pointed out that if he is right about what the teacher wants, then hitting the teacher is a way to make sure that the teacher wins. I said we needed to think together about what to do.

However, I had no idea what to do. He seemed to have no ideas either. Silence. Out of the blue, I asked him what his father does for a living. He told me in a matter-of-fact way that his father had legal training and had worked in a number of fields. Almost as an afterthought, he mentioned education. 'Education? Have you spoken to him at all about the situation at school?' 'No.' 'Well why not?' I asked. 'If he has held important posts in education and knows the law, he would have a better idea than me or you about what might be the best thing to do now.' Collin looked at me: 'Do you think so?' I imagined supervisors and colleagues rolling their eyes with irritation, telling me that I am 'in the wrong place', that I should be concerned with his internal world or the unconscious meaning of his communications, that due to who I am, I am too caught up with my client and race. And yet, I certainly thought he should speak to his father about it, and I told him so.

Slowly, the father who had been in the background moved into the light, and I began to see a man who had held quite senior posts in a number of fields. Perhaps in response to my remark about how well his father has done and how little Collin had said about him, Collin remarked, 'Oh, didn't I tell you? My father is white'. Dad had invited Collin to come and live with him. A number of things fell into place for me at this point, and Collin readily agreed when I suggested that all this was very important, and that he had all sorts of feelings about Dad's offer. (Why did I think that I knew this? Why did I express this to him rather than wait for him to tell me about his feelings about his father? I had a sense of being in a hurry, of our both needing to get on with it.) What came out quickly and easily, perhaps because of my directness at this point, and because I suddenly felt that I understood something based on what he had already said about his relationship with his mother, was his concerns about disloyalty to his black mother (leaving her all alone when she has tried so hard to bring him up by herself), leaving his friends and his area in London to begin a new life in a place where there are few black people, and joining a family in which everyone else would be white. He readily agreed and elaborated on each of the points I made, seeming as if he was articulating them clearly for the first time. Although I flagged these things as important for us to talk about, I expressed the view that contacting his father was his priority. It is unusual for me to know so much and be so directive. He left saying that he would contact his dad right away.

Collin was beaming when I saw him the following week. Dad's response had been supportive, clear and immediate. He had phoned Collin to reassure him that he would sort it out, then he had phoned the Headmaster and written officially to the school, threatening to visit the very next day. His view, expressed to Collin and to the school, was that this sort of thing happens too often to black boys, and that they were not going to do this to his son. The school certainly knew of Dad, but seemed to have no idea that he was Collin's father; they were suddenly afraid and did not want him to visit. The Headmaster suddenly found himself confronted by a powerful white man, legally astute and knowledgeable about education, politically well connected, and making it clear that if they persisted in harassing his boy then they would be tangling with him. The school could not backtrack fast enough. Collin was summoned to the Headmaster's room and told clearly and definitely that of course they were never going to exclude or demote him, as he is an excellent pupil. The school insisted that Collin misunderstood: The whole matter had been a misunderstanding. There was never any question of this happening. Laughing at the idea that this was just his misunderstanding, rather than expressing anger at more lies, Collin said he did not really care how they tried to wriggle out of it, as long as it was clear that he was not going to be demoted or excluded and that he could get on with his education. It is hard not to wonder what he learned from this incident.

He was, he said, very grateful, not only for my encouraging him to get his father involved but also for some of the other things we spoke about, such as his relationship with his mother and his loyalty to her, his friends and the part of London he grew up in. He had clearly been thinking about this. He told me that his father repeated his offer: his wanting Collin to come and live with him, whilst he finishes his education. Dad said he would be able to keep a closer eye on him and help to see him through it. Collin was clearly pleased that Dad had said this again; he wanted to go and live with Dad, but he still had a lot to sort out about guilt and loyalty before he could do this. We spent the rest of our time together speaking about these issues.

Discussion

In the accounts above, it is perhaps easy to see that both my literal return to school, and my return in my thoughts to my returning to school for the purpose of writing this chapter, facilitated a return to school in terms of reflection on what I am doing in the consulting room, what I have been taught, about concepts, ideas, practices and writings, as well as the sorts of considerations referred to in the introduction to this chapter as my 'partiality'. In this way, if we are fortunate and do not habitually assume that the world must be as we see it, all our work with clients may serve as doorways that lead us back to our schooling as practitioners, which includes the life we have lived up till now, our everyday lessons as well as the more formal ones. As I have stated above, these accounts of my work indicate how what happens in the consulting room partially rests on me, my words, tendencies, intuitions, thoughts. I cannot claim to be an objective observer of phenomena I partly create, and what I tend to create owes much to what I am here referring to as 'my schooling'. I have just stated that literally going back into schools inspired me to reflect and write this chapter, and that each client we see might invite us to reflect on our schooling. Another path that often leads me back to school is my encounters with the unique work of some psychoanalysts and philosophers, who, as I hear and read them, often provoke me and remind me of much that seems to be related to my task as a psychotherapist.

These three accounts can be rewritten making more explicit and laboured use of terms such as *identification, transference, countertransference, projection* and *projective identification,* and it might be thought that more explicit and extensive use of psychoanalytic terms, for example, would improve this attempt to write about my work as a psychotherapist. Is it not obvious, for instance, that what I have to say about 'partiality', as my discussions with myself, my capacity to turn against or reflect on myself, could be redescribed or explained in terms of there being different parts of me, different forces, or agencies in my psychic apparatus, or different identifications? It could be said to be partly identified with each of these boys, with their parents, with the teachers in the schools and with the psychotherapeutic groups and schools who taught me that doing what they do is a good thing, and I may face exclusion in one form or another, if I do not follow the rules or fall foul of someone in a position of power. This could be said to be about my 'superego'. The reader who is familiar enough with psychoanalytic concepts and ways of working will see psychoanalysis in these accounts, and he or she will be right; for psychoanalysis is useful and important to me, but it is not my intention here to insist on my place in this school, and to show this explicitly and conclusively. It is important, to me at least, that the psychoanalysts I am fondest of were not people who fitted easily into the rules of the existing schools, who allowed what they had been taught in school to come between them and phenomena: I mean Freud, Sandor Ferencz, Donald Winnicott, Charles Rycroft, R.D. Laing and Peter Lomas. Fitting well into a school, being a good pupil or disciple, may not sit so easily with trying to think for ourselves, or to allow that there might be other things in heaven and earth than are dreamt of in our system.

In Nietzsche's work there are warnings about our tendency to bring our education 'in between' as if this education is a 'secure measure and criterion

of all things', and a hope that we might be educated enough to think little of our education, 'indeed to despise it'. This, he tells us, will allow us to
abandon ourselves to where the author (we might add 'or speaker') leads us,
'exactly from not knowing' (Nietzsche, 2004/1872, pp. 19–20). I read this as
a warning about bringing my education in between me and my client, and as
a challenge to become educated enough to think little of what I can claim to
know. When Heidegger makes a distinction between the 'thirst for knowledge and *greed* for explanations' on the one hand, and on the other, 'the will to
abide in hope before what is worthy of thought' (Heidegger, 1982, p. 13), I
read this as a lesson about being too interested in explanations and knowing in
psychotherapy, as opposed to being willing to try to stay with what is. I read
Bion's 1967 'Notes on Memory and Desire' (Bion, 1988) in a similar way.
These potential lessons about the task of therapy, encouraging staying with
rather than trying to run on ahead by means of what we think we know, are
also similar to Freud's teachings in his 1912 recommendations. In what I have
written about my work, I try to stay with the particular, I do not try to go
much beyond the unique encounters with these three boys to generalisations
about schools, race, racism and black boys. Wittgenstein equates the 'craving
for generality' with 'the contemptuous attitude towards the particular case'.
This craving for generalities or contempt for the particular, he warns us, leads
to 'complete darkness'. He continues, 'I want to say here that it can never be
our job to reduce anything to anything, or to explain anything. Philosophy
really *is* "purely descriptive"' (Wittgenstein, 1980, p. 18). I am wary of trying
to reduce one thing to something else, to present myself as giving explanations rather than redescriptions.

However, being concerned to give a flavour of each individual encounter
with each boy, to emphasise uniqueness and be wary of generalisations, does
not mean that similarities and issues in common can not be acknowledged
and thought about.

Here are three concluding remarks. First, in the past, following Winnicott's,
'There is no such thing as a baby' (Winnicott, 1992, p. 99), I have argued that
there is no such thing as a black boy. For when we encounter a black boy, we
are also encountering and have to make room in our thinking for his relationships in his family, with his peers, his school and the wider society of which he
is a part. I worry now, though, that this may be a mistake. It might be better
to say that we usually make use of the convenient fictions of race, as if 'black'
and 'white' are straightforward, objective ways of saying how the world is,
rather than at least potentially problematic terms and political. We do generalise, but we need to watch our 'craving' for generalisations and 'explanations'.

Second, it should be obvious from the above that when I work in a school
I try to leave my door open to the school, in that I present myself as someone
who wants to hear what concerns the school has, what is being said, what has
happened. It is important for both pupils and adults in the school to have the

experience of someone listening and responding to their anxieties. It is not usually difficult to make it clear to the school that although you are willing to hear what others have to say, you cannot actually say much about the content of your sessions. In the examples above, I keep in mind the concerns voiced by representatives of the school. I am partial toward my client and careful about the contents of the sessions, but our conversation is at least partially porous to the concerns being expressed outside of the room.

Third, it should be obvious that for all three of the boys discussed above, his relationship with his father is very important. Alan struggled with becoming the sort of man who dished out beatings and might find himself in trouble with the law for this. Bill clearly identified with his engineer father, and, I feared, in becoming frustrated and slapping his son, his father was reinforcing rather than helping to loosen Bill's tendency to become frustrated and hit people. As for Collin, one of the things about him that seems to be implicated in his reputation as 'a bit of a character', had, it seemed to me, from a position that I have acknowledged is 'partial', much to do with his being seen as a 'black', working-class boy in a rough school, but his being strongly identified with a very successful and confident white father. Identifying with your father can be experienced as transgressive and strange, particularly if your behaviour is regarded as dissonant with your race, class and school.

I wish to end this chapter with three invitations rather than questions. First, I invite the reader to think about the claim that there is somewhere outside of or other than 'partiality' from where we might see, and to try to elaborate on this. Second, I would like the reader to think about how race and culture, a sense of things being unfair, as well as poverty and class, are at work in these three accounts as matters that need thought, but what would be lost or left out if we focused only on one or all of these terms. Third, I would like the reader to think about where I might have overstated the case or been too accepting of what was said to me or not critical enough of the thoughts I found myself with. If this reader finds him- or herself wanting to say that this is an indication of my 'partiality', in the sense of where I am coming from, my 'schooling', I would like the reader to think of how his or her own views, including views about where this chapter could do better, might be related to his or her own 'partiality'.

Bibliography

Bion, W. (1988). Notes on memory and desire. In E. Bott Spillius (Ed.), *Melanie Klein Today, Volume 2*. London, UK: Routledge.

Freud, S. (1912). Recommendations for physicians on the psycho-analytic method of treatment. *Collected Papers, Volume 11*, 323–333.

Freud, S. (1924). An autobiographical study. In P. Gay (Ed.), *The Freud Reader* (pp. 3–41). London, UK: Vintage.

Gay, P. (1995). *The Freud Reader*. London, UK: Vintage.

Gomez, L. (1997). *An Introduction to Object Relations*. London, UK: Free Association Books.

Heidegger, M. (1982). *A Dialogue on Language*. San Francisco, CA: Harper & Row.

Nietzsche, F. (2004/1872). *On the Future of Our Educational Institutions*. South Bend, IN: St Augustine's Press.

Paton, G. (2013). 'School expelling too many ethnic minority boys', *The Telegraph*, 21 March.

Saito, N. (2009). Ourselves in translation: Stanley Cavell and philosophy as autobiography. *Journal of Philosophy of Education*, 43(2), 253–267.

Winnicott, D. W. (1992). *Through Paediatrics to Psychoanalysis*. London, UK: Karnac Books.

Wittgenstein, L. (1980). *The Blue and Brown Books*. Oxford, UK: Basil Blackwell.

Chapter 3

A case of missing identity

Working with disassociation and 'multiple selves' in the countertransference

Mario Marrone and Nicola Diamond

Introduction

In the course of a seminar one of us facilitated some years ago, a student told us a joke. A patient arrives to a psychotherapist's consulting room for an initial consultation and says, 'Doctor, before I sit and start my first session with you, I need to know if you have experience and expertise in the sort of problem I have. I feel internally divided. I feel as if I am two persons living in the same body'.

The therapist replies, 'Yes, of course. Sit down and let's have a conversation between the four of us'.

In response, the seminar leader said, 'Maybe we can modify the joke':

A patient says, 'Doctor, before I sit and start my first session with you, I need to know if you have experience and expertise in the sort of problem I have. I feel internally divided into multiple bits. I feel as if I am many persons living in the same body'.

The therapist replies, 'Yes, of course. Sit down and let's have a group therapy session'.

This joke may be a metaphor for pathological dissociation, that is to say, the experience of feeling internally fragmented. However, paradoxically, there is another possible interpretation of this joke.

Every day we all have to reconcile and integrate different thoughts and feelings, which often coexist in contradiction or dissonance with each other. Decision-making processes are the result of such reconciliation and integration. The development of creative thinking and psychological insight are facilitated by 'hearing different voices'. Group therapy and teamwork depend on allowing and using free expression of different voices. Our own personal identity is composed of multiple aspects, based on different sources of identification. Similarly, our internal working models have different sources, and they coalesce in different ways in different individuals according to their early attachment experiences.

However, there is a sharp contrast between using internal voices as a source of reflective thinking, on the one hand, and the manifestation of pathological dissociation, on the other. We can call the first *associative multiplicity* and the latter *dissociative multiplicity*. The latter expresses itself in a variety of forms, such as dissociative amnesia, dissociative fugues, dissociative identity disorders and many other manifestations, described or not as *dissociative pathology* by the psychiatric nomenclature. In our clinical experience, dissociation stems out of traumatic events in childhood attachment relationships, associated with a lack of reflective dialogue. Reflective dialogue is what happens in families able to share knowledge of attachment-relevant events and explore them in a thinking manner.

The therapist's ability to deal with countertransference feeling in response to dissociative multiplicity depends to a large extent on his or her ability to engage in associative multiplicity. Before we venture deeper into this idea, we refer to a clinical example.

Louise

The patient we would call 'Louise' for reasons of confidentiality was referred to one of us following an unsuccessful therapy with another practitioner. Louise, at the age of 40, was wondering if she had early Alzheimer's because of the recurrence of episodes of dissociative fugues and amnesia. A typical situation would be that she would take a train to a distant city, travelling in a state of confusion. Once in her destination, she would not remember anything about the preceding hours: how she got there and what was she doing there.

She had a traumatic attachment history. Her mother was a narcissistic woman who was self-involved and preoccupied. As a mother she was emotionally distant and neglectful. She grew up in Australia, in her father's large farm. Her father was in charge of planting and harvesting the fields and, of course, raising pigs and cows. With his profits, he kept upgrading and expanding his farm. He was an angry man, frequently aggressive, at times violent. She thinks that her father bullied his employees in the farm. She suspected that he killed employees he had in the farm and buried them, as she noticed that some workers often disappeared without leaving any trace.

Her father was also a gun collector. He used to repeatedly sexually abuse her and threaten her that he would fire one of the rifles at her if she ever disclosed their sexual activities to other people. Furthermore, as one would expect in such a family, there was no open communication, no sharing of information or reflective dialogue. She felt that her perception of real events in the family and the farm were disconfirmed by her parents and her emotional responses invalidated. She ended up doubting her own perceptions. In one session she confided: 'If I saw clotted human blood on the floor and my parents said that it was spilled chocolate, I would end up believing that it was spilled chocolate'.

In adolescence, Louise was severely disturbed and had to be admitted to a psychiatric unit and later sent to a mental health halfway house. She engaged in self-harm and also committed acts of arson. During that period, she had psychotherapy with a hospital psychiatrist with whom she established a good enough therapeutic alliance and who seemingly helped her. At the age of 19 she had become a prostitute and lived in a brothel in Sydney. She said, 'What I liked about the brothel was that we all belonged to an underculture: Since birth I belong to an underculture'.

In her early twenties, in the brothel, she and a regular client, an English man, fell in love with each other. He proposed marriage and brought her to live with him in London. Soon after her arrival, she started therapy, had twin children and began training as a psychiatric nurse and, concomitantly, as a Suzuki violin teacher. Her life reached a certain degree of stability. However, she started showing multiple symptoms of dissociation. Further, she could only enjoy sex with her husband if he tied her up in bed and simulated a rape. She believed in the goodness of being a submissive spouse and opened an Internet site to promote her ideas. She dedicated a great deal of time to looking after her children, but was seriously lacking in confidence in relation to her maternal skills. Professionally, she felt torn between different professional interests. She wanted to work as a nurse and a music teacher, and she was even exploring the possibility of applying to a psychotherapy training course (although she was aware that her chances of being accepted were slim).

At one time, she was having four individual sessions a week. One day she came to a session in a very good mood. She told her therapist that she was very happy because one of her neighbours, a musician at a London-based symphony orchestra, was having a party with well-known London-based classical musicians and had invited her and her husband. As the session went on, at a certain stage in the session, her general verbal and nonverbal communications sharply and dramatically changed. She then suddenly said, 'I have brought something with me'.

She suddenly opened her handbag and produced a large kitchen knife. Then she said, 'You know what? I came to kill you!'

The therapist was shocked and terrified but said, 'You want me to feel empathy towards your plight as a child! You want me to feel the same fear you felt when your father was pointing his rifle at you!'

In response, she opened her hand and let the knife drop on the floor.

The therapist took the knife and said, 'I am going to put it in an A4 envelope and keep it to discuss this issue in future sessions'.

Now we can understand that her acting out was the result of a dissociative reaction, partially based on identification with the aggressor, partially based – as the therapist said – on her wish to evoke empathy.

She was extremely upset, and, as the therapist had another patient to see, the therapist suggested she could stay in the waiting room until she felt ready to drive. So she did.

A few hours later, the therapist received an email from Louise, saying, 'I apologise for not having been able to attend our session today'.

Obviously, the revival of pain she experienced was of such intensity that she needed to shut it off from consciousness by using dissociative amnesia.

During the analysis of this patient the therapist developed the concept of 'representational constellation'. What does it mean? It means that internal working models with their associated emotions and episodic memories may remain dormant in a person's life, yet be reactivated by current triggers, or intimate situations with a therapist, in one way or another.

If we carefully read Bowlby's trilogy *Attachment and Loss*, we will see that he uses a control system model to understand psychic functioning. This model can also be described in terms of cybernetics. It refers to the way in which systems and subsystems (both in biological and psychological terms) can be activated and deactivated in response to interpersonal triggers. Internally, we have many representational constellations that coexist, often in a dormant, subliminal or unconscious way. Each system can be reactivated in particular circumstances, like computer programmes at the click of the mouse.

For instance, when Louise had a dissociative fugue, it was unconsciously triggered by a present-day event that reactivated representational constellations of early traumatic events. This involved an unconscious set of defence mechanisms and strategies to deal with pain.

Dissociation and its various manifestations reflect the way representational constellations operate as cybernetic units and mainly at an unconscious level. The therapist's response largely depends on his or her capacity to have a wide repertoire of potential responses. This, in turn, depends on the therapist's capacity for what we call *associative multiplicity*. This is a term we borrow from John Southgate (personal communication).

When Louise came back to hold her next session, the therapist showed her the knife and a printout of her email. She recognised the knife and email as hers, but did not remember how they reached the therapist. However, gradually, in the course of the following sessions, she gradually began to remember some traumatic episodes of her childhood and adolescence, together with their associated emotions. She not only remembered and reexperienced traumatic scenes of her childhood and adolescence but also developed the capacity to tolerate painful emotions associated with those scenes. She gained a good understanding of her family dysfunctionality, and was able to make meaningful links between past and present experiences in her life.

As her therapy progressed she began to play with the idea of travelling to Australia and visiting the farm where she lived and was abused by her father. When she finally made the decision to go ahead with her plan, the therapist asked her if she would like to videotape the place so that that they could both watch it together on her return to London. Eventually she carried out her plan. When she and her therapist watched the video together in the consulting room, she was able to remember the abuse without needing to use dissociative mechanisms to shut off her feelings. A couple years later she, her husband and her twin children went to live in Australia.

Some theoretical considerations

The way a patient acts in the context of a therapeutic relationship is the result of complex mechanisms. Firstly, it is the result of transference phenomena. Transference has been interpreted in different ways by different schools of psychoanalysis. In terms of attachment theory, transference is the result of the operations of internal working models whereby the patient expects to be treated by his analyst (or other group members in group therapy) as he was treated by his attachment figures in childhood and adolescence. Secondly, it is the result of unconscious identification with early attachment figures: The patient treats the analyst (or other group members in group therapy) as he or she was treated.

The coexistence of various internal working models and identification systems leads to multiplicity. The greater the degree of insecure attachment and trauma in childhood and adolescence, the greater the dissociative mechanisms at play will be.

A therapist who is duly acquainted with these processes will be in a better position to identify and effectively deal with multiplicity. This involves a theoretical understanding of attachment trauma, internal working models and related issues. Furthermore, adequate work on him/her would be necessary.

Increasingly, in attachment theory, it is being recognised that the body plays a crucial role in the transference, because what occurs is a reenactment whereby the person automatically and without reflective awareness acts out the unresolved memory and experience with their body. Complex processes take place, whereby dissociation becomes the result of both a developmental failure due to early traumatic experiences and a defence against pain. Defence mechanisms at play include dissociation and identification with the aggressor. Louise became the father with the gun (knife) and acted out the painful and terrifying scene again in reverse roles, the therapist becoming her as the victim. In Louise's case there is a complete dissociation, the memory of her enactment is deleted; her defence is the most extreme, not involving denial or repression, but complete cutting off, an ejection of experience. In the case of 'multiple dissociation', she presents different 'part-selves'. Louise does present with an extreme disassociation because there is no central self. The different fragmented part-selves remain dispersed and unintegrated. The bringing together of the evidence of the email and the knife helps us to revisit and begin the arduous task of making relational links for the first time.

The fact that Louise was affectively engaged with the therapist and trust had been built allowed for the connective process to begin; the therapist was the empathetic parent to the vulnerable child in Louise that she had never had, who recognised her plight as a child with the father. In the countertransference, the therapist did not react defensively or with aggression as her father had done.

Internal working models are not merely mental representations but are also part of procedural bodily based memory laid down as part of our deepest infant and childhood recording of the lived interaction with our attachment figures.

The memory is not just recalled; it is reenacted. This enactment involves movement – the muscles and the limbs. It activates the neural and nervous system. For a reworking of the internal working model, this embodied enactment is necessary in order to get to the more profound bodily held experience that is part of the memory, which is not consciously accessed at all.

We now know there are two kinds of related memories: declarative, which has more conscious access, and has the capacity of remembering facts and logical thinking; and procedural memory, which is action-based, 'doing'-bodily memory, and is prereflective, similar to learning to ride a bike without consciously thinking, or typing, playing a musical instrument or dancing. Procedural memory characterises the internal working model of the lived self with attachment figure, the memory of enacted interactions. Schore (1994) argued that bodily memories have to be accessed and reworked in reenactments for real change to take place in thinking and experiencing.

Episodic and semantic memory that Bowlby refers to had been aligned to declarative, more consciously accessible and conscious memory, but later thinking is recognising the way procedural internal working models are where the more profound level of prereflective, nonconscious experience is rooted. Where Louise is concerned, it is the procedural mode of memory (that is only recovered through enactment) that is so central and important to work with. Bowlby explained (1988) how the person could access an episodic memory in analysis. For example, the adult may remember how, as a child, his parents had been arguing and he had overheard them. Bowlby would encourage the patient to talk about this memory and describe what he could recall. The patient could reply 'I remember mother said "she was leaving for good"'. For Bowlby, a memory like this would be experienced as threatening for the child, as in the child's experience it could mean abandonment and loss of his or her key attachment figure. The semantic memory, however, could be entirely in contrast, the semantic memory being what the parents tell the child the reality is, even though it is a hiding of the true experience for the child. In this case, the parents may say 'We were just having a lively conversation; no physical row took place'; so the child may start to disbelieve what they truly know (see Bowlby, 1988, chapter 6: 'On knowing what you are not supposed to know and feeling what you are not supposed to feel').

Such is the case for Louise, who started to believe dry blood was in fact spilt chocolate, or that her father never abused her. However, in Louise's case, the trauma was so great and the parents so disorganised in their dysfunctionality that dissociation became the key mode. The semantic memory was so powerful that it negated any awareness of her actual experience. Only later the episodic memory of her father and his actions could be recalled in therapy, and it was only at the deeper mode of enactment at a procedural level in a state of dissociation that the reworking and working through could begin. In the context of the therapist's embodied countertransference, the therapist who had a knife pointing at him resisted responding with fear and terror.

The difficulty of working with the embodied countertransference is that the line is so thin between reacting defensively or with insight. The analyst only has a split second to decide what to do, and this is therefore largely unconscious for the analyst also. It would have been so easy for the therapist to have reacted with self-preservation and feel aggressed by Louise, who was pointing the knife. Yet, instead, the therapist retained a sensitively attuned responsiveness and offered an insightful interpretation that captured Louise's experience as a child. The only way the therapist managed this situation was by accumulating an attachment understanding of Louise's history over many sessions and staying in touch with this in the moment of reenactment with the knife. This understanding had been thoroughly integrated, so any spontaneous response was immediately accompanied with reflective understanding of Louise's plight.

When Louise points the knife she is immersed in the act and is in the 'doing' prereflectively; this is her transference enactment, to tell the therapist what it feels like in the only way she knows how because she cannot reflect on the unthinkable. For Louise, her act is more than unconscious, due to her dissociation; the act is not registered or stored in her autobiographical memory. It is the role of the analyst to take up the embodied countertransference and bring what Bion (1962) referred to as *beta elements* into contact with alpha processing. The therapist links the bodily experience (beta elements) that she picks up with thoughtful reflection (alpha function) and this is a step toward greater integration. Neurobiologically, the brainstem, rooted in bodily states, is linked with the prefrontal cortex, and the analyst has access to cortical processing to provide insight into his response. This lays the foundations for Louise to eventually have the possibility of integrating these different levels of cortical and subcortical functioning together.

With patients who 'multiply dissociate', making links in experience is very difficult, because there is no coherent autobiographical memory of the self to tap into or build upon; the importance of the analyst as a witness, who is on the side of the damaged 'multiple selves', cannot be overemphasised, nor the importance of the analyst offering a corrective style of empathic parenting. With 'multiple disassociation', the creation of a 'coherent self' is something that gets cocreated and constructed through the dialogue with the analyst. This can take many years. It is created by the analyst keeping in mind the many 'multiple selves' that are in play, something in the analysand that is 'multiply disassociated'. As part of this process, the analyst is linking experience and memory, with the attachment history and childhood trauma, consistently keeping the links together in mind and body, when the analysand cannot.

As a way of creating relational links, contextualising the analysand's experience, it is necessary to create tangible ways of establishing orientation, hence the re-print of the email, the show of the knife in the analytic session, the encouragement of Louise to take videos of the farm house in Australia (where the traumatising events took place), and to bring these to the therapy sessions, to help ground the experience in concrete events that are shared and hence witnessed by another. When experience has been systematically negated by the parents, resulting in annihilating any possibility of a self, when blood is called chocolate, when hate and destruction is called life and love, and so on, when reality is so eschewed and any validation of experience is made impossible, then to ground experience in concrete ways through reconstruction with the analyst is vital. The analyst can be the witness in this locating of the experience, a shared reality and truth can then be established and sustained. This is all necessary for the analytic process of reworking the unbearable trauma into a more bearable experience which is this time based on truth and an integral relationship.

As a general rule, from an attachment perspective, contextualisation (not de-contextualisation) is an absolute requirement for therapeutic technique and practice (Diamond & Marrone, 2003). This is where the attachment approach radically differs from a traditional psychoanalytic orientation which is influenced by the Kleinian orthodoxy. Let us give an example to illustrate this point.

Marsha, who was in analysis, remembered when her analyst said to her 'you have an internal persecutor inside you'. Marsha felt somewhat persecuted by the analyst's statement, she felt bad as it seemed to her it was her fault. Even if not consciously so, she believed she was the origin and creator of the problem. This is what she thought the analyst implied. She felt stuck, helpless and lost, since she could not stop feeling aggressed and undermined. However hard she tried, she could not get rid of this 'felt sense'. In this case example, the analyst had located the source of the problem from within, and having heard her patient complain of feeling emotionally abused by certain significant others, she concluded that the analysand was externalising the persecutory feelings that nonetheless originated from an internal source. This interpretation concerning the 'internal persecutor' was something that the analyst never strayed from. She never explored the analysand's attachment history, and in fact when Marsha brought it up she said it was irrelevant.

The 'persecutory state' was left decontextualised, as a pure intrapsychic phenomenon. Marsha left the analysis and went to one of us for a second go at therapy. When she told the therapist this story, the therapist asked questions, and noted that Marsha had got involved with an abusive and undermining partner. Yet, Marsha also hated this situation and felt retraumatised and did not quite understand how she found herself there again. On deeper exploration, the wider situation became apparent. Marsha was a Jew, her mother from Germany, a holocaust survivor, and she learned that her mother's side of the family had virtually been extinguished by the holocaust. Suddenly, to Marsha things started to make more sense, she understood the context of her persecutory feelings, their intensity and dominance, and remembered when she had been brought up, how her mother had been a bully as she had been bullied in the numerous foster homes she had been brought up in as a 'refugee child'.

By contextualising the experience, and making attachment links, Marsha could locate her persecutory states in an immediate, historical and relational context, to understand herself and stop repeating the pattern of what had been done to her and had happened in the wider historical cultural context.

From an attachment perspective 'multiple disassociations' are the outcome of profoundly disturbed disorganised parenting and an intergenerational history will inevitably be part of that context. However the 'self' and 'identity' are problematic for us all, as we all have diverse, differing and divided aspects of the 'self' or 'selves'. It is a matter of degree, particularly when there is no reference point from which to orientate and integrate in extreme cases of 'multiplicity'. So what has been discussed also has applicability for other analysands we may work with, particularly where trauma and more extreme defences come into play, where disassociation is the only way 'how to survive'. Countertransference not only can involve enactments but requires them in order for the relational disturbance to be identified and ultimately repatterned, as it is only when we find a way of mobilising procedural memory that therapy can begin to touch the parts that the 'pure talking cure' has failed to reach.

Bibliography

Bion, W. (1962). *Second Thoughts*. London, UK: Sage.

Bowlby, J. (1988). *The Secure Base*. New York, NY: Basic Books.

Bowlby, J. (1999/1969). *Attachment: Attachment and Loss* (2nd ed., Vol. 1). New York, NY: Basic Books.

Diamond, N. (2013). *Between Skins: The Body in Psychoanalysis – Contemporary Developments*. Chichester, UK: Wiley & Sons.

Diamond, N., & Marrone, M. (2003). *Attachment and Intersubjectivity*. London, UK: Whurr.

Marrone, M. (2014). *Attachment and Interaction*. London, UK: Jessica Kingsley.

Panksepp, J. (2004). *Affective Neuroscience: The Foundation of Human and Animal Emotions*. Oxford, UK: Oxford University Press.

Shore, A. (1994). *Affect Regulation and the Repair of the Self*. New York, NY: Norton Books.

Siegel, D. (2015). *The Developing Mind*. New York, NY: Guildford Press.

Sinason, V. (2011). *Attachment, Trauma and Multiplicity*. London, UK: Routledge.

Chapter 4

Countertransference, art psychotherapy and the prediscursive abject

Janek Dubowski

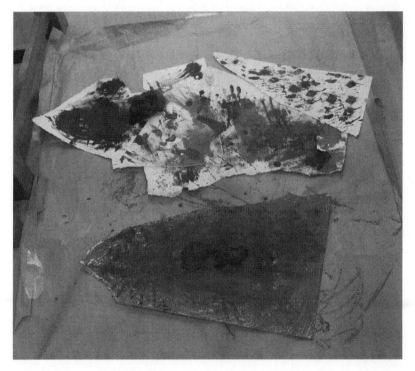

Figure 4.1 Art-making image 1

In this chapter it is my intention to exemplify how countertransference might be understood in respect to art psychotherapy, through the utilisation of an illustrative case study involving the making and exploration of a single image (see Figure 4.1, above).

In much the same way that the mother, in anticipating her infant's psychological needs, actively encourages and welcomes his projections in order to better help process them with him and for him, or if this is not possible, to accept them into herself – as therapists we actively encourage and welcome the client's projections and transference. Analytic art psychotherapy, underpinned by Jungian theory, provides clients with the opportunity to explore and make concrete (through the use of art material), these unconscious processes. Schaverien (1999) described the dynamics of the therapeutic relation in art psychotherapy, in which the image made by the client constitutes a 'third element'. She goes on to suggest that artworks themselves can embody the transference and subsequently evoke a countertransference response. She distinguishes between 'diagrammatic' and 'embodied' images, the latter containing ideas and feelings that require verbal exploration whereas the 'Embodied Image' is itself imbued with feelings and ideas which could not have been expressed in any other way. I would add that these ideas need to include the performative aspects of the making of the image, as well as the analysis of it once it is finished.

When the making process takes place in such a way that it can be directly observed by the therapist, it becomes a form of enactment. *Analytic enactment* has been defined as 'to . . . refer to the (non-verbal) events occurring within the dyad that both parties experience as being the consequence of behaviour in the other' (McLaughlin [1991] in Ellman & Goodman, 1998, p. 80). Both transference and countertransference elements might be enacted in this way including what Joseph Cambray (2001) referred to as *countertransference enactments*:

> [T]he ability to attune to enactments thus offers access to the flux of unconscious contents as they are constellating. Observation of the context in which these events emerge, through self-analysis of the countertransferential components can shed light on meaning as it evolves in analysis.
>
> (Cambray, 2001, p. 278)

In art psychotherapy, therefore, elements of these processes are conducted through the art-making by the client, under the therapists gaze, and the subsequent exploration of the finished object or objects by the client and therapist working together. This distinction between finished image and process is important and this chapter is designed to exemplify how witnessing a client's image-making process is a specialised form of enactment countertransference. The example I have chosen is taken from an art psychotherapy workshop that was conducted at the University of Tokyo during the summer of 2016. This was a group session with 12 participants but what made this particular case stand out was how the 'artist' positioned herself in respect to the therapist in his direct gaze. The art-making process within the context of art psychotherapy can be highly personal and it is not uncommon for clients to find a place to work that is unobserved. Occasionally the contrary happens, even if it is not done as an intentional act, that the client positions themselves so as to be in the direct gaze of the therapist, as was the case in this example. What ensued was experienced by the therapist as a ritualised performance (this realisation occurred to me later, after taking part in a traditional Japanese tea ceremony).

As the therapy develops, the client becomes increasingly aware of the therapist's ability to help in bringing the unconscious elements of the image into the light of awareness. This includes an element of 'unconscious awareness', by which I mean that the client's unconscious processes become aware of the therapist's potentiality. The therapist's active participation in welcoming the client's projections play an important part in this. In respect to art psychotherapy, we see this unfolding in the '*performative*' aspects of the art-making process. To understand the central importance of this we need to first of all explore the image-making process as a *narrative*.

Figure 4.1 shows a completed image but no matter how studiously or analytically one might view it, in itself it can only reveal a fraction of what it contains. In other words, the narrative of its making, which might reveal elements of unconscious process, are no longer wholly at our disposal. Some aspects of this narrative might be deduced: some elements overlay others, for example, so we can deduce which came first and which followed. A line of paint might be stronger in colour to one side than the other and from this we can deduce the direction of the paint brush as the line was made. But the amount of overlaying of paint or drawing, the order of tearing, the full sequence of the use of colour, these and many more vital elements of the process are hidden and lost.

Now we can start to see that the way that the image is created under the gaze of the therapist becomes so vital to the psychotherapeutic-art process, and can be considered as a form of countertransference. There are instances, of course, when the client (either through conscious choice or unconsciously) actively discourages the therapist's gaze, choosing instead to work privately. For our purposes here, I will be focusing on instances where the therapist's gaze features as an important and integral part of the therapeutic endeavour.

Below I have included my unedited process notes, taken during the session, in order to provide as accurate an account as I am able of the client's art-making process. I follow this with an account of my thoughts and feelings during the session itself together with my postsession analysis, including the process of amplification. The client is a young woman in her late 20s, a psychology graduate with an interest in art psychotherapy. Later I learned that she was in her fourth month of pregnancy at the time of the session (through correspondence in the form of an email she sent me announcing the birth of her child).

The session took place over the course of a full day which included theory lectures that preceded the art psychotherapy session itself. The session was for 2 hours and took place in a well-equipped university classroom. A wide range of art materials were made freely available.

The narrative of making

Territory with large wrapping paper is established on the floor, achieved by laying a large sheet of roughly torn brown wrapping paper on the floor in order to protect the floor covering.

A large sheet of white paper is torn, then torn again, then again several times, some fragments relatively large, some smaller.

Red paint directly applied with both hands is smeared on some of these fragments.

Then black paint, again with both hands, first the right then the left, smearing then smacking.

I notice the use of black leaves very different marks from that with the red but both appear primitive, nonfigural, abstract.

She looks at her hands noticing how the red and the black paint mixes, reacts with one another.

Fragments of paper torn from the whole are thus smeared and slapped then moved aside to be replaced with other, at first smaller fragments of white paper. On these occasionally paint is dripped directly from the tube then only afterwards smeared with the flat of her hand; I sense she is predominantly right-handed but she uses both hands at this stage.

Then she gets up and washes her hands. I note she takes great care with the washing, using soap to make sure both hands are clean and free of the paint. This seems important.

She returns to her territory, perhaps a part of her senses my attention as she now sits on the floor facing away from me. I am no longer able to witness her working so directly but I see her picking up the fragments of smeared paper, some with her hand printed clearly on them and I note she is applying glue to the edges and now she is gluing fragments together – is this some form of reparation or repair? There does not appear to be an effort to make the original sheet of paper whole again. Now I notice it wasn't glue at all but some form of red marker. (I managed to see later that indeed she had used glue *and* the red marker. The glue was used to stick some of the fragments together but one was left separate – she spoke about this fragment later referring to it as 'shit and anger' that 'needed to be expelled, thrown away, got rid of', but added that she would keep it – the paper representation of her feeling states.) She uses this to make spirals then zigzags on one of the fragments, again using both hands. Predominantly the right, forcefully using the implement almost obliterating the black paint underneath with the red marker. This whole fragment is becoming entirely red; there is a force used in applying the marker, again spiral movements, clockwise spiral movements.

Round and round and round and round all clockwise, sometimes moving inwards sometimes outwards but remaining confined to this one fragment, at times going over the edge and marking the brown paper that marks her territory.

She keeps up this red spiralling for some time, many minutes pass, it seems important that she keeps this up. Now more red paint is poured onto this fragment and forcefully applied with a brush before she gets up for a second time and goes to the sink to wash, carefully, all remnants of pigment from her hands. Also the brush is cleaned before she returns to her territory. She uses the brush first to mix some of the red paint with water on a palette then she uses the brush to splash the wet paint onto her fragments but only for a short while before getting up and walking away to the materials table returning with a ball of fabric, a light grey/white in colour, about the size of an apple. Then she goes back to the sink to wash her hands yet again.

Crouching down again she seems to know exactly what to do, first clearing up the implements, tidying up her territory. The palette and brushes are washed – it is important they are made very clean.

The drawn on and painted fragments are piled up one over another and now she returns, her left hand is cupping something, it is black paint or ink, something black and the ball of wool is now black with the same stuff – which is dropped onto the main fragment. Black on red, or first black, then red now black again. Then to the sink one more time and now it's not just her hands but one of her feet that need washing, where black paint has splattered. Now back to the territory for more tidying, taking art materials back to the (materials) table and coming back with glue which is applied to the black wool to glue it down to the predominantly red fragment. Then the fragments are re-arranged, moved together (but not glued), arranged together but *not* joined.

Then back to the sink for more washing of hands. Much soap is needed but all traces of paint have to be removed.

She returns to her territory and picks up some of the smaller un-worked fragments, they are squashed together then dropped but not removed – are they still an integral part of the whole?

Now she is at the material table again selecting some more paper this time carefully cutting it with scissors. She returns holding a small carefully cut rectangle of white paper and the scissors, together with a box of coloured pencils. Now she cuts the edges away from the rectangle to make an oval which she places down then picks up again – a shape emerges – is it a cat?

She gets up and leaves the room after a while returning, looks towards me, she bows, with a smile on her face. I notice the cut out shape of the cat laying on top of the unopened box of coloured pencils – she is back at the materials table.

The enactment countertransference

Here I expand the 'narrative of making' by including my feeling states in response to witnessing it as well as to some retrospective analysis of my countertransference.

Territory with large wrapping paper is established on the floor.

This is not uncommon when someone intends to use paint or other potentially 'messy' materials in order to avoid staining the floor. What was more unusual was that she positioned herself very close to where I was sitting. The room was very large with lots of opportunities for finding a more private space in order to work. My immediate thought was that something was about to happen that was required to be witnessed by me.

A large sheet of white paper is torn, then torn again, then again several times some fragments relatively large, some smaller.

There is something primitive about tearing, unlike cutting, it is less precise and more uncontrollable. In this instance there was something very deliberate about the tearing, and as she tore she allowed the fragments of paper to fall from her hands, only later delicately picking them up and placing them in some kind of arrangement on the large sheet of paper on which she was working. By sitting and working on the floor she positions herself to me in a very particular way, with me 'looking down' on her.

Red paint directly applied with both hands is smeared on some of these fragments.

This feels very primitive, visceral, I reevaluate the tearing I had just previously witnessed, the paper becomes flesh being torn and made bloody. I notice the blood on her hands. I know it is only paint, but it represents blood to me.

Then black paint, again with both hands first the right then the left. Smearing then smacking.

She has briefly looked up and we have made fleeting eye contact. I consider that my gaze is important to her. She turns her attention fully back to her work, I might not exist, her concentration is on smearing and smacking black paint onto the torn fragments. There is a primitive violence taking place but it is a controlled primitive violence and I am transfixed by it.

I notice the use of black leaves very different marks from that with the red but both appear primitive, nonfigural, abstract.

I am witnessing a primal act. There is something violent about the juxtaposition of black on red. I have seen this combination before, anger and sadness perhaps? I am very aware that I am in a foreign land and do not understand the culture here, what might these colours signify in Japan? I am more certain of the abstraction, is it nonfigural or prefigural? It is certainly primitive.

She looks at her hands noticing how the red and the black paint mixes, reacts with one another.

She is fully involved in the work, sitting on the sheet of paper she has put down to mark her territory and protect the floor from spillages. Her hands are covered in red and black paint and in looking at them they become part of the making that she is involved with. She may not be consciously aware of my gaze but I feel that my gaze is important to her and her process.

Fragments of paper torn from the whole are thus smeared and slapped then moved aside to be replaced with other, at first smaller fragments of white paper. On these occasionally paint is dripped directly from the tube then only afterwards smeared with the flat of her hand, I sense she is predominantly right handed but she uses both hands at this stage.

Why is noticing whether she is right- or left-handed important to me? In using both her hands and in such a primitive way is she revisiting a time before she developed handedness? Is this a form of primal regression? I am getting a sense of the primitiveness that I am witnessing from a developmental perspective.

Then she gets up and washes her hands. I note she takes great care with the washing, using soap to make sure both hands are clean and free of the paint. This seems important.

I experience an anxiety of a premature ending of something. In washing her hands is she putting an end to a process that has hardly begun?

She returns to her territory, perhaps a part of her senses my attention as she now sits on the floor facing away from me. I am no longer able to witness her working so directly but I see her picking up the fragments of smeared paper, some with her hand printed clearly on them and I note she is applying glue to the edges and now she is gluing fragments together – is this some form of reparation or repair? There does not appear to be an effort to make the original sheet of paper whole again. Now I notice it wasn't glue at all but some form of red marker, she uses this to make spirals then zigzags on one of the fragments, again using both hands. Predominantly the right, forcefully using the implement almost obliterating the black paint underneath with the red marker. This whole fragment is becoming entirely red, there is a force used in applying the marker, again spiral movements, clockwise spiral movements.

Relief that she has returned to the work and now a second stage is beginning, one that is perhaps more private for her. I am not disappointed that she is no longer facing me but I am aware that there is a difference in affect now. I think I see that what has been torn is being joined back together but am I mistaken? Do I have a wish for some kind of reparation for her?

Round and round and round and round all clockwise, sometimes moving inwards sometimes outwards but remaining confined to this one fragment, at times going over the edge and marking the brown paper that marks her territory.

In noticing the direction is clockwise am I making an association with time passing or is it a mental acknowledgement of her right-handedness? I have seen this kind of spiralling before and take note of whether it is spiralling inwards or outwards and noticing it is both – I cannot know what this means, if anything.

She keeps up this red spiralling for some time, many minutes pass, it seems important that she keeps this up. Now more red paint is poured onto this fragment and forcefully applied with a brush before she gets up for a second time and goes to the sink to wash, carefully, all remnants of pigment from her hands. Also the brush is cleaned before she returns to her territory. She uses the brush first to mix some of the red paint with water on a palette then she uses the brush to splash the wet paint onto her fragments but only for a short while before getting up and walking away to the materials table returning with a ball of fabric, a light grey/white in colour, about the size of an apple. Then she goes back to the sink to wash her hands yet again.

Using the brush is something new but the way she uses it is also very primitive. She uses it to strike at the paper, drumming movements to splatter the paint (it is later that I notice the marks that are left look like sperm or tadpoles (Figure 4.2). I am increasingly aware of just how visceral what she is making is becoming. My association is still with torn flesh and blood. It brings to mind (in retrospect) witnessing the birth of my son, or much earlier, entering my parents room to see the bed is covered in blood. The original sheet of paper covering the floor now becomes a placenta with a bloodied object laying on it. When she gets up to wash I think it must be finished but then she returns with the ball of fabric and places it on her work. In retrospect it looks like the stuffing they use in upholstery, stuffing coming out, becoming stuffed, unstuffed.

Crouching down again she seems to know exactly what to do, first clearing up the implements, tidying up her territory. The palette and brushes are washed – it is important they are made very clean.

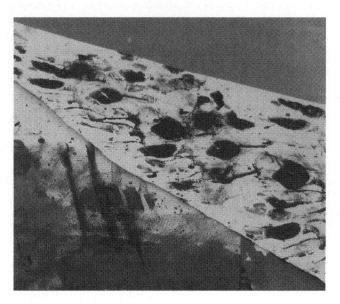

Figure 4.2 Art-making image 2

This feels very ritualistic to me – perhaps a ceremony to mark the ending of something?

> *The drawn on and painted fragments are piled up one over another and now she returns, her left hand is cupping something, it is black paint or ink, something black and the ball of wool is now black with the same stuff – which is dropped onto the main fragment. Black on red, or first black, then red now black again. Then to the sink one more time and now it's not just her hands but one of her feet that need washing, where black paint has splattered. Now back to the territory for more tidying, taking art materials back to the (materials) table and coming back with glue which is applied to the black wool to glue it down to the predominantly red fragment. Then the fragments are rearranged, moved together (but not glued), arranged together but not joined.*

This is unexpected – another stage in the making. Whatever is being 'exorcised' is not yet finished. Something cathartic is taking place – something very primitive and primal is being given form. She playing with that form, arranging and rearranging it – 'it' has to be made 'just-right' before she is permitted to wash away the evidence that 'it' was made by her hand – that she is 'red-handed'.

> *Then back to the sink for more washing of hands. Much soap is needed but all traces of paint have to be removed.*

I notice how much effort she makes in the washing but later, when the group returns to the circle I notice how she is sitting, how curiously she holds herself, especially her arms, with both hands turned outwards so I can see that the red staining that the soap has not been able to remove.

> *She returns to her territory and picks up some of the smaller un-worked fragments, they are squashed together then dropped but not removed – are they still an integral part of the whole?*

I seem to hold a wish that some form or wholeness is achieved, or that reparation to the primitive violence I have witnessed is possible. After the 'disintegration' through the tearing to pieces I wish for some kind of reintegration.

> *Now she is at the material table again selecting some more paper this time carefully cutting it with scissors. She returns holding a small carefully cut rectangle of white paper and the scissors, together with a box of coloured pencils. Now she cuts the edges away from the rectangle to make an oval which she places down then picks up again – a shape emerges – is it a cat?*

This is something very different and my initial feeling is one of disappointment – there is something very childlike in the making and presenting of this cat, it feels sentimental to me. Likewise the coloured pencils I associate with materials a young child would choose to use. Using scissors instead of tearing is such a departure from what I have been witnessing. This use of 'collage' is childlike and the juxtaposition of this sentimental imagery on the primitive bloody visceral substrate is jarring for me.

> *She gets up and leaves the room after a while returning, looks towards me, she bows, with a smile on her face. I notice the cut out shape of the cat laying on top of the unopened box of coloured pencils – she is back at the materials table.*

This marks the ending of the transference enactment – the 'bow' marking the ending of the ritual, the ceremony is over and she can return to normality.

The embodied image

What I have attempted to demonstrate is how the way that the image is created under the gaze of the therapist becomes so vital to the art psychotherapeutic process, and can be considered as a form of transference. (There are instances, of course, when the client [either through conscious choice or unconsciously] actively discourages the therapist's gaze choosing instead to work privately). Schaverien (1999) divided how an image might be considered within psychotherapy into three areas: 'its objective nature, its aesthetic qualities, and the imagery it reveals'. Accordingly, the primary focus is on the finished image rather than the processes that led to its creation. Schaverien did go on, however, to state: 'At times these combine to offer psychological mediation in states which are otherwise inexpressible' (1999, p. 420). Later she does reflect on the creative act itself when she adds:

> The point about the *embodied image* is that, in the process of its creation, feeling becomes 'live' in the present. This may be understood to be a result of an unconscious, transference-of 'attributes and states'. Very often the aesthetic quality of such a picture is commensurate with he engagement of the artist/patient within the transference.
>
> (Schaverien, 2007)

So while the importance of process is acknowledged, the analytical focus remains mainly on the finished 'object' which itself is referred to as either an 'image' or as a 'picture', with the assumption that it contains some kind of revelatory content and aesthetic qualities. When Schaverien focussed on the process, as she did later in the same article, she referred to it as *enactment*; such enactments, she suggested,

> embody the transference, bringing otherwise unspeakable imagery out into the light and so transforming the psychological state of the analysand. This is because previously unconscious material becomes conscious and is seen first in the picture. Such pictures deepen the analysand's relation to herself and also profoundly influence the countertransference.

An embodied image, as we have seen, might involve the making of something that expresses an early, primitive presymbolic state (as witnessed in the making process I have chosen as the focus of this paper). Julia Kristeva (in Beardsworth, 1993) described the 'presymbolic' as a form of

> 'visceral' reactivity . . . : an ontological domain that both precedes and exists in opposition to the realm of language and the 'symbolic'. . . . The body is indispensable to this theory; the ego is never wholly autonomous its corporeal basis – indeed, it is the body within this account which stakes out the limits not only to the physical experience of the subject, but to social identity as well.
>
> (Beardsworth, 1993, p. 68)

What Kristeva was working towards here, is her formulation of 'abjection', literally something to . . . 'cast out, or off – in speaking of the abject we have in mind the contemptible, the repugnant, the wretched, that which is unwanted, filthy, contaminated'. In Butler's (1990) terms, 'the abject, at its most literal, designates that which has been expelled from the body, discharged as excrement, literally rendered "other"' (p. 169). Here, Butler referred to ideas of the 'maternal body', following Kristeva herself, who linked abjection to the earliest affective relationship with the maternal body.

My countertransference as I observed her painting, cutting, tearing and sticking back together involved an instance of witnessing something essentially 'pre-discursive' being born into the world. Julia Kristeva (1982a) referred to this idea as something that is 'neither subject nor object':

> There looms, within abjection, one of those violent, dark revolts of being, directed against a threat that seems to emanate from an exorbitant outside or inside, ejected beyond the scope of the possible, the tolerable, the thinkable. It lies there, quire close, but it cannot be assimilated. It beseeches, worries, and fascinates desire, which, nevertheless, does not let itself be seduced. Apprehensive, desire turns aside; sickened, it rejects.
>
> (Kristeva, 1982a, p. 1)

Later when the group returned to sitting in a circle I asked whether anyone would like to share their image by placing it in the centre where we could all look at it together. The artist whose work I have described set to my left and I noticed the way she was sitting displayed both her hands which were laying on her lap palms upwards. No amount of washing has been enough to completely remove the red staining and there was something in the way that she displayed them that appeared to me to be deliberate. She chose to share her work, I was working with an interpreter and how she described her paining was in her native Japanese. As she pointed to various parts of her work she described them, saying that the 'Red – blood', the 'Purple – cuts/wounds', and the 'Black – creep up (crawl up)'. She added, 'I wanted irregular shapes of paper so that I have torn it. I have tried to stick small pieces together but I didn't like it so I only chose to stick relatively big piece of paper. After I painted red, purple and black, I put some felt fabric too' (on the paper). 'I felt something was missing so I coloured white felt fabric with red, purple and black and I put it there' (pointing). Now looking at her image and with a slightly raised voice she added 'Go to hell (Fuck you!)'. When she said 'Go to hell' she made a tight fist with her right hand and indicated through miming how she had moved the paintbrush when she had painted with the red. I asked her what she wanted to do with her images and she replied, 'I want to throw them away but I will take them to my home'.

Conclusion

I consider what I witnessed to be a form of non rather than prediscursive expression, or as Butler put it, 'that lie/reside beneath discursive consciousness'. Butler went on to ask, 'What can we make of the way in which discourses not only constitute the domains of the speakable, but are themselves bounded through the production of a constitutive outside: the unspeakable, the unsignifiable?' (Butler, 1997, p. 94). In permitting the art materials to be regarded and remain as primitive and 'visceral', form has been given to something essentially 'abject' and its expression was 'embodied' under the direct gaze of 'another' in an attempt to permit the holding space necessary for such potentially violent, primitive and presymbolic material to surface. What I have demonstrated in this vignette is an instance of *enactment transference* and my countertransference to this, as mediated through the creative process, permitting the expression of something that was otherwise an instance of the 'inexpressible abject.' How was this made possible? An important element was that the art materials that she manipulated possess almost limitless possibilities in the ways that they can be manipulated. They inherently possess what Daniel Stern (1973) called 'vitality affects'. For example, the visceral qualities of the paint, glue and other substances used, together with her 'tearing' and 'cutting' constitute what Stern calls an 'activation contour', this combination of the vitality effects and associated activation contours created through her actions formed a major contribution to the countertransferential witnessing and holding that I experienced. Stern points out that the infant starts to pay active attention to both vitality affects and accompanying activation contours during the first weeks of life (so they constitute primitive precursors to the eventual genesis of symbolic functioning much later on in the baby's development). Essentially these primitive interactions involve the mother (or primary caregiver) and we can consider the parallel to this in the active welcoming of the artist's projections by the therapist and through what the medium of art allowed to give form to – the otherwise formless *abject*. In introducing the term *abject* I refer to Julia Kristeva, who defined the idea thusly:

> There looms, within abjection, one of those violent, dark revolts of being, directed against a threat that seems to emanate from an exorbitant outside or inside, ejected beyond the scope of the possible, the tolerable, the thinkable. It lies there, quite close, but it cannot be assimilated. It beseeches, worries, and fascinates desire, which nevertheless, does not let itself be seduced. Apprehensive, desire turned aside; sickened, it rejects.

A certainty protects it from the shameful – a certainty of
which it is proud – holds on to it. But simultaneously, just
the same, that impetus, that spasm, that leap is drawn
towards an elsewhere as tempting as it is condemned.
Unflaggingly, like an inescapable boomerang, a vortex of
Summons and repulsion places the one haunted by it
Literally beside himself.

(Kristeva, 1982a)

She constantly relates abjection to the 'maternal body', the "mother". She
stated, the mother 'is gradually rejected through rituals of cleanliness, toilet
training, eating habits and so on. Although through these lessons in "horror",
the mother is abjected, in signifying horror, reconciliation with the maternal
body is possible'. This for me relates to the washing that it was important for
me to witness – abjection is not only about a woman's own pregnancy and
giving birth, it is also about that earlier and forgotten struggle to separate
from one's own mother – in order to separate from the mother, the mother
must herself be abjected.

I understand the enactment countertransference as part of the ritual act
necessary on the part of the subject to permit herself to expel what Lechte
and Zournazi (2003) considered to be a liminal condition, neither inside nor
outside of the body, but which stems from the maternal or the presymbolic.
Kristeva explained more of this idea:

The chora (a term she borrows from Plato) is not yet a position
that represents something for someone (i.e., not a sign); nor is
it apposition that represents someone for another position (i.e., it
is not yet a signifier either); it is however, generated in order to
attain to this signifying position.

(Kristeva, 1982b)

What we have been exploring is the creative expression of something that
is primal, primitive and presymbolic and that required an external witness.
It is through the processing of the countertransference, the participation of
the other, which allows it to emerge in the space between and to be shared.
The making narrative included the establishment and maintenance of a
performative space that I likened to a shared placenta, suggestive of our
connection. It involved tearing and cutting of paper that represented flesh.
It involved menstrual blood and excrement in the smearing of red and black
paint. It involved gluing or joining/rejoining, healing and repair. Washing
involved both the removal of 'abject material' and a ritualistic act, a ceremony that involved some form of relationship to the masculine in relation
to the therapist's gaze.

Bibliography

Beardsworth, S. (1993). *Julia Kristeva: Psychoanalysis and Modernity*. New York, NY: SUNY Press.

Butler, J. (1990). *Gender Trouble*. New York, NY: Routledge.

Butler, J. (1997). *The Psychic Life of Power: Theories in Subjection*. Stanford, CA: Stanford University Press.

Cambray, J. (2001). Enactment and amplification. *The Journal of Analytical Psychology*, 46(2), 275–303.

Ellman, P. L., & Goodman, N. R. (1998). Enactment: Opportunity for symbolising trauma. In J. Ellman & M. Muskowitz (Eds.), *Enactment: Towards a New Approach to the Therapeutic Relationship*. Northvale, NJ: Jason Aronson.

Jung, C. G. (1947/1954). On the nature of the psyche (*Collective Works*, Vol. VIII). London, UK: Routledge & Kegan Paul.

Kristeva, J. (1982a). *Approaching Abjection: Powers of Horror*. New York, NY: Columbia University Press.

Kristeva, J. (1982b). *Revolution in Poetic Language*. New York, NY: Columbia University Press.

Kristeva, J. (1993). *Nations without Nationalism*. New York, NY: Columbia University Press.

Lechte, J., & Zournazi, M. (Eds.) (2003). *The Kristeva Critical Reader*. Edinburgh, UK: Edinburgh University Press.

McLaughlin, J. T. (1991). Clinical and theoretical aspects of enactment. *Journal of the American Psychoanalytical Association*, 39(3), 595–614.

Schaverien, J. (1999). *The Revealing Image: Analytical Art Psychotherapy in Theory and Practice*. London, UK: Jessica Kingsley.

Schaverien, J. (2007). Countertransference as active imagination: Imaginative experiences of the analyst. *Journal of Analytical Psychology*, 52, 413–431.

Stern, D. N. (1985). *The Interpersonal World of the Infant*. New York, NY: Basic Books.

Chapter 5

CBT versus the unconscious

Ignore countertransference at your peril

Angela Devon

Anna was referred with symptoms of severe depression. Her marriage ended 12 years ago. She was upset that her ex-husband no longer had contact with her. She was distressed that she only had two children and her husband had refused to have a third child. Anna had seen many therapists. She stated that her parents were good parents but had been busy and had not given her enough attention. She did not want to explore possible childhood issues. She wanted to use cognitive behaviour therapy (CBT) and explore her thoughts and behaviours but it was very difficult to develop an effective formulation as she did not want to explore the past.

We agreed to use behavioural activation in an attempt to lift her mood and determine if this would then facilitate more meaningful discussions. She engaged well and began increasing her social activities. She found it hard to stay on an agenda and wanted to talk about issues in her day to day life.

She was always late for sessions. It was a struggle for her to accept the end of sessions. When we discussed the difficulty relating to ending, she had an explanation in terms of practical issues but could not recognise the psychological significance of her behaviour. She increased her activities but was always dissatisfied with every activity she tried. My feelings of counter-transference were that I felt she was very negative and complaining. I felt irritated and frustrated. I discussed the possibility of counselling for her and I recognised that I wanted to stop seeing her. She then started ring-ing between sessions and asking to change appointments and to discuss emergencies. Attempts to discuss the past were blocked. She stated she had connected with me and found the sessions really helpful and that her mood was better. My countertransference was that I felt trapped and wanted to push her away.

When I focused on my feelings, I saw I had become embroiled in reac-tions which I was not consciously noticing. Based on my reactions I suggested that she never got enough attention from people, that what she wanted was someone to be available all the time for her and it was so hard when they were not. She tried to get their attention but they ended up getting irritated and left her. Her dissatisfaction with all her activities was that they were not enough for her. She always felt nothing was enough and she was constantly disappointed and withdrew. This was significant for Anna who was then able to explore her past experiences with her mother who she felt did not give her enough attention and who pushed her away. We were able to explore her behaviours that pushed people away. We were then able to engage in more meaningful discussions about her core beliefs, her thoughts and behaviours and progress was made.

My feelings towards her (countertransference) were the key to change. Without this, I would have discharged her as many therapists had done and repeated her experience of being rejected. Working within a cognitive behavioural approach, recognising and understanding countertransference is important and I would suggest that it is helpful to pay attention to such feelings.

In this chapter I am going to examine the historical commonalities of CBT and psychodynamic approaches and the relational aspects in CBT. I will draw attention to the issues which draw people into becoming therapists and the importance of integrating an awareness of counter-transference in CBT work, so increasing therapeutic efficacy. Looking at some CBT work I have undertaken, I will illustrate how an integration of approaches is helpful.

'CBT versus psychodynamic? No!' (Henriques, 2014)

Traditionally CBT and psychodynamic (PP) approaches were seen as very different and many people had allegiance to only one of these approaches. Psychologists and psychotherapists behave like members of competing tribes, with different esoteric languages and rituals (Magnavita, 2013).

Many therapists define themselves as CBT therapists or psychodynamic psychotherapists and discussions about which is the better therapy abound. In the NHS in particular, these approaches have been competing for legitimacy and funding. CBT has been more amenable to randomised controlled trials enabling recognition in NICE guidelines which has strengthened the use of CBT in NHS settings.

In recent years, it has been recognised (Prasko et al., 2010) that there are significant commonalities and that the 'CBT versus PP' framing of training, approaches and practice is unhelpful.

'It is wrongheaded to define CBT against PP as if they were horses in a race' (Henriques, 2014). Transference and countertransference were seen as cornerstones of psychodynamic approaches, not of CBT. It is now recognised that irrespective of approach, attention to the therapeutic relationship and the feelings it engenders is critical. Transference and countertransference are likely to be experienced in all therapeutic relationships.

Historical perspective of commonalities between CBT and PDP

Saul Rosenzweig (1936) suggested that different types of therapy had the same effective factors in common. His paper is one of the earliest to integrate therapies. Weinberger (1995) mentioned five possible common factors: the therapeutic relationship, expectations, confronting problems, mastery, and attribution of outcome. Lambert and Ogles' (2004) common factors account for a substantial amount of improvement attained in psychotherapy.

Many psychological theorists recognised the commonalities and the importance of integration (Larson, 1993). Skinner (1953) and Wolpe (1958) recognised that the quality of the therapeutic relationship is the most important factor leading to effective therapy of any kind. Skinner (1953) showed an early interest in theoretical integration.

Rogers (1957) discussed the importance of the therapeutic relationship. Rogers saw great similarities between the different forms of psychotherapy. They could all be effective or ineffective depending on the therapist's personal skills. His view was that different kinds of therapists used different methods to do the same thing. Beck, Rush, Shaw, and Emery (1979) reported, 'Cognitive and behaviour therapies probably require the same subtle therapeutic atmosphere that has been described explicitly in the context of psychodynamic therapy'.

CBT has evolved over time and many variants exist. The first wave of behaviour therapy concentrated on changing behaviour. The second wave added changing of thoughts, and the third wave of behaviour therapy is directed at changing the function of the thoughts, not their content.

The third-wave therapies include schema therapy (Young, Klosko & Weishaar, 2003), dialectical behaviour therapy (DBT) (Linehan, 1993), mindfulness-based cognitive therapy (MBCT) (Segal, Williams & Teasdale, 2001) and acceptance and commitment therapy (Hayes, Strosahl & Wilson, 1999). They acknowledged the importance of the relationship and the importance of processes occurring in the therapeutic relationship even more than earlier models.

CBT has evolved and developed. First-wave CBT examines the relationships between thoughts, feelings, and behaviours. Its purpose is to help people overcome emotional problems, make patients aware of automatic thoughts, and how those automatic thoughts affect how patients feel and behave. In schema therapy, third wave CBT, schemas are seen as 'deep, unconscious cognitive structures seated in long term memory that give meaning to events'. These affect our appraisal of events and our behaviours. This can be seen as similar to the unconscious (Cottraux & Blackburn, 2001).

Leahy (2001) focused on the importance of the relationship in CBT and many approaches combine CBT with a focus on the corrective emotional experience and the therapeutic relationship (Beck et al., 2004; Young et al., 2003; Beck, Freeman & Davis, 2004). Some CBT therapists use terms typical of psychodynamic theory, such as *transference interpretation* (Safran & Segal, 1990);

countertransference (Hayes et al., 1999); and *resistance, transference* and *counter-transference* (Leahy, 2001).

However, not all CBT therapists acknowledge the importance of these experiences. I would suggest that if CBT therapists could include thinking about transference and countertransference, the therapeutic efficacy would be enhanced.

The differences between therapies decreases when therapists are more experienced (Wiser, Goldfried, Raue, & Vakosh, 1996). Larsson (1993) commented that it is hard to find unique characteristics of different therapies in the empirical literature, with the exception of the use of homework and outside-of-session practice.

PP and CBT have different theoretical rationales. In PP, the client is encouraged to develop a greater understanding and insight of themselves through the exploration and discussion of the past and early childhood. By bringing the unconscious into consciousness and through their interaction with the therapist within the therapeutic relationship, corrective emotional experiences occur. CBT focuses on challenging our assumptions, patterns of thinking and behaviour, but also on developing a greater understanding of our core beliefs, derived early in life but which influence the present, all within the context of a trusting therapeutic relationship.

Interestingly, a recent client of mine, towards the end of the assessment sessions, was powerfully struck through the Socratic questioning process exploring his earlier life and then developing the formulation, that he reported feeling amazed about how the childhood experiences were affecting him now. He had a core belief of being 'not good enough' which affected his appraisal of situations and his behaviours. He had no awareness of this before the sessions. It really was bringing the unconscious into the conscious.

Countertransference

Therapists have unresolved conflicts from our earlier experiences. This leads us to repeat earlier patterns in the transference relationship. We have core beliefs that affect our thoughts, behaviours, physiological responses and emotions (Prasko et al., 2010).

The importance of relational aspects and of countertransference has also been explored in attachment theory where the therapist's early attachment experiences can affect their ability to function effectively in the therapeutic relationship (Berry & Danquah, 2015). This is manifested as countertransference and they recommended that from the beginning of their careers, therapists should receive training and supervision to enhance their awareness of their own and their client's attachment experiences and how these become apparent in therapy. An awareness of our own attachment histories can assist us. Attachment style influences caregiving ability (George & Soloman, 1999). There is an association between therapist's attachment style and the working alliance (Degnan et al., 2015). This affects the therapist's ability to function as an attachment figure for clients and their ability to provide a secure therapeutic relationship (Berry & Danquah, 2015). Bowlby (1977, 1988) highlighted that the therapist can be drawn into reenacting the client's attachment experiences with their primary caregivers. Berry and Danquar (2015) referred to papers which discuss the importance of therapist awareness of their attachment histories (Eagle & Wallin, 2009; Pearlman & Courtois, 2005). Heard and Lake (1997) reported that clients' experiences of inadequate care can remind therapists of their own, and therapists can respond unempathetically.

In CBT or PP, one could expect that such aspects of relationships need to be understood to increase our effectiveness and to stop us from engaging in behaviours which are unhelpful to our clients.

The psychopathology of the helping professions

Many people go into the caring professions because of unresolved personal conflicts. Tillet (2003) referred to a number of writers who have discussed this psychopathology:

1   Lief (1971), who suggests that at least a third of medical students are motivated by unconscious neurotic drives and unresolved conflicts from childhood.
2   A medical career may serve as a defense against feelings of anxiety or impotence resulting from the experience of illness or death in family members (Feifel et al., 1967; Pfeiffer, 1983; Gabbard, 1985).
3   Tillett (2003) stated that choosing the helping professions may be an attempt to resolve early emotional neglect by giving the care and attention to others that was never received as a child. Bowlby (1977) talked about: 'the typical childhood experience of such people is to have a [parent] who . . . was unable to care for the child but instead welcomed being cared for . . . the person who develops in this way has found that the only affectional bond available is the one in which he must always be the care giver, and that the only care he can ever receive is the care he gives himself'. Bowlby described this as 'compulsive caregiving'.
4   Malan (1979) referred to 'helping profession syndrome', in which the professional 'compulsively gives to others what he would like to have for himself, which . . . leads to a severe deficit in the emotional balance of payments'. He speculated that such professionals perceive other people's needs as demands, rendering them vulnerable to depression.
5   Johnson (1991) suggested that deficiencies in parenting or illness in oneself or in family members might result in a narcissistic disturbance of personality that he characterises as 'fragile grandiosity' leading to emotional detachment and denial of personal vulnerability.

6   Psychotherapists commonly report disturbed attachments to their own parents, especially their mothers, and this might form a significant unconscious part of their interest in psychotherapy as a profession (Storr, 1979, 2012; Prodgers, 1991).
7   Rycroft (1993) suggested that some people become psychotherapists to ablate the memory of their own (unsatisfactory) parents, replacing this with an idealised projection of their own caring.
8   Jacobs (1991) used the notion of 'constructive vengeance' to suggest that many health professionals are motivated by a desire to put right perceived wrongs of the past, sublimating a wish for revenge into a conscious wish for reparation.
9   Zigmond (1984) described the symbiotic relationship between patient and doctor, in which the doctor has many parent-like qualities and the patient has correspondingly childlike ones: 'When we deny powerful needs or impulses in ourselves we will either be intolerant or compulsively solicitous of these attributes in others. If it is the latter then we can professionalise this problem by working in one of the caring professions . . . our needs may then be fulfilled in an illusory and vicarious way through a state of mutual dependence . . . such dependence on our patients for our sense of power, self-esteem, worthiness and vicarious expression of locked up feeling is often not conscious'.

I suggest that CBT therapists would benefit from exploring their unconscious motivation for being a therapist, and this should be included in training programmes.

If a therapist is aware of transference and counter transference, they will understand and deal with feelings towards the client more effectively and will be able to use this insight to develop the formulation and to enhance the therapeutic relationship to effect change.

Watch out for strong feelings in therapy (e.g., boredom, wanting to stop therapy, feeling caring, maternal, unwillingness to stop therapy).

Notice physiological reactions such as heart pounding, anxiety.

Analyse your feelings and if they are related to the client.

Do they make you think of previous times you have experienced such feelings in relation to clients or in your past?

Take it to supervision to explore possible countertransference.

Leahy (2003) discussed schemata in therapists and supervisors. A common schema is the need for approval. Therapists can be empathic and caring but not raise difficult issues. This can occur in therapy or supervision and is unhelpful. Negative emotions or behaviours are not addressed. They may miss sessions or come without homework but this will not be addressed as conflict will be avoided. The difficulties caused by an abandonment schema are that the therapist will avoid difficulty due to subconscious fears of abandonment and that the person will leave therapy.

My countertransference with Maria

Maria was referred by her GP, who described her as 'a really lovely woman'. The GP said she was sure she would work well with me. Maria came for one session and said she was going to see another therapist as she really wanted someone closer to where she lived. After a month, she contacted me again saying she had seen the other therapist and was aware that she really wanted to work with me as she had a better connection with me. I felt pleased that I had been chosen.

Maria's husband had committed suicide. She had three young children and she told me that the family had been very close. She could not understand why he had committed suicide. She spoke of feelings of loss; she experienced no negative feelings towards her husband who had left her with financial problems and three small children to care for. She was sad that the children had lost their father.

I was aware of strong positive feelings towards Maria and looked forward to the sessions. I became aware that we were only talking of how wonderful her husband had been and of her loss and shock.

I noticed that I had not taken much history as she wanted to talk about her husband. I caught myself explaining the process of grief which caused me to reflect as this was very different from my usual approach. Noticing when one has strong emotions and behaving unusually is often an indication of counter-transference. I reflected on being pleased that I had been chosen and of the GP describing her as a lovely woman.

I consciously refocused, took a detailed history, and guided the therapy session so we did not avoid more difficult subjects. She described her childhood as perfect and her parents as 'wonderful'. They were caring, giving and supportive. She worked in her father's company and loved it. She met her husband who was handsome, popular, and charismatic. Her children were born and were delightful. Her husband had some financial difficulties and was feeling low but she had felt he would be alright.

My formulation recognised her grief but also the idealisation of her family and the core belief that everything had to be perfect. She worked hard to maintain that belief. Her belief was that her family was perfect, ideal, supportive, and caring and she was lovable only when all was perfect.

At the end of sessions she said how helpful the session had been and how grateful she was that she had found me. It was when I explored my countertransference in terms of the warmth I felt towards her and my positive experience of the sessions, that I was able to appreciate my collusion with her creation of idealised relationships. I noticed that I wanted to help her to find a cleaner and a gardener to support her. These are clearly not actions that would normally spring to mind in my work! I wanted to be the perfect therapist but also to be the special one who would care for her and rescue her.

Once I became aware of my feelings I realised that she cared for everyone and felt she had to be positive and how hard that must be for her. This can be interpreted in terms of her core belief or the transference that occurred in all her relationships: her belief that she was unlovable unless she was perfect and that family members had to be perfect or the family would be at risk.

I was aware that my countertransference issues were linked to my need for approval due to my childhood issues, years of threatened loss and the early death of my father. I have anxiety about loss and an idealisation of my father which led me to avoid facing issues with Maria. I identified with Maria in terms of the loss and was acting out issues relating to pleasing people. In terms of CBT my belief was that I could be abandoned and my conditional assumption was that if I cared for and pleased people I could rescue and protect them. I wanted to rescue Maria in order to rescue the child within me.

Realising these issues meant I could then step back into the therapist/adult mode. We addressed difficult issues, and I was more challenging. We dealt with the formulation in CBT terms, the core belief of being unlovable, the conditional assumption of having to be perfect to be loved and the behaviours of ignoring and avoiding difficult discussions. We focused on behavioural experiments to test out whether addressing difficult issues would lead to abandonment. Over time she was able to discuss her feelings towards her husband, his selfishness and that he had let her down on many occasions. She was able to understand her beliefs and her need to be perfect and was able to become much more balanced and integrated.

Countertransference 'can be used as an open window into the interpersonal relations of the patient' (Prasko et al., 2010, p. 1). With Maria, my countertransference feelings clarified issues which were preventing effective therapy.

A CBT formulation of countertransference reactions is illustrated in Figure 5.1 showing early childhood experiences leading to the creation of core beliefs. The beliefs lead us to have unhelpful thoughts leading to unhelpful therapist behaviours. This can easily be seen as transference where conflicts and unresolved issues from the past are being repeated in present relationships, in this case the therapeutic relationship. Understanding issues from the past is essential in our work and is a good illustration of the need to integrate approaches and helpful concepts from other therapeutic models.

It is important to recognise that while the therapeutic relationship in CBT is not regarded as the agent of change (as in psychodynamic therapies) it is seen as vital in creating the right conditions for enabling a change.

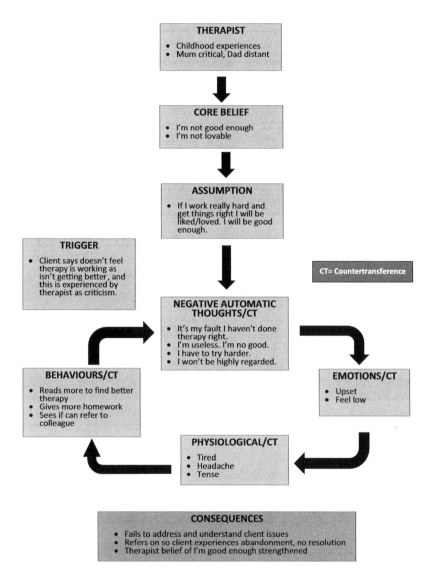

Figure 5.1 CBT formulation of CT

Transference and countertransference

Unlike in PP, transference is not the central tool in CBT. However, automatic thoughts and emotions related to the dynamics of the therapeutic relationship have now become a part of treatment for more complex disorders (e.g., personality disorders), providing a valuable opportunity to test and modify dysfunctional attitudes to people as in schema focused therapy.

Our experiences with important people in our childhood such as parents or siblings result in needs relating to for example security, acceptance and appreciation. Experiences of hurt, abandonment and rejection occur and these then set up expectations as to how people will behave in the future. We develop avoidance or compensatory strategies (excessive caregiving, competitiveness or direction). Leahy (2003) discussed narcissistic therapists with schema relating to perfectionism and competitiveness which can be linked to a core belief of incompetence or not being good enough. The compensatory strategy is perfectionism and high standard and demands. Such therapists or supervisors can be hypercritical *of themselves and others.*

In CBT, countertransference occurs and is understood when the relationship with the patient triggers automatic thoughts and schemata in the clinician. This can affect the therapeutic process. Transference and countertransference occur in any relationship and of course will occur in any intense therapeutic relationship.

In my first session with Sue, she said she was always disappointed by people. They always let her down and she became really angry and hurt. She gave me examples. She had experienced strong feelings of her parents not being there for her, of her feeling unimportant and felt they didn't really love or care for her. She reported that they had always been critical of her and did not value her. From a CBT perspective, her core beliefs were about being unlovable. Childhood experiences and transference reactions are seen as important in CBT and we also need to work with difficult transference reactions.

As she told me more of her previous experiences of people letting her down and of the rage she felt, I felt highly anxious and stressed. I was aware of my heart pounding; I was tense and felt hot. Being aware of emotions, physical changes and behaviour in response to thoughts are helpful in picking up countertransference issues. I became aware that it was likely she would experience the same feelings of disappointment and rage about being let down by me. I was thinking 'this is going to be really difficult, she is going to get really angry'.

We developed our formulation of her feeling unlovable and not being able to trust people, her consequent negative appraisals of people letting her down. We identified her negative thoughts that people were awful and horrible, they were critical of her and that people never treated her properly. We identified her behaviours of withdrawing from people and cutting them off and of her feelings of rage. At this point I raised the possibility that she could experience these feelings in relation to me and that we could expect such feelings to develop, and that it made sense given her earlier experiences.

I asked that if she experienced these feelings in relation to me to try and alter what she usually did in that typically she would withdraw and cut off. In therapy, it would be helpful if she talked about it so she could learn from it and address it in a different way. She agreed with this. We worked on her negative automatic thoughts and behaviours. She came late to the next few sessions and I was aware that I was relieved. I was not looking forward to the sessions. I anticipated difficulties with her as it was inevitable that she would get angry and be disappointed and I was bound to fail. I did not address her late attendance. The next session she said she needed to talk about a difficulty with one of her children. She had been shouting at him as he was not working hard doing the extra lessons and tuition she had arranged. She said she wanted to consider how she was dealing with him. We explored this in the session and looked at ways of reacting to her son and of her feelings. To me it had felt to be a positive session.

She did not attend the next session. I tried to contact her. She did not respond. After a number of weeks, I called her again and her husband picked up the phone and passed it to her. She was very angry and told me that I clearly had the view she was a rubbish parent and that I had no idea how good she was and that she did not want further sessions. She would not come to a session to discuss further.

On reflection, my own core belief about feeling not good enough and the desire to please others had led to my anxiety about knowing that I would displease Sue. I knew she would become angry with me. I also therefore let us be distracted into talking about child management approaches rather than keeping my focus on the main issues which led me to walk into a scenario whereby she would view my reactions as negative to her. I am sure this would have occurred in other sessions with other issues but I was blinded and did not see what was happening quickly enough within the session.

My countertransference issues affected the therapy process. My core beliefs about not being likeable and a fear of being abandoned are combined with a conditional assumption that if I try really hard I can please people. I recognised that she was likely to get angry and reject me. Many therapists enter the profession as they have a belief about being unlikeable or unlovable (Storr, 2012). I had felt that I understood these dynamics but the force of her anger had created a block in me.

I had not used my feelings to deal with her therapy-interfering behaviours which could have helped us to deal more effectively with her (and my) unconscious processes. An intellectual understanding of course does not stop the unconscious processes in the room and hence the importance of some understanding of the unconscious and one's own therapy for all practitioners.

Schema therapy

Schema therapy is used with people with personality disorder, and utilises many techniques to help weaken the maladaptive schemas and coping styles and rebuild the patient's healthy side. In a sense, schema therapy works with the patient's inner child to help correct the emotional difficulties experienced during childhood. Schema therapy works to rectify past emotional disturbances and change long-term patterns.

Vyskocilova and Prasko (2013) talked of the client modes or styles in schema focused CBT and talk of the vulnerable/abandoned child which is characterised by a complaining, helpless and hopeless stance and this can evoke in the therapist the countertransference response of:

1   hypercompensator where the therapist gives advice and overemphasises or empathises;
2   detached protector who talks about medication and detaches;
3   punitive parent who criticises lack of homework or little endeavour;
4   vulnerable, abandoned child where the therapist becomes helpless, feels guilty and reviews personal competencies;
5   angry child who criticises the client, punishes them and feels angry.

An awareness of countertransference issues is at the heart of such work and can facilitate therapeutic effectiveness and help our understanding of the client's experiences and behaviours. It can also prevent us from addressing issues which can sabotage progress.

Conclusion

I suggest that our cherished allegiance to Purity of CBT or PP is not of absolute importance. What is important is that attention is paid to the feelings and behaviours of the therapist and that this is used to help us get a greater understanding of our clients. This can prevent us engaging in unhelpful reactions and being blind to important things happening in the therapeutic process. The relationship is critical in all therapies and so it is inevitable that countertransference issues will emerge. These can be used to enhance our understanding or can prevent effective therapy if they are not noticed and addressed. Using supervision to explore such issues is helpful as otherwise our unconscious processes will interfere with our practice of CBT.

It is helpful that clinical and counselling psychologists receive training in both CBT and PP. However, it is apparent that some CBT therapists who focus more on manualised CBT, such as High Intensity IAPT workers, do not receive training in PP, and this has the potential for these important processes to be missed.

I have not reflected in this chapter on the differences and similarities between more classical PP and CBT approaches, but our knowledge of the importance of nonspecific factors and the evidence that experienced therapists using different therapeutic approaches achieve similar outcomes suggests this is not as important as the *quality of the therapeutic relationship* (Wiser, Goldfried,

Raue & Vakosh, 1996; Messer & Wampold, 2002). Research demonstrates that the most effective therapists are those that recognise transference and utilise it therapeutically, regardless of what types of therapy they are practicing, including CBT models (Albion & Jones, 1998; Jones & Pulos, 1993, quoted in Shedler, 2010, 2006).

Gomez (2004) argued that it is the atmosphere and intention in which the interpretation, *or therapeutic intervention*, is made which is important; the containing and being contained which promotes change as seen in Klein's 'containment' and Winnicott's 'facilitating environment'. This is true of all therapeutic approaches.

I recommend that all trainee and practising CBT therapists pay attention to the relational aspects in therapy and integrate an understanding and awareness of transference and countertransference into their work. Enhancing our understanding of our own dynamics can reduce therapy interfering behaviours and increase our effectiveness.

Bibliography

Beck, A. T. (1995). Beyond belief: A theory of modes, personality, and psychopathology. In P. Salkovskis (Ed.), *Frontiers of Cognitive Therapy* (pp. 1–25). New York, NY: Guilford Press.

Beck, A. T., Freeman, A., & Davis, D. D. (2004). *Cognitive Therapy of Personality Disorders* (2nd ed.). New York, NY: Guilford Press.

Beck, A. T., Rush, A. J., Shaw, B. F., & Emery, G. (1979). *The Cognitive Therapy of Depression*. New York, NY: Guilford Press.

Berry, K., & Danquah, A. (2015). Attachment-informed therapy for adults: Towards a unifying perspective on practice. *Psychology and Psychotherapy: Theory, Research and Practice*, 89(1), 15–32.

Bowlby, J. (1977). The making and breaking of affectional bonds. *British Journal of Psychiatry*, 130(3), 201–210.

Castonquay, L., Goldfried, M. R., Wiser, S., & Hayes, A. M. (1996). Predicting the effect of cognitive therapy for depression: A study of unique and common factors. *Journal of Consulting and Clinical Psychology*, 64(3), 497–504.

Cottraux, J., & Blackburn, I. M. (2001). Cognitive therapy. In W. J. Livesley (Ed.), *Handbook of Personality Disorders: Theory, Research, and Treatment* (pp. 377–399). London, UK: Guilford Press.

Degnan, A., Seymour-Hyde, A., Harris, A., & Berry, K. (2015). The role of therapist attachment in alliance and outcome: A systematic literature review. *Clinical Psychology & Psychotherapy*, 23(1), 47–65. doi:10.1002/cpp.1937

Eagle, M., & Wolitzky, D. L. (2009). Adult psychotherapy from the perspectives of attachment theory and psychoanalysis. In J. H. Obegi & E. Berant (Eds.), *Attachment Theory and Research in Clinical Work with Adults* (pp. 351–379). New York, NY: Guilford Press.

Feifel, H., Hanson, S., Jones, R., et al. (1967) Physicians consider death. *Proceedings of 75th Annual Convention of the American Psychological Association.* Washington, DC: American Psychological Association.

Gabbard, G. (1985). The role of compulsiveness in the normal physician. *Journal of the American Association, 254,* 2926–2929.

George, C., & Soloman, J. (1999). Attachment and caregiving: The caregiving behavioural system. In J. Cassidy & P. R. Shaver (Eds.), *Handbook of Attachment: Theory, Research, and Clinical Applications* (pp. 649–670). New York, NY: Guildford Press.

Gluhoski, V. L. (1994). Misconceptions of cognitive therapy. *Psychotherapy: Theory, Research, Practice, Training, 31,* 594–600.

Gomez, L. (2004). Humanistic or psychodynamic: What is the difference and do we have to make a choice? *Self and Society, 31*(6), 5–19.

Hayes, S. C. (2004). Acceptance and commitment therapy, relational frame theory, and the third wave of behavioral and cognitive therapies. *Behavior Therapy, 35,* 639–665.

Hayes, S. C., Strosahl, K. D., & Wilson, K. G. (1999). *Acceptance and Commitment Therapy: An Experiential Approach to Behavior Change.* New York, NY: Guilford Press.

Heard, D., & Lake, B. (1997). *The Challenge of Attachment for Caregiving.* London, UK: Routledge.

Henriques, G. (10 January, 2014). *CBT versus psychodynamic? No! It is wrongheaded to define CBT against PP as if they were horses in a race* [Online]. Retrieved from www.psychologytoday.com/blog/theory-knowledge/201401/cbt-versus-psycho-dynamic-no

Holder, J. B. (2013). *What are they? Comparing and contrasting three of the main counselling approaches* [Online]. Retrieved from www.counselling-directory.org.uk/counsellor-articles/what-are-they-comparing-and-contrasting-the-three-main-counselling-approaches

Jacobs, M. (1991). The therapist's revenge: The law of talion as a motive for caring. *Interdisciplinary Journal of Pastoral Studies, 105*(1), 2–11.

Johnson, W. (1991). Predisposition to emotional distress and psychiatric illness amongst doctors: The role of conscious and experiential factors. *British Journal of Medical Psychology, 64*(4), 317–329.

Jones, E. E., & Pulos, S. M. (1993). Comparing the process in psychodynamic and cognitive-behavioural therapies. *Journal of Consulting and Clinical Psychology, 61,* 306–316.

Lambert, M. J., & Ogles, B. M. (2004). The efficacy and effectiveness of psychotherapy. In M. J. Lambert (Ed.), *Handbook of Psychotherapy and Behavior Change* (5th ed., pp. 139–193). New York, NY: John Wiley & Sons.

Larsson, D. G. (1993). *The Helper's Journey: Working with People Facing Grief, Loss, and Life-Threatening Illness.* Champaign, IL: Research Press.

Leahy, C. (2001). Bilingual negotiation via email: An international project. *Computer Assisted Language Learning, An International Journal, 14*(1), 15–42.

Leahy, R. L. (2003). *Overcoming Resistance in Cognitive Therapy*. New York, NY: Guilford Press.

Lief, H. (1971). Personality characteristics of medical students. In R. Coombs & C. Vincent (Eds.), *Psychosocial Aspects of Medical Training*. Springfield, IL: C. C. Thomas.

Linehan, M. M. (1993). *Cognitive-Behavioral Treatment of Borderline Personality Disorder*. New York, NY: Guilford Press.

Magnavita, J. (2013). *Handbook of Personality Disorders: Theory and Practice*. New York, NY: John Wiley & Sons.

Malan, D. (1979). *Individual Psychotherapy and the Science of Psychodynamics*. London, UK: Butterworth.

Messer, S. B., & Wampold, B. E. (2002). Let's face facts: Common factors are more potent than specific therapy factors. *Clinical Psychology Science & Practice*, 9(1), 21–25.

Perlman, L. A., & Courtois, C. A. (2005). Clinical applications of the attachment framework: Relational treatment of complex trauma. *Journal of Traumatic Stress*, 18(5), 449–459. doi:10.1002/jts.20052

Persons, J. B. (1989). *Cognitive Therapy in Practice: A Case Formulation Approach*. New York, NY: W. W. Norton.

Pfeiffer, R. (1983). Early adult development in the medical student. *Mayo Clinic Proceedings*, 58, 127–134.

Prasko, J., & Vyskocilova, J. (2010). Countertransference during supervision in cognitive behavioral therapy. *Activitas Nervosa Superior Rediviva*, 52, 251–260.

Prasko, J., Diveky, T., Grambal, A., Kamaradova, D., Mozny, P., Sigmundova, Z. et al. (2010). Transference and counter-transference in cognitive behavioral therapy. *Biomedical Papers*, 154(3), 189–198.

Prodgers, A. (1991). On hating the patient. *British Journal of Psychotherapy*, 8, 144–154.

Rogers, C. (1957). The necessary and sufficient conditions of therapeutic personality change. *Journal of Consulting Psychology*, 21, 95–103.

Rosenzweig, S. (1936). Some implicit common factors in diverse methods of psychotherapy. *American Journal of Orthopsychiatry*, 6, 412–415.

Rycroft, C. (1993). Why analysts need their patients' transferences. *British Journal of Psychotherapy*, 10, 83–87.

Safran, J., & Segal, Z. (1990). *Interpersonal Process in Cognitive Therapy*. New York, NY: Basic Books.

Segal, Z., Williams, J. M., & Teasdale, J. (2001). *Mindfulness-Based Cognitive Therapy for Depression*. New York, NY: Guilford Press.

Shedler, J. (2006). *That was then, this is now: Psychoanalytic psychotherapy for the rest of us* [Online]. Retrieved from http://psychsystems.net/shedler.html

Shedler, J. (2010). The efficacy of psychodynamic psychotherapy. *American Psychologist*, 65(2), 98–109.

Skinner, B. F. (1953). *Science and Human Behavior*. New York, NY: Macmillan.

Storr, A. (1979). *The Art of Psychotherapy*. London, UK: Secker & Warburg.

Storr, A. (2012). *The Art of Psychotherapy* (3rd ed.). New York, NY: Routledge.

Tillett, R. (2003). The patient within-psychopathology in the helping professions. *Advances in Psychiatric Treatment*, 9, 272–279.

Vyskocilova, J., & Prasko, J. (2013). Countertransference, schema modes and ethical considerations in cognitive behavioural therapy. *Activitas Nervosa Superior Rediviva*, 55(1–2), 33–39.

Weinberger, J. (1995). Common factors aren't so common: The common factors dilemma. *Clinical Psychology Science and Practice*, 2(1), 45–49.

Wiser, S. L., Goldfried, M. R., Raue, P. J. & Castonguay, L. G., & Hayes, A. M. (1996). Predicting the effect of cognitive therapy for depression: A study of unique and common factors. *Journal of Consulting and Clinical Psychology*, 64(3), 497–504.

Wiser, S. L., Goldfried, M. R., Raue, P. J., & Vakoch, D. A. (1996). Cognitive and psychodynamic therapies: A comparison of change processes. In W. Dryden (Ed.), *Research in Counselling and Psychotherapy* (pp. 101–132). London, UK: Sage.

Wolpe, J. (1958). *Psychotherapy by Reciprocal Inhibition.* Stanford, CA: Stanford University Press.

Young, J. E., Klosko, J., & Weishaar, M. E. (2003). *Schema Therapy: A Practitioner's Guide.* New York, NY: Guilford Press.

Zigmond, D. (1984). Physician heal thyself: The paradox of the wounded healer. *British Journal of Holistic Medicine*, 1, 63–71.

Part II

Countertransference in the wider context in supervision, teaching, group therapy and in organisational work

Chapter 6

"Impossible to do, but possible to say"

Using countertransference in the trainer-trainee relationship

Russel Ayling, Egle Meistaite and Paola Valerio

> Even the most experienced psychotherapist will discover again and again that he is caught up in a bond, a combination resting on mutual unconsciousness. And though he may believe himself to be in possession of all the necessary knowledge concerning the constellated archetypes, he will in the end come to realize that there are very many things indeed of which his academic knowledge never dreamed.
>
> (Jung, 2013/1969, p. 178)

This chapter is co-written with two colleagues (one a fellow trainer, and the other a counselling psychology doctoral student, whom we trained), and concerned with countertransference in the supervisory and teaching environments. In introducing it, I find myself reflecting on some of my own experiences in education. I recall one incident as a small child during religious instruction, when the head teacher urged us to remember that God made us all. Striking my hand into the air, I enthusiastically asked, "But Miss, Miss . . . who made God?" She silently, purposefully strode to my side, whacked me around the head and strode off again without a response. This instilled in me a great sense of shame but also injustice. Interestingly, it also instilled in me not the hoped-for compliance, but the beginning of a rebellious defiance. I also recall, many years later at my comprehensive school, my History teacher who was a bit "scruffy", skinny with long unkempt hair, striding towards me during one lesson in which I was fooling around. He simply asked me in a concerned manner if I intended to continue wasting his and my time and thus, without him trying to shame me, curiously I felt shame.

Now I imagine my comment about God seemed blasphemous, or perhaps even perverse, in an environment that was all too restrictive. Yet, is it possible to speak about what is different, unusual, or doesn't fit in somewhere neatly (such as a little girl asking the teacher who made God, if God made everything); what is interesting, novel, risky, but potentially opens a door to somewhere else? "Perverse" may be all too knowing, as what one considers perverse may be another's preference, and it is certainly not a timeless concept.

Yet in becoming trainers, we get invested with all sorts of qualities, hopes and expectations. As Lacan termed it, we are "the subject who is supposed to know" (Rizq, 2009, p. 369), and indeed this is how we come to be invested with power and exert great influence in ways that may indeed later surprise us. Would the reader be surprised that I read History and not Religious Studies at university?

We are probably fairly comfortable with the idea that the supervisory process, to an extent anyway, mirrors the analytic one. As in the clinical situation, supervision takes place within the transference–countertransference matrix. It is an intimate relationship, conducted within the safety of the relationship's confidentiality, whether in group or individual format, and follows its own, mutually determined course. The difference between analysis and analytic supervision perhaps lies in the agreed-upon scope of the endeavour or "ground rules". In supervision, the field of inquiry is essentially seen as relating to the supervisee's analytic work. There are specific regulations laid down by the BACP/BPC/UKCP/BPS that are attached to the frame, regarding competency and a requirement for continual assessment, hence an inequality that is rarely available for negotiation. Yet, and notwithstanding such limits, the process is the mutual creation between the participants, just as it is in the analytic encounter. However, the scope of the enquiry ensures that there is a fine line between what the trainer should and should not say to the trainee about the trainee's unconscious defences or "blind spots" or the trainer's own countertransference, and that line relates to the task of learning, which is not necessarily the aim of analysis itself.

Although the role of the trainer cannot be divorced from the vicissitudes of organisational dynamics, this is not the main scope of this chapter. Transference and countertransference are equally alive and co-created between trainers and trainees, but we believe that countertransference is still acknowledged rather uneasily in training environments. Rather, it appears as the shadow in the seminar room, in the knowledge that it was only relatively recently invited in. Yet academic settings, where we are most often in dual roles as teachers and supervisors, demands of us as much self-reflexivity as in our therapist roles, as Lemma (2012) highlighted:

> As clinicians we take it for granted that we need to discuss our clinical work, but as far as psychotherapy trainers are concerned – a role that has such far-reaching consequences for future generations of therapists and hence for our discipline – we do not systematically institute a requirement to evaluate and monitor the process of teaching in this more self-reflexive manner, which is quite different from evaluating teaching through feedback from candidates.
>
> (p. 458)

As lecturers and supervisors, we each bring radically different styles of training to the mix, influenced by our own histories, experiences of education, analysis and supervision. Some of us instill and inspire more than others; some of us will inspire some and disappoint others, and that is never easy. Of course, we have most willing partners in our endeavours: anxious trainees and supervisees who have invested a great deal of time, money and effort in their training. The unconscious situation is ripe for much trouble, false conformity, conflict and trickster-like games. It is thought that many of us choose this profession because of less-than-ideal early environments. Many of us teachers, supervisors, therapists and trainees alike are grappling with our own wounds: we are often referred to as "wounded healers" (Guggenbühl-Craig, 1971). Throw in a big dollop of anxiety about successfully completing a professional training and/or an academic degree, whilst trying to work with vulnerable clients, often for the first time. Indeed, it's hardly a surprise that so many psychotherapy and psychology trainings are renowned for encouraging regressed states in our trainees, who scramble for our approval in forging a professional identity and hopefully ending up with a qualification.

As Egle suggests, supervised practice is much more than teaching, but less than treatment. However, it is still the case that the focus is all too often on learning for the trainee, or what supervision might *produce* (through the "parallel process" for example) in the service of the trainee's patient. All of this sets up an uncomfortable dynamic, one where it becomes harder for trainers and supervisors to acknowledge the not-so-knowing bits of ourselves and our learning, with trainees. I suggest therefore that we should place much more focus on the learning opportunity for the trainer or supervisor. Perhaps an idea of some sort of "parallel process" between the supervisor-as-trainer and the trainee, as well as the more usual trainee/client dyad. Hence what follows is an endeavour by a counselling psychology trainer (working both as lecturer and supervisor-tutor) and his trainee to share their experiences of a process of mutual learning and growth.

Paola Valerio

Russel's story

As Egle goes on to say, this piece of work signifies something new, and it was new for me as much as it was for her. This was not my first academic role as a psychologist, but it was my first since qualifying as a psychoanalytic psychotherapist. It was my first course team role as a clinical tutor, my first time writing about my work in a chapter of an edited book, and definitely my first time interpreting my countertransference directly with one of my trainees with the explicit aim of trying to disrupt a process. Egle and I are taking the unusual step of sharing an account of our journey in the latter, in the hope that it might be helpful for others too.

The setting was a professional doctorate in counselling psychology. The role was to lead the clinical practice module and work with a team of four

clinical tutors who were responsible for authorising trainees' clinical placements, managing any issues that arose on placements, and convening a weekly
clinical discussion group where trainees were required to take turns presenting material from their clinical work to a few of their colleagues and receive
feedback. This was the second of three years in the programme, a year exclusively devoted to learning how to work psychodynamically.

I only came to know Egle half way through the academic year. She had
begun her year in another tutor's group, and this group had run into difficulties with their tutor. The programme director and I had taken the decision to
disband the group and distribute the trainees across the groups of the remaining three tutors, of whom I was one. The difficulties in the other group had
resulted in a rather aggressive verbal attack on their clinical tutor, and from
the correspondence I had sight of, I made a judgment that Egle had been
one of the louder voices. Therefore, I decided to place her in my group in
order that I would be able to take up proactively and directly any issues that
were not resolved by, or indeed might be provoked by, the change of group.
Interestingly, I made this decision without having had personal experience of
being with Egle, and I found that I did not know her by sight. I had taught
the year group a few times but had not had reason to "put a face to the name".

The second half of the year progressed seemingly uneventfully; my group
accepted its new members, and the new members seemed to accept their new
group. Egle remained quiet, contributing a little discussion to others' presentations and asking a few questions. When the time came for Egle to present
her work, I listened with interest. I understood from the presentation that
Egle's patient was difficult to be with, struggled to receive interpretations,
and was contemptuous of the work and Egle's attempts to help. I felt that
Egle's responses to this were to be more challenging, perhaps intrusive, and
to attempt to out-manoeuvre her patient's thinking. It seemed to me that
they were tying each other up in knots. In the client session, a minute or two
away from the end, Egle had opened up the session again quite provocatively
in response to something her patient had said to her, and the session then
over-ran by ten minutes. On discussing this with Egle, I felt that she was
disinterested in the time boundary and was actually quite excited by the over-
running session. My own fantasies turned towards some kind of triumphant
retaliation by Egle over the patient and the regaining of some control by
breaking the frame. I felt quite frightened at the idea of them joining together
into some kind of sadomasochistic pact that neither of them seemed very conscious of. I found myself conflicted: I wanted to discuss the idea of a perverse
transference but it felt dangerous. On the one hand, it seemed intrusive and
unwelcome to label a relation in this way, in a group, with a trainee I knew
very little about. On the other hand, it felt remiss to ignore it, and I felt a
need to protect the client and the trainees by trying to educate them about
this particular kind of transference pull. I felt vaguely aware of my own perverse positioning here: an apparent black-and-white choice to either intrude

or watch helplessly. Grimly aware that neither would win, I opted to say what I could about what I felt was going on. In preparing to share my thoughts, it seemed impossible to conceive that they would be well received. My assumption, based on my history of engaging in similar work with other trainees in the past, was that I would be challenged, perhaps attacked. My knowledge of the events in Egle's previous group only added to my foreboding. But, to my surprise, I was met with acceptance rather than resistance from Egle. However, while my thoughts didn't seem new to her, neither did they seem particularly useful. I was left unsure what impact, if any, I had made.

In every tutor group meeting, there was some time reserved for discussing and troubleshooting practical and contractual issues that arose in placements, for documents to be signed, and the like. Egle brought an issue she had encountered on her placement, where she had been left on her own in the building seeing a patient, and she had not been aware of this until a member of security staff attempted to lock up the building. I was quite perplexed by the issue, as it seemed to represent another boundary breach. I struggled to understand from Egle's account how this situation had occurred, but I felt that whatever Egle's part in it, she shouldn't have been left in the building on her own. I advised her to establish what the service's policies were for evening working, and ensure that she followed them. No more was mentioned about the issue the following week, so I assumed all was well, and when I remembered to enquire about the issue a further week later (unhelpfully from my side, right at the end of the session) Egle told me, quite jovially, that it hadn't really been sorted out but that she would be leaving the placement soon anyway. On reflection and with the benefit of hindsight, I'm surprised that I didn't take what she said more seriously. Looking back, I think I fell into being as unconcerned as she seemed to be, and I chose not to intervene further here.

A couple of weeks later, the programme director received an angry e-mail from Egle's placement supervisor. Egle had told her that she was intending to leave the placement, but had done so in a manner that the supervisor felt was unprofessional. I had sight of the correspondence, and looking back now, the style was unconcerned and off-hand – just as I had experienced her when she told me about it. The supervisor raised other issues too, including the issue with the lone-working, and the chief complaint was that she felt Egle hadn't taken any of these seriously. She was most inflamed by Egle's writing that "no one [in the placement] knows what they are doing". At this point, all of these stories connected up for me, and I decided that it was time for me to take Egle seriously and to think with her about what she was doing.

I decided to invite Egle to a meeting with me. It felt vital for me to understand the position I wanted to take in relation to her and the issues, and I met with the programme director in advance of my meeting with Egle. Here, I clarified what "law" was available to me and to the supervisor, and found that in the current course regulations, the worst-case real outcome for Egle was that she would not be able to count the hours that she had spent on this placement. It wasn't very many, so while such an outcome would be inconvenient, it would have little impact on her training. I did feel that there were potentially graver consequences for the programme, as if the supervisor didn't think that we had taken her concerns seriously, she might well complain formally about our programme leadership. Personally and professionally, I felt the only outcome where I would be satisfied would be one where Egle took me seriously. I realised that this could only happen within our relationship, and that my next move would be a complex relational task.

I reflected privately on what resources I had to make this move, and realised that they were all inside me. In my own psychoanalytic training, one of my supervisors had helpfully offered me a perverse formulation to help me with my work with a very difficult patient where enactments were abounding. This had led me to take a particular interest in perverse dynamics, to write up my patient for my clinical paper, but most importantly and productively, to take my own perversity, as I saw it, to my own analysis and think seriously about its origins. I wondered if I could achieve part of this with Egle. I was most pressingly aware of, and anxious about, the potential of a boundary breach in overstepping my role, and generating a further complaint, from her about me. I didn't like the idea of treating Egle as a patient, by interpreting her unconscious from her behaviour, yet I wasn't sure how to avoid this. I wasn't Egle's analyst, and although I had some information both first-hand and second-hand about some of her behaviours, I certainly couldn't diagnose her as perverse! But I wondered, if I used all of my countertransference so far (which felt pretty perverse) to symbolise "as if" Egle were my perverse patient, could I at least avoid too much of my own enactment in my meeting with her? My understanding of Lacanian theory told me that there were transferential positions to be labelled yet avoided: the merging, seductive mother (or first-other) who would only be satisfied if her desires were met by the child; and the impotent and absent father (or second-other) who either looks away or looks on uselessly, powerless to intervene in the dyad. Could I be a symbolic father who could represent otherness: the law, our shared profession and its required practices, professionalism? A piece of relational analytic theory also came to mind, the idea that transformation happens when the analyst refuses to take a single position: when they can be in a duo, yet also external to it — as a third. Perhaps here, I could be an authoritative, symbolic trainer representing "other" but also a supportive, well-meaning and caring real person, trying to help Egle. To support and condemn at the same time. I wondered if a mixture of laying down the law, alongside disclosing my own identifications with her position and telling her my story about my perversity, might help Egle to use me in solving her problems with her supervisor, and perhaps too her problems with her patient.

Our talk that day seemed to move back and forth between discussing Egle's feelings about her supervisor and her reasons for taking the positions she took. I tried to respond in the same vein, talking explicitly about my feelings about the events and the position that I was trying to take. I entered a teaching place, sharing a nugget of theory and trying to link it with Egle's behaviours while also illustrating it with my own dilemmas, from when I too had been a trainee, but also from my own position now as a trainer. Looking back, the number of positions that it had been possible to both occupy and describe feels remarkable, although the boundaries between them felt very unclear, perhaps absent. Beyond this, the precise conversation we had that day is hard for me to remember; perhaps what was said is not as important as how it felt. I did feel like both a mother and a father. I felt close yet distant. I felt identified yet radically different. I felt useful and useless; understanding yet incomprehension. The conversation was circular, repetitious and unending. I remember the point that we both decided was time to stop – we had both done enough and had enough. I left the conversation feeling very unsure what had actually gone on, but quite sure that something had shifted, a connection had been made, and something had transferred from me to her, and from her to me.

In practical terms, other things shifted. Egle was able to meet her supervisor and come to an amicable ending, which allowed her to count her hours. She was able to write up the patient in question for her coursework that year, which Paola and I marked. Paola, who only been aware of part of the story, was most impressed with the reflexivity and I felt proud to have been part of it. Most importantly for me, Egle was no longer quiet. She joined me more in discussion in class, she asked my advice when a further ethical issue presented itself, and she agreed to contribute her story to this chapter to help others learn and develop, which I experience as a generous gift to others' process, as well as hers and mine. I also know that, in the writing of this chapter both together and separately, Egle and I have learned more about each other, ourselves and the space-in-between.

Egle's story

"Tyranny is the absence of complexity."

(Gide, as cited in Bonn, 2010, p. 1)

As I began to reflect on this chapter, I felt a familiar disorganisation. I was rapidly oscillating from order to chaos and back again in order to intermingle and connect my different levels (old and new) of experiencing, with explanatory constructs to produce understanding. What is my change? How did it happen? Who was contributing what? And why is change so difficult? At times, my loss of space for interweaving thought and feeling sank me into total confusion. I wondered, of all I perceived, what belonged to the client and what to me, and engaged in constructing familiar repetitive problematic interactions. My clinical work has been punctuated with self-destructive enactments and empathic blockages, and I am thankful that some of my countertransference scotomas were recognised through the encounter with my clinical tutor Russel.

It is important to mention that I will use the terms *tutor* and *supervisor* interchangeably in this text. The boundaries between the two roles felt blurred, the focus on matters of theory and technique intermingled with unconscious contents, and thoughts of how psychodynamically informed supervised practice in the second year of my doctoral training in counselling psychology affected my personal growth and clinical work.

So let me move on to what I think about my resistance against inner transformative dynamics!

"Towards pleasure. Away from pain. Pain. Pain. Spit it out. Squirm. Cry. Sleep. Dream. Pictures of fulfilment, pictures of rage." Here, Mary Shepherd (2015, para. 1) depicts babies' primary ways of coping with frustrating situations. We repeat negative impulses because it is easier; it does not require us to give up the pleasure involved, but it diminishes the ability to distinguish between ourself and others. And when something that the client or an Other says or does, connects with the aspects of the archaic self, "the awakening of sleeping tigers is not a welcome prospect" (Jacobs, 1996, p. 316).

My client Claire[1] had a long history in which she experienced marked cruelty and destructiveness from others. She was intensively preoccupied with what was in my mind, she Googled and analysed me, and for her, intimacy did not herald comfort and safety. Claire was skilled at making jokes and, at first, I naïvely colluded with her sense of self-deprecation. But my fascination with her narrative gave way to a feeling of being flooded and swamped. Moreover, each time I tried to say something, she immediately closed down and cut off. She countered all my attempts to intervene and anything I tried to offer by way of interpretation. Claire's enthusiasm abruptly transmuted either into detailed stories about her sexual experiences or into a reminder to me that my reflections were merely manifestations of projections. Something took place that was not spoken about, but bound us together. The rigid and controlling script was that of one person treating the other as a puppet in order to defend against the unbearable psychic pain of repeated experiences of early traumatic rejection (Welldon, 2009).

The experience of my tutor group, which was client-centred and both dialectic and didactic in style, greatly facilitated my cognitive-contextual learning. However, I wonder if in part it could have contributed to my resistance in becoming aware of the wounds of unconscious conflict in myself. On the one hand, due to my critical demeaning superego projections onto the group, and realistic concerns about evaluations of my work at the university by my tutors, I felt quite hesitant to reveal anything that I imagined might jeopardise my status. On the other hand, I am guessing that the clinical tutor is not meant to treat the aspects of the unconscious motivations and fantasies of the trainee, thus the presence of my perverse defences allowed me to stay immune to the effects of Russel's primary indications about some of my blind spots. Of course, I am not suggesting that I would have wanted to openly discuss my countertransference difficulties in the group. Training is a time of turmoil, and primitive feelings like envy and persecution can be easily stirred up in trainees.

Firstly, training for me was initially, in part, a regressive experience. I joined the doctoral programme in my thirties and I had to put aside my achievements in a former field. After years of successful management of my own company, it felt very unsettling to be a student again. A loss of power and status elicited strong needs for being admired and idealised. Secondly, as a beginner, I was in constant uncertainty: did I know anything at all about what I was doing? However, one thing was definite: my future career depended on getting good evaluations. Thirdly, most trainees see tutors, supervisors and the organisation as having great authority, thus it is not unusual for trainers to receive, and identify with, trainees' projections of parental transference. It can feel very uncomfortable knowing that a tutor could realise that an issue is less to do with the client than with my own lack of empathy. Finally, some of my anxieties lay at a much deeper level. It became apparent that I found it extremely hard to feel dependent on someone. Thus, in relation to the Other of authority, I enacted my sado-masochistic mother–child inner object relationships and evacuated my powerlessness in order to defend myself against my dreaded black holes of non-existence (Welldon, 2009), perhaps echoing my client.

While I was resisting to co-operate, I think it took patience and courage for Russel to try something new. As McWilliams (2013, p. 624) wrote, "When the amygdala erupts with red alerts, is not an abstract of theoretical notion to me". I received a direct prohibition to act out and a warning that I would lose Russel's support if I continued fighting. Three words – prohibition, support and loss – created the portentous moment of a real meeting, breaking out the confines of the academic ritual.

First, Kernberg (1987) noted that in upholding limits we present ourselves to be separate objects that are beyond the power of others' omnipotent reach.

Second, Russel set the constraints and placed my countertransference reactions in perspective with a tight and firm monotone, but in a supportive manner. He was neither an over-controlling moraliser, nor an anxious and resentful victim. This shattered some basic organising fantasies about the world or, as Phillips (2006, p. 219) put it, "being caught off guard" led to a sense of turmoil and brought a brief loss of my sense of self. The dyadic exchange felt messy and painful, in which anything unexpected could occur at any time. It took only minutes, but it felt like hours, for the emergence of an increased awareness of something new: call it a separate mind, the inner observe, a space to think or the emergence of the present.

Third, possibly my immigration status, as I am a foreign student, could have also contributed to the maintenance of insecure relatedness. Moving to a new country can leave one feeling robbed of safety and connectedness to the primary object – the mother country of symbiosis – and a strong yearning for a third identification with a new country – a fatherland (Pourtova, 2013). Meanwhile, the offer of genuine help mirrored my own lack as an imaginary form of castration and dependence on the Other. Finally, when Russel shared some personal views in regards to perversion, the dynamics in the room shifted again. Somehow it felt ultimately empty, released from some sort of inner tension. It felt more real and most importantly interdependent, now between what is *impossible to do but possible to say*, and this perhaps generated a hope that by being a little more conscious of my motives, I might need to enact them less.

I think the most helpful experience was when Russel was able to combine a holding environment with placing my countertransference in perspective with his own experience. Russel enabled an affective learning but did not overwhelm me and did not go too far; instead my problems were referred to my personal analysis. I offered my self-observations; Russel suggested his insight into the process and some useful meta-theoretical guidance without exploring or interpreting the roots of my issues. I think the supervision entered a "quasi therapeutic analysis" (Doehrman, as cited in Pegeron, 1996, p. 697), and this enabled:

- further development of self-awareness and a capacity to reflect upon myself. The "third" position brought a greater ability to contain the paradox of seemingly conflicting or discrepant understandings and perceptions of internal and external reality, allowed empathy and tolerance of other perspectives, affective experiences of change, uncertainty and confusion;
- thinking about the impact of the client upon myself and of my own reciprocal impact upon the client. It increased my ability to take up the projections and make sense of them without being too drawn into them. Hopefully it will help my client to think about her subjective experiences of me; and
- a facilitation of deeper examination of the unconscious motivations, fantasies, conflicts and breakthroughs in my personal analysis.

The experience of immediate change can be particularly extreme and painful, but I am doubtful if less intense experiences would have elicited the

emergence of very estranged aspects of myself. After all, it is compre-
hensible that for some clients, initially tolerating a great deal of anxiety,
uncertainty and "mess", as the systems theorists would say, makes little,
if any, sense at all. In this messiness, or non-sense, the disorganisation of
old meanings in the dyad became the source for new meanings to emerge
(Tronick, 2004).

Finally, my case illustrates that approaching the countertransference in
supervision and teaching can facilitate personal growth and new relational
experiences. Of course, I am not suggesting that this is the only catalyst for
the change. Complexity theory views "self" as a complex system that is a
part of other, larger complex systems. My transformation occurred and continues as a result of specific interaction in supervision, clinical placements,
personal therapy, and the training itself. Nor do I believe in a seductive simplicity of the change process: it is not some sort of healing linear
increase formula. Our analysis is an open-ended exploration and emotional
growth carries on throughout life. However, I hope that even a little bit of
change can go a long way. As Cwik (2006, p. 209) wrote, "Just one ounce
of the tincture, or stone, could transmute its own weight over a hundred or
thousand times".

Key learning points:

- For some trainees, training may inevitably encourage limited and momen-
  tary regressions, which can be destabilising and uncomfortable, but have
  the potential for an enriching experience.
- Running a tutor group/supervision space as suggested in this chapter
  could be thought of as a system of "triadic mundus imaginalis" (Cwik,
  2006). Firstly, it offers a cognitive/intellectual area, which creates a space
  to think, integrate theory and increase skills; secondly, it provides containment and management of countertransference difficulties; thirdly, a
  co-creation of the unconscious intersubjective third serves as a new relational learning experience.
- Supervised practice is more than teaching, but less than treatment. Perhaps
  at this level, academic input should not separate cognitive learning from
  trainees' sensitivity and personality and, if needed, to a certain extent,
  should facilitate movements in their personal therapies or analyses.
- In this way, change can involve surprise, chaotic anxieties and a heightened awareness in the dyad. It offers potential to continue to affect other
  areas of personal and professional development. Firstly, it increases the
  ability to reflect on subjective experiences; secondly, it enables the exploration of clients' mental and relational patterns; thirdly, hopefully it helps
  the clients to develop their own inner supervisor or ability to interweave
  thoughts and feelings.

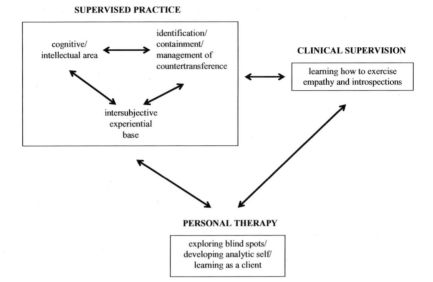

SUPERVISED PRACTICE

cognitive/
intellectual area

identification/
containment/
management of
countertransference

intersubjective
experiential
base

CLINICAL SUPERVISION

learning how to exercise
empathy and introspections

PERSONAL THERAPY

exploring blind spots/
developing analytic self/
learning as a client

Figure 6.1 Simplified reciprocal cycle of training that influenced Egle's change (after focus placed on the supervised practice)

Paola's reflections

I initially found this process difficult to reflect upon, being both inside and outside; inside in writing with my colleagues about the group; outside in that I was not a member of this tutor group nor the intimate dyad within the tutor group. I was Egle's lecturer (as I convene the psychoanalytic module on the doctoral programme, which was a group of 18 trainees that year) and was clinical tutor to another group of five trainees. I was initially concerned about a scapegoating process in Egle's original group (perhaps something had been transferred from the larger teaching group) but I also experienced a gut reaction of concern, perhaps even outrage, on behalf of my colleague who was clinical tutor to Egle's original group. On the final day of teaching that year, in the large group seminar, we talked about endings and I facilitated an experiential group. Interestingly, Egle and another trainee (who had been largely silent members of this large teaching group), were able to talk about their experience of being scapegoated or ignored by the others and there was at least the beginning of an idea that this might have stirred things up in the small supervision group. I wondered if Russel's timely disclosure in that chosen moment represented the "something more" that was needed to break the perverse coupling (Stern, 1998). Yet perhaps the place to end is to remark that there is no ending: The trainer tries to facilitate thinking, sharing and learning, which often involves acknowledgement of the importance of complexities, subtleties and imponderables, without claiming to be the one who knows or having to say the final word.

Questions for further reflection

How can exploring enactments in trainees' work with clients and colleagues aid their personal and professional development?

How should trainees' blind spots in the work with a tutor or a tutor group be taken up with them?

What are the primary tasks of the three different sources of training (i.e., academic tutorial group, clinical supervision and personal analysis)? What might be advantages and disadvantages of working at or beyond the boundaries of these roles?

Under what conditions might Russel's intervention with Egle have been unhelpful? How could he have used or responded to his countertransference differently?

What might have been happening in the organisation or in the large teaching group that could have been enacted in the small group? Was there another way to address this? Can you relate this to your own teaching and supervision groups?

Note

1 Claire is a pseudonym.

Bibliography

Böhm, T. (1992). Turning points and change in psychoanalysis. *International Journal of Psychanalysis*, 73(4), 675–684.

Bonn, E. (2009). Turbulent contextualism: Bearing complexity towards change. *International Journal of Psychoanalytic Self-Psychology*, 5(1), 1–18.

Brown, L. (Ed.) (1993). *The New Shorter Oxford English Dictionary on Historical Principles* (Vol. 2). Oxford, UK: Clarendon Press.

Cwik, A. J. (2006). The art of the tincture: Analytical supervision. *Journal of Analytical Psychology*, 51(2), 209–225.

Freire, P. (1970). *Pedagogy of the Oppressed*. London, UK: Penguin.

Guggenbühl-Craig, A. (1971). *Power in the Helping Professions*. Dallas, TX: Springer.

Jacobs, T. J. (1996). The patient as instrument of change in the analyst. *Psychoanalytic Inquiry*, 16(3), 314–339.

Jung, C. G. (2013). *The Psychology of the Transference*. New York, NY: Routledge.

Kernberg, O. F. (1987). *Psychodynamic Psychotherapy of Borderline Patients*. New York, NY: Basic Books.

Lemma, A. (2012). Some reflections on the "teaching attitude" and its application to teaching about the use of transference: A British view. *British Journal of Psychotherapy*, 28(4), 454–473.

McWilliams, N. (2013). The impact of my own psychotherapy on my work as a therapist. *Psychoanalytic Psychology*, 30(4), 621–626.

Pegeron, J. P. (1996). Supervision as an analytic experience. *The Psychoanalytic Quarterly*, 65(4), 693–710.

Phillips, A. (2006). *Side Effects*. London, UK: Hamish Hamilton.

Pourtova, E. (2013). Nostalgia and lost identity. *Journal of Analytical Psychology*, 58(1), 34–51.

Rizq, R. (2009). Teaching as transformation: A psychoanalytic perspective on psychotherapeutic training. *British Journal of Psychotherapy*, 25(3), 363–380.

Shepherd, M. (2015, April 23). *Why psychoanalysis?* Retrieved from https://bgsp.wordpress.com/2015/04/23/why-psychoanalysis/?iframe=true&theme_preview=true#more-280

Stern, D. N., Sander, L. W., Nahum, J. P., Harrison, A. M., Lyons-Ruth, K., Morgan, A. C., Bruschweilerstern, N. & Tronick, Z. (1998). Non-interpretive mechanisms in psychoanalytic therapy: The "something more" than interpretation. *International Journal of Psychoanalysis*, 79(5), 903–921.

Tronick, E. Z. (2004). Why is connection with others so critical? The formation of dyadic states of consciousness: Coherence-governed selection and the co-creation of meaning out of messy meaning making. In J. Nadel & D. Muir (Eds.), *Emotional Development: Recent Research Advances* (pp. 293–316). Retrieved from http://nicolettacinotti.net/wp-content/uploads/2014/06/NADEL-FEB-16-04.pdf

Welldon, E. V. (2009). Dancing with death. *British Journal of Psychotherapy*, 25(2), 149–182.

Chapter 7

'Just don't get involved'

Countertransference and the group – Engaging with the projective processes in groups

Cynthia Rogers

Introduction

The secret to conducting analytic groups is to monitor countertransference reactions, think about them and use them sensitively and reflectively to provide feedback to the group. I hope to interest the reader in using their countertransference to work with the projective processes in a group. The group therapist who employs a delicate form of free-floating attention will be able to tune into these unconscious communications in the group and reflect on the nuanced interactions. Staying calm and able to think in the heat of a group exchange is not easy. A therapist finding herself lost in the complexity and distress of the content of a group's narrative would be well advised to switch their attention to the unconscious communication. I hope by the end of this chapter you will understand why I recommend taking into the group with you, in your imagination, a large Gladstone bag, a tennis ball, a baby, a glove puppet and your favourite satirical cartoon.

Thinking about transference relations in groups

Transference is complex in groups. Transference relationships exist not only between the group members and the therapist but also between individual group members and subgroups. The therapist can observe, highlight and work with these relationships by reflecting on their countertransference in the moment. It is also helpful to think in terms of which split off affects are being projected in the group. For example, where a woman experiences a man in the group as if he were her aggressive big brother, this might also be interpreted as her denying her own aggression and locating it with him. In either case the therapist uses her free-floating attention and countertransference to relate to these unconscious communications.

Early group processes

A common unconscious fantasy among new patients is that an analytic group will provide a womb-like experience where they can regress and be totally understood without having to explain anything. Naturally the therapist who cannot provide this will start to have countertransference feelings around trying to live up to these demands. The frustrated patients will experience feelings of hate towards the depriving mother and group, whilst the therapist may fear being devoured by the group. If the therapist can take a step back in her mind and reflect on these feelings she may be able to disentangle herself from the identification with the overwhelmed mother that so many of her patients have experienced. She can then talk with the group about how disappointed they are to have to struggle to engage, and perhaps wonder whether there is any point. She might even share how useful it is that the group have given her a glimpse of what their experience has been and what they long for. The group may not be ready to talk about these feelings but the feelings have been noted.

The group looking at the unconscious communication involved and putting it into words usually works through this early stage with great care. However, this same process is needed throughout the life of the group. At a superficial level a group may appear to be communicating freely, but close attention by the therapist to her countertransference feelings of perhaps 'feeling defeated and not being quite good enough' will often reveal a group still struggling with the dilemma of how to say what it thinks, and still wishing that just for once it could be given the cup of coffee with the right number of sugars without having to ask for it.

Asking the group to do the work

> Why would a group do the work themselves, if they can persuade the therapist to do it for them?

In the early stages of a group, the members are often adept at behaving in such a way that the therapist carries their anxiety for them. A therapist starting a new group would be right to be anxious. Will anyone come? Will the members see what they have in common or just their differences? Will they engage with the process and one another? What will they make of him or her?

In some groups the members will talk about their anxiety as a way of bonding. They identify something they have in common and, together with the therapist, deal with their anxiety. However, in a group where a significant number have had unreliable parenting and they have learnt to rely on themselves, they may deny their anxiety and test out the therapist. They might plunge into very personal disclosure behaving like an apparently brilliant group unafraid to talk about anything and appearing not to have any qualms. The therapist might initially think she does indeed have a rather special group to conduct. Only later would it become clear that their anxiety had been dealt with through a projective process. If there is no anxiety shown and they feel no need to exercise caution, she might start to feel concern on their behalf about the risks they are taking and wonder what she will say or do if the group hits the rocks at full speed. The group can afford to be unconcerned because she is worrying and so they do not need to worry and they are free of their anxiety. Of course, being out of touch with the cautionary influence their healthy anxiety might have exerted, they are likely to behave in an increasingly cavalier fashion and the therapist becomes increasingly anxious. It feels like her anxiety; it looks like her anxiety and it would be natural for her to be anxious. However, if she can be encouraged to think about countertransference she might wonder why she is quite so worried, while they are quite so unconcerned and she might wonder whether the feelings go beyond her natural response to a new group and are a reflection of their early experience of not having their anxiety attended to. Commenting benignly on how surprised she is that no one has mentioned anticipatory anxiety is likely to enable the members to reconnect with, and share, their fear. I would expect the therapist to return to a normal, appropriate level of anxiety.

How it plays out in the group

> It is tough coming to terms with how like our parents we are.

Avoiding the critical parent

Many people are desperate not to be like their parents. Someone who grew up with critical parents is likely to be ashamed of their own critical aspects and try desperately to keep them hidden from others and themselves. One way of doing this is by provoking someone else into being critical and then sitting back reassured that they are not the critical one. Of course, it is a dysfunctional solution and the criticism is now both internal and external so the process has to be repeated endlessly. Take the scenario of a colleague who is furious about something but instead of expressing it goes around behaving in such a way that everyone gets frustrated and angry with them and then they can say 'I do not know what you are getting so uptight about'. Their anger has been expressed for them and no one is destroyed by it.

The important thing is that it is a way of dealing with parts of ourselves that we wish to deny or distance ourselves from, for whatever reason. There is a big element of control and manipulation in the interaction, all be it unconscious. It is not that people actually transfer feelings from one person to another but simply that they behave in such a way that the recipient feels the feelings that the projector can then deny or distance themselves from.

A therapist who finds herself in the grip of potentially overwhelming feelings, which the group are disowning and expecting her to deal with, might want to think about a glove puppet and reflect on whether the group has got inside her and is controlling her like a glove puppet by behaving in a certain way. Recognising it as dysfunctional will enable her not to collude with it and free everyone from what could become a stuck dynamic.

Group roles

> Group roles that appear to be helpful can become defensive and entrenched. The helpful group member; the group historian; the risk taker who gets things started; the kind, sensitive member; the reliable regular attender; the critic; the cynic; the catastrophiser; and the dreamer all might need to explore the unacknowledged and disavowed aspects of themselves. It is counterintuitive, but probably essential, for the therapist to explore members hiding behind roles.

A group can become stuck when group members assume roles for the group. The individuality disappears and members hide behind familiar behaviour rather than trying out neglected parts of their personality. A group member who is not used to taking responsibility will look around the group for another whom she imagines might be more competent than herself and behave in a way that invites the second person to step in. Whether she is successful in passing the responsibility on depends whether the recipient identifies with being responsible, in which case it becomes difficult to resist. Someone who has a tendency to rebel will find it easy to resist helping out, but when invited to attack the group leader he or she will probably find they have done so before the thought even registers. In other words, the projection 'lands' because the recipient has the valency for the split off attribute. They identify with it, introject it and then act it out. It would be easy for the therapist not to see this but if they can develop a kind of free-floating attention and become aware of their countertransference irritation about the predictability and 'stuckness' of the group they are better placed to work with it and question why 'James' allows the group to exploit his willingness to rebel. I think of it as the group throwing feelings in the air and seeing who will pick them up and deal with them for them, which is creative if it keeps moving but not if it gets stuck.

Much of the work in a group is sorting out 'whose feelings are they anyway?' Not everyone is equally susceptible to projective processes. Those who are empathic tend to be readier to take on others' split off and denied feelings. Reflecting on countertransference feelings critically is essential if one is to distinguish one's own feelings from those of others and wonder aloud where they belong. Group members who have a history of internalising and identifying with their parent's feelings, will naturally take on other group member's feelings if they are not careful. Equally someone who has always protected her younger sister may unhelpfully draw any group conflict to herself, relieving the others of the opportunity to learn to engage with tension and disagreement.

Not knowing

Being comfortable with not knowing is the beginning of learning something in the countertransference.

Central to conducting groups is recognising how little we know. Where eight people are of necessity giving us the minimum of information, we simply cannot know what is going on between groups. It is extraordinary what fails to be mentioned for one reason or another, accidents, suicide attempts, new relationships etc. However, resting in blissful ignorance is not an option. Taking countertransference feelings seriously allows a sense of fishing in the unconscious and letting information fall into its own pattern rather than risking premature closure. Noticing projections is a rich area for these fishing expeditions.

Asking patients to become aware of their response to transference and projective processes

Psychotherapy patients are asked to tread the delicate balance of regressing sufficiently to get in touch with unconscious processes whilst retaining the adult functioning necessary to deal with it. This is particularly so of people in group analytic treatment who have a clear role as therapists to one another. We are all the recipients of projections. Our friends and colleagues draw on their experience of life to predict how we might behave. It would not be surprising if a group member with an unkind sister is cautious around new women they meet, while someone with a supportive twin might be naively confiding in newcomers and find themselves surprised to be repeatedly let down. In a group these projections can be recognised and tested. The challenge is to ask the group members to recognise that they operate in a world of projection where we largely sleep walk and that their certainty about others is probably misplaced. Often, we do not even know what other people project onto us except through our countertransference experience. Group members can become aware of subtle incongruent feelings that alert them that this projective process is in operation and think about it together. Clearly in a situation like an approaching break or where a member is holding the group to ransom there can be excessive splitting and projection that are experienced as an attack on thought processes, destroying dialogue and needing very particular attention from the therapist who will reflect on her countertransference and interpret the projections.

Containing the projections

Group members with mothers who have failed them will tend to recreate this scenario in the transference with the therapist, who experiences the despairing dilemma of the mother. Wilfred Bion (Bion, 1984) described such a situation, where the mother could only respond to her baby by either denying the baby's feelings ingress or becoming prey to the anxiety. A therapist who is reconciled to the fact she is not perfect may be able to hold these feelings long enough to find a way of feeding them back but also modelling not taking on more than she can handle. We can hold and tolerate a lot but there will be issues that are too close and we have a duty of care to ourselves and our patients not to collude in this unhelpful experience. A recently bereaved therapist who omnipotently makes herself available to engage with her patient's sense of loss, rather than trust the group to deal with it, may find herself out of her depth and the patient knowing his feelings have damaged her.

> The path to hell is paved with good intentions. Beware the impulse to rescue.

Looking in the mirror

One cannot take it for granted that group members want to see split off denied parts of themselves. Show someone a photograph of themself and they usually dislike it. Mirrors are almost as bad. Our image of ourselves derives from the mirrors our families and wider society have held up to us that are designed to suit their purposes and idiosyncrasies. By each group member comparing the glass they see the world through they can begin to identify some of the distortions that have developed over the years. I think there are four types of mirrors:

1. The plain glass – simple reflection

Groups can act as a plainer glass with some of the distortions picked up through our family experiences ironed out. The patient uses the group as a mirror that she can hold up to see herself as the group simply gives feedback, about their reaction to her. Maybe simply that she is not unattractive or demanding.

2. The concave mirror – seeing ourselves in others

What happens when one meets one's twin? Imagine someone who is somewhat self-righteously tolerant and kind, watching someone else who is being sweetly reasonable, when it is quite obvious from the train of events they should be hurt and angry. She will see with extraordinary illumination, the falseness of her own suffocating kindness and how much simpler it would be if she could be direct.

3. The convex mirror – seeing the mirror image of oneself

It might be helpful to have someone timid in a group, together with a member who cannot resist acting rather like a 'bull in a china shop'. With help, they might come to recognise that they are the mirror image of one another and explore withdrawing the mutual projection of, and identification with, split off aggression to reclaim their rightful assertiveness and manage better their own aggression.

4. The magical mirror – the family come alive

The group can come alive, almost like a psychodrama, and seem to embody one member's whole family or perhaps reflect a joint inner world fear of total abandonment near a break. Staying calm and interrogating the countertransference can open up the possibility of a whole reworking of past struggles in the present and the development of some real intimacy.

Locating the projective processes in groups

In a group, there are a multitude of configurations whereby disowned and split off feeling can be projected into others. They can be located in the therapist, other members of the group, sub groups of the group, the group as a whole or pushed right out of the group into the external environment. Each will look plausible.

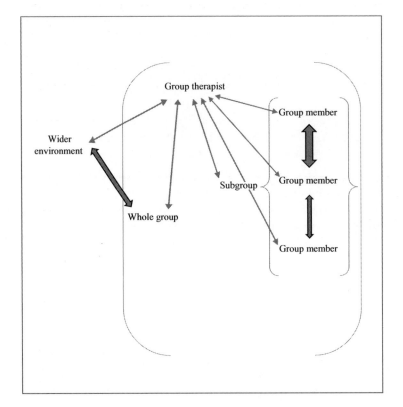

Figure 7.1 Transference relationships in a group

The therapist

If the therapist is the recipient of projections he or she can monitor this by their countertransference reaction as you would in individual psychotherapy. She may simultaneously be experienced and experience herself as the nurturing grandmother to one patient, the intrusive mother of another and critical father to a third. One member will be desperate for the therapist's undivided attention while another will be dismissive of any connection, certain they will be let down. It is complex for the therapist to inhabit this multiple role not simply sequentially but simultaneously.

Interestingly therapists can be required to carry the group members' good feelings. People who are prone to splitting try to keep the good aspects of themselves away from the destructive bad aspects and sometimes project their strengths into others who they hope will look after them. Patients come to therapy looking for help and in order to believe the therapist can help they may idealise the therapist. The patients do this by projecting onto the therapist their own strengths. This has some perceived advantages: the therapist is seen as wiser, kinder, more intuitive etc. The hope is that the therapist is then more able to tackle the very real problems the patient is bringing. The therapist who starts to feel over confident and brilliantly intuitive would be wise to wonder whether this is real or a countertransference reaction. A satirical magazine might come in handy here to remind the therapist not to believe her own image.

> A highly dependent group, where in the countertransference the therapist feels it is all down to her, might be indicative that the group members are denying their potency and locating it safely away from their own aggressive impulses in the therapist.

The denigrated therapist

In contrast, at times the therapist will be denigrated and it is important that she resist this projection. By embodying the transference relationships where she becomes experienced as the neglectful, competitive or critical parent, a window opens on the group member(s)'s experience. The therapist speaking in an unexpectedly aggressive tone to an apparently shy and silent group member might be put down to frustration on the therapist's part, or it might indicate the level of hidden passive aggression in the particular group member that needs to be explored. Determining whether the aggression belongs with the therapist or the group member is a countertransference exercise. A triumphant and yet more silently compliant group member might hint at a projective process that the therapist has fallen into. Equally if the therapist has simply got out of bed on the wrong side, lost patience or has slipped into a transference role as the critical mother, it would be important to acknowledge that to herself and possibly the group. It can be a real turning point because that gives a measure of the strength of the feelings the group member is struggling with, which the therapist needs to respect.

Members

Naturally most of the projective processes occur between the members of the group with endless possibilities for the open expression of denied feelings. Group members will readily accept roles they are unconsciously assigned provided such a role complies with their own fantasy. At the simplest level one member might relate to another as if she were her big sister who always knew best and did not listen. Simply allowing this to go on and each group member eventually coming to understand and respect one another allows the projections to be worked with and withdrawn. However, there can also be a more lethal subtle continuous process, which if unaddressed, results in one member of the group carrying feelings of inadequacy for the whole group and eventually leaving. Groups are often reluctant to give up their scapegoats and will resolutely deny any identification with the patient carrying the projections, especially if they are fulfilling the important function of making others feel superior. Behr and Hearst (2005) described how 'monopolising and victim behaviour are particularly deceptive manifestations which can lead to scape-goating, since they all too easily invite the self-justifying collusion of the group, including at times, the conductor' (p. 155).

Groups are very talented in identifying who will hold what feelings for them. A 'rule bound' member who likes to patrol the boundaries will probably be set up by the group to act out their aggression towards the therapist, leaving the rest of the group free to disapprove and disowning the part of them that would like to behave unreasonably. Others will be allocated the role of crying, or talking excessively. Drawing attention to this exploitation may be more helpful than addressing the monopolising or the distress. 'I wonder why the group is leaving X to do all the work?' or gently suggesting to Y 'I don't think you are alone in feeling sad but I worry that the group are using you to express it for all of us which is why it feels so endless'.

In a common example a group member projects their wish to be brought into the group in such a way that others feel the need to include that member. The compulsion that is felt to ask 'How are you this week?' is an indication that projective processes are at work rather than simple kindness or curiosity. It is not a healthy position for the quiet member since they are not only projecting the need to be included but also the strength to bring them in that they endow other members with. The danger is that if people resist the impulse to include them they are left high and dry and further weakened. If the group can become aware of this and wonder about the way the member got what they needed, they may be able to help the patient re-own their own strength and begin to move forward to more mature forms of communication, such as asking, rather than staying in the terribly vulnerable dependent position. Most exciting is when members are able to notice feelings derived from early experience which tend to take them over and, in the very special atmosphere of a group, resist acting them out and instead talk about them.

Subgroups

Subgroups can be supportive and creative, making strong connections and exploring difficult feelings together. In a healthy group the subgroups will be fluid, establishing new connections and morphing into patterns of relationship that will move the work forward.

Subgroups are more problematic when they become stuck in malignant mirroring. The established members of a group rejecting the intruding new members, or the men and women behaving as if they come from Mars and Venus.

Men are not always familiar with talking about their feelings and it is not unusual for them to feel increasingly inadequate as the women want more from them than they feel they can give. As the men become more passive the women become increasingly strident and the two subgroups despair as they fulfil each other's predictions. It would be easy to mistake the women for harridans and the men as withholding but the therapist's countertransference reaction will give a clue as to whether it is reality or whether the women are caught up with increasingly passive men who are disowning and projecting their potency into the women who as willing recipients become emasculating. Most likely both are true but the group needs to explore it rather than each subgroup hold the other in contempt.

Whole group

Feelings that cannot be contained by individuals can be projected into the whole group. At one point the group might be idealised perhaps in the face of an ending, or it might be seen as a frightening dangerous place, a mirror of the members' inner worlds, which they do not wish to tolerate and hence they stay away. Through mutual projection a new member can come to embody the fears and fantasies of the existing members. A man joining a group, who is hyperaware of but unconfident of his sexuality will stir up sexual anxiety in the group. Where group members have been abused physically or sexually the fantasy may become so alive that they are unable to see him and he is unable to disentangle himself from their history. The safest place for the overwhelming fear and rage to go is towards the therapist who might be attacked ferociously for failing to protect the new member, or the group, and has allowed the group to become a dangerous place. It would be easy for the therapist to get caught up in the projections and feel she had made a terrible mistake and wonder how she could have been so neglectful. If she can resist enacting the transference and take a moment to reflect on the careful selection she made and wonder why the man is presenting himself as he is, she may be able to see that what has come into the room is their mutual fear. When a group projects all their rage and fears of sexual violence into the group as a whole it is a rather scary place to be. In the therapy situation, early fears and phantasies come into the room and the experience is not simply repeated but approached differently. The group members are not alone, they can share the feelings, think together and ultimately there is a new and different experience. For this to happen the therapist uses her countertransference experience to fully name the fears and fantasies but also to assert that it is what they are there to deal with, that she trusts them to deal with it and introduces the reality that what they are engaged with are negative predictions, not violence that has happened in the group. For a while the group had become the patients' inner worlds made manifest. Clearly if the therapist believed the reality was that she had made a selection mistake she would take a different path; explain to the new member that she had misjudged the appropriateness of him joining this group at this time and help him understand the complex interplay at work.

It is the therapist's responsibility to distinguish fantasy from reality and insist on thinking about what is happening not simply carry on acting it out. It is helpful to nudge the group at one moment towards engaging at a primitive unconscious feeling level and at the next to reflecting on the experience thoughtfully to avoid getting stuck in a malignant mirroring of past experiences.

> A therapist using free-floating attention can enable group members to examine and re-own difficult and valuable disowned aspects of their personality that might otherwise be located in the therapist, other group members, subgroups and the group as a whole.

Staff groups and large groups

In a world of social media and globalisation, relationships are increasingly multifaceted and individuals are challenged to engage simultaneously on many levels. Staff groups, student groups on courses and median groups provide support for these activities by addressing the shared culture and how it can be made to work, rather than be the individual's difficulty. It is a place where an individual can acquire the skill to follow multiple conversations simultaneously whist holding on to their own thoughts, experience how differently others think and become aware of the culture they are operating in.

Conducting these groups is tricky. Frequently no personal family history is forthcoming and even catching up with events is likely to be sketchy. However, if each session is treated like an assessment where the therapist without memory or desire focusses on their countertransference reaction to the material it can provide a clear elucidation of the underlying dynamics that drive the decisions the team or group engage with (Rogers, 2013). Understanding why this dynamic predominates and what comfort it gives, is essential before trying to frame a supportive intervention that might help the group think about their situation from a different perspective. These groups are not stranger groups and the individuals are bringing a complex field of external interactions to the group. Even defining the purpose of the group and what the members would like to get from it requires considerable activity on the therapist's part. Simply leaving it to see what happens results in considerable dissatisfaction when people do not get something useful. Some psychotherapy student groups are conducted to maximise the projections so students experience being on the receiving end of powerful projections and start to learn to listen to their countertransference while their thinking capacity is under attack. If they develop a real respect for unconscious processes they can draw on this experience when they are with patients, provided they have properly understood their own countertransference experience and not simply withdrawn from it or been frightened by it.

Teaching reflection: Images

I would like to leave the reader with the images which sum up the ideas in this paper.

The Gladstone bag

The Gladstone bag reminds me that the group as a container needs to have plenty of room for manoeuvre, giving flexibility but also good boundaries. If a group can contain difficult feelings, they will be able to think and reflect and they will be less likely to revert to projective processes. If I insist on a tight briefcase or let it become loose like a laundry bag no one will feel safe.

The tennis ball

If a ball is thrown towards a group of people one of them will catch it almost on a reflex. Anyone who has been to a pantomime will see the way people elbow each other out of the way to catch the sweets thrown into the audience. What I am suggesting is that feelings are just the same. If split off disowned feelings are bouncing around in a group someone will pick them up. They may get stuck with them but the therapist and the group can learn to encourage one another to own the feelings, pass them on or share them.

A baby

In the presence of a baby there can be no doubt about the power of projective processes as a form of communication. When a baby cries, I would be utterly unable to resist doing what was necessary to meet the baby's needs. His crying would mobilise in me feelings commensurate with his feelings of life and death, such that I would have to do what he needed, in order to reduce my own levels of anxiety, which of course in turn reduce his. The challenge to group therapists is to know how to handle communication that uses projective processes. Also, to sensitively allow the group to regress sufficiently to get in touch with primitive material while moving forward to more mature ways of communicating which are less dependent and more articulate, i.e. dialogue and free-floating discussion.

A glove puppet

Conducting groups is hard work but immensely rewarding. One has to develop respect for the power of unconscious processes or one can be open to quite serious attack from the group's split off unmanageable emotions. The glove puppet is here so that on a bad day a therapist in a group, feeling powerless and controlled by the group, might not berate herself or contemplate giving up but she might have an image of a glove puppet and recognise that the patients have got inside the therapist's mind. That might allow her to stop and think 'What are the unconscious split off feelings that I am both feeling and acting out? How can I give them back to the group?' People are amazingly reluctant to do this and somehow feel safer blaming themselves, rather than acknowledging the power of the unconscious forces that the group has stirred up, and the real fear of the feelings that are being denied.

The satirical cartoon

It is important for the therapist to acknowledge and think about feedback from the group whilst being wary of completely believing either their idealised, or their denigrating view of the therapist. The satirical cartoon of what happens to politicians who believe their own image can keep the therapist grounded.

Bibliography

Behr, H., & Hearst, L. (2005). *Group-Analytic Psychotherapy: A Meeting of Minds.* New York, NY: Wiley.

Bion, W. (1984). *Second Thoughts: Selected Papers on Psychoanalysis.* London, UK: H. Karnac.

Rogers, C. (2013). Engaging with the median group. *Group Analysis*, 46(2), 183–195.

Chapter 8

Can organizations use countertransference to reflect?

Suzanne Weeks

Introduction

Countertransference is how I feel when I am with "you", because of "you". In this chapter, the "you" is the organization. I have many years' experience coaching in and consulting to organizations. However, there are times when I walk into an organization and find myself lost for words and doubting my competence.

A simple example to explain what countertransference in organizations can feel like is when I stand outside the building, feeling confident and competent about my abilities and experience, compared to when I am in that organization and I lose that feeling and sense of competence, often within the first hour. We can use our understanding of these dynamics that are emerging within the organization, and between the organization and the consultant, as an essential element of our interpretative work. As an example, imagine that you have never been into any shop or restaurant, so you have no expectation of what happens inside. Now imagine you go into McDonald's for the first time. What do you see, what do you feel, what is your experience? Now imagine walking into a Tiffany store for the first time, with no previous knowledge of the brand. Again, what do you see, what do you feel, what is your experience? One has tiled floors, the other carpet; the lighting is different; the ratio of staff to customers is different; waiting time is different and so forth. If we put aside our expectations from knowing these brands, and focus only on our experience as we enter – we start to get a sense of the countertransference in organizations. What do I experience on the inside? This is what we explore in this chapter.

The use of the concept of the analyst's countertransference has always been viewed as a key element of clinical practice in psychoanalysis. Yet, countertransference is not exclusive to the clinical domain, and is an equally valid concept in organizational and coaching work, offering as it does "data" about unconscious communication.

Organizational consulting to organizations

In working with and consulting to organizations, the framework we use in this chapter to interpret and learn from these cases is that of Hinshelwood and Skogstad (1994). They take into account the following four dimensions of observation.

1   **The recognition of the unconscious dimension.** In order to address the unconscious dimension in an organization, we use the metaphor of the iceberg – **what** is above the surface, seen, heard and known? More importantly, what is under the water surface – the unconscious level, including the irrational, emotional – and unknown? We can try and explore the **why** of what we see and hear. These hypotheses can be shared with the client, and this is one way in which the consultant can help bring forth the unconscious of the client into the conscious mind.
2   **The observer's subjective emotional response (countertransference).** I share my own experience of my emotional responses, and how I used them in the service of the work with the client, sometimes as they arose, and sometimes after several weeks or months had elapsed.
3   **The consultant's capacity to reflect and think.** In considering our capacity to reflect and think, we use two specific lenses here, through which we collect and subsequently interpret our data.
4   **Interpretation.** This is used during the consulting assignment when the feelings, experiences, countertransference and reflections are shared back with the client as part of the ongoing work together. In the case studies that follow, we share examples of what happened when the interpretations were given to the client.

The different levels of analysis

Wells (1985) identified various levels of analysis, including the intrapsychic, interpersonal, group, intergroup and system levels:

- The intrapsychic (individual) level is what happens either inside ourselves (as the therapist, coach or consultant) or in the individual client.
- The interpersonal level is what happens in the intersection of any two individuals.
- The group level is what happens in a particular group, which is composed both of individuals and multiple interpersonal dynamics. From Bion's work (1961), we know that a group has an unconscious in the same way that an individual has an unconscious – and that individuals and subgroups can be triggered to act in particular ways "on behalf of the group". Similarly, groups may need scapegoats, rescuers, harmonizers

and persecutors, many of the same roles we see emerging in interpersonal and family systems.

- The intergroup level is what happens between two groups – and how might some of the behaviors and actions change, and what might happen in the unconscious of both groups.
- The final level we consider in this chapter, and based on the Wells' definition of levels, is the system level, or level of the organization, which can be composed of many different groups and subgroups, hence each individual may be a member of multiple groups and subgroups in both the formal and informal systems within the organization. The unconscious of the organization is, at times, visible in its' culture (Schein, 2004), and we address the organization level in all four case studies.

The second lens we consider is the consultant's capacity to think and reflect in the context of organizations. It is what happens to a specific person in a specific role in a specific organization. How does that relate to the person's history, and how does it relate to the history and expectations (and job description) of the role? In most cases, the role has a history from previous people in the same role. The organization has its own history and culture, and expectations both of people in the organization and what is expected of particular roles. As an example, most organizations have both a human resources director and a finance director. However, what is included (and excluded), the level of autonomy, the scope and the level of the role compared to other directors can vary enormously by organization. Based on the work of Newton, Long and Sievers (2006), we will leverage their organizational role analysis suggestions to consider the individual, role and organization.

In our first case, we look at a person (in a role) in his organization. The second case considers how the organization may influence the behavior of the individuals. The third case looks at the impact of role and organization on the individual, as we follow one man through three roles in two organizations. Finally, the fourth case study is used to show how the person, the role and the organization all impact how the person is seen both in role and by the organization when the organization is under stress.

Consulting to organizations

Projections are as prevalent in work in organizations as they are in any other group you may work with. In the case studies in this chapter, we distinguish between the projections onto the individual and those onto the role that person occupies. For example, a school child may come home and describe to her parent how the teacher is a monster. In most cases such as this, the child is identifying with the authority of the role, and not with the individual herself.

In working with organizations, we place an increased importance on the "task" when compared to working with individual clients. Clarity about the task for which the consultant is hired is essential. For example, when a coach is hired by a company, the individual's goal (task) may be to get promoted and increase salary, while for the role that he occupies, the task (and therefore success) might be in better controlling his department and getting better results from his staff. However, for the organization, the most important task might be to stop him being a micromanager. Of course, all three are linked, yet they are not the same. Hence, the importance of a clear, agreed task. If the task (and therefore goal) is not clearly stated and agreed up front, confusion in terms of task and role are inevitable, and the chances of success are reduced, while the chances of potential damage to one of the individuals concerned increases.

Case study 1: Andrew, regional director of Dog Care, Inc.

The first case takes place in a major food company; part of a multinational, we shall call Dog Care, Inc. I was hired as a coach for the regional director, Andrew. I agreed to shadow him and work with his senior management team for a day. I would observe and feedback my experiences and observations, so he could improve his own leadership development and team working.

When I first walked into the offices of Dog Care, Inc., I was greeted by the receptionist with a smile. While sitting in reception waiting for Andrew, something felt familiar and comfortable. I noticed there were many photos of cats and dogs on the walls along with familiar corporate values. I noticed two bowls of water for dogs, there was much evidence that dogs were as welcome as humans. The water, photos and friendly face left me feeling very comfortable and "at home". It was a feeling I had never experienced sitting in the reception of a factory or corporate office.

When Andrew arrived we passed through a number of open spaces – I was initially amazed at the presence of dogs in baskets under the desks. I felt comfort and familiarity, and my associations were around being in homes with dogs; my associations were of more freedom in this organization and the ability to choose rather than being dictated to or rigidly enforced rules.

In Andrew's office, a traditional and easily recognizable senior manager's office, I felt comfortable, and as if I were meeting people and not only the role (the "marketing director" or "sales director" for example). Being in such an environment where the person as well as his role was evident had a direct impact on the work together.

I spent the morning with the senior management team. While the objectives of their meetings were (mostly) achieved, the manner of interaction was cordial and collaborative: Voices were not raised and there were no direct contradictions.

Following the meeting, I asked Andrew to describe himself and other members of his team in metaphors, as a way to surface some of the unspoken dynamics, projections and transferences within the senior management team and the organization.

The senior manager used mostly animals for his metaphors, seeing himself as the "lion". Other members of the management team included the "ghost", "monkey", "rhinoceros" and "cat", with his two key direct reports as the "fox" and the "elephant".

When I returned nine months later, the building, surroundings and people remained the same. However, my experience in the management team meeting, and the relationships and conversations between them, had shifted significantly.

Interpreting case study I

If we look at what happened within the senior management team (a group) my own emotional response was that, at times, I was almost bored and sleepy and struggled to maintain full attention: The edginess, contradictions and direct challenge I experience in many senior management meetings was reduced. I felt more like I was with a group of tired, old dogs and not with young, ferocious hunting dogs who want blood. My subjective emotional response and the impact on my own work, questions I asked (and did not) and hence countertransference was in being more careful than normal, avoiding asking critical questions and not pointing out all the unfinished business at the table. It was much later that I understood my reaction of sleepiness as fitting with the group and company culture, which later emerged as being very consensus driven, often much more important than fast decision making.

This culture of consensus was also significant in how this group worked together, how Andrew works as an individual, and the impact on my emotions. By being able to understand the intersection of the person, role and organization, I was able to help Andrew interpret what might be happening, to improve the effectiveness of the team meetings.

We used Andrew's metaphors for the individuals in his team, and the way they work together in the team, to explore his associations onto these characters. Bringing in my own countertransference, we were able to surface a number of unaddressed dynamics – the "elephant in the room" in terms of what was never talked about in the management meetings. The accepted absence of the ghost – who was physically present in meetings, but rarely spoke, was often ignored or dismissed, and, as later became clear, often felt invisible. This is an example of how we were able to consider the individuals at the table as well as the roles they represented in how the group worked together.

Over the next six months, I met with Andrew every two weeks and we worked with his associations to address some of the unhelpful dynamics which were initially a part of the life of this particular team. Andrew later asked the ghost about his presence (and absence) in management team meetings, and the ghost shared how he felt invisible and unheard. Together they agreed a way for Andrew to actively include him and solicit his opinion more in such meetings. In a later discussion with the "elephant in the room", the difficult negotiations around budgets were addressed directly, Andrew expressed his frustration about what was seen but not spoken, and asked the elephant to speak more and address the specific issues (with supply chain). Over the following months, the tension around budget discussions and what could be said was notably improved.

How I used countertransference

The comfort I felt in the organization setting may have contributed to my own avoidance of asking more difficult questions, or sharing more controversial hypotheses and observations. I was able to understand my own sleepiness as avoidance, as countertransference mirroring group avoidance. By sharing my observations and my own emotional response with Andrew, he was able to consider both his own avoidance in general and the avoidance in his regional director role in particular.

When I returned for my second visit, my experience was different. I did not feel sleepy in the meeting, but more energized. Difficult topics were addressed and discussed. Everyone was on time to the meetings and there was more informal banter between them. Using my own experiences as well as those of the senior manager who was my client, we had been able to have a significant impact on the nature and productivity of the meetings.

> In your experience as a consultant (whether as coach or therapist), how has the external environment impacted on your emotional response and your work?
>
> In what organizational settings do you experience yourself as at your most effective, and when do you experience yourself as less effective? Reflect on how the countertransference from the organization contributes to your experience.

Case study 2: Senior leaders working for a tobacco company

What was your first reaction to a case from the tobacco industry? It attracts many projections – it can be vilified, hated, seen as a killer. Yet for some individuals it is the provider of one of their favourite products (tobacco) and for others, it can be the employer of choice, paying above-market-average salaries. Given my own ambivalence about working with the tobacco industry, when I first started working with a group of senior managers I was curious about how I might relate to the organization and the people.

My role was as an executive coach. My task was to help them learn about themselves and their leadership in the context of the group that week, and as individuals over the coming months in individual coaching sessions.

In the first encounter, I met six senior managers. I was surprised by how anxious I was – unusually so, and uncomfortable. I felt compelled to explain every detail of the "what" we would do, with much less emphasis on the vision for the work together and potential leadership development.

By the end of the second hour, we had conducted an introductory exercise: drawing a picture to represent their personal and professional identity, past, present and future. Everyone has an opportunity to first draw and then share their own story. The group is then encouraged to be curious about each other and to look at similarities (or differences). The purpose is to be able to learn not just about ourselves but also to consider what might be some of the organizational issues in the recurrent themes. Their drawings were all very precise, often angular, and many were drawn in boxes.

A dynamic which surfaced was consistently asking questions with tangible answers, a reluctance to be curious, and an unwillingness to answer "I don't know" or "I am not sure". The conversation was very much above the water surface of the iceberg. When I first asked the question about these patterns, I was met with denial and dismissal.

Interpreting case study 2

The drawings were a way to access the unconscious of the individuals. The themes across drawings surface some of the unconscious dynamics of the organization. I found myself focusing on the words (the rational) and not on the drawings (the access to the unconscious). I was in a very rational world of absolutes, and felt deskilled in looking at the images and unable to access my emotional response. When I reflected, there were many clear signals to the unconscious needs of the group, including control and safety. Initially, I could not access my own emotions and I felt I needed to protect myself. I came to understand that this was exactly what the group were also doing. The hypothesis I shared with the group was that they were transferring onto me their own need to protect, and with a hope that if I could become one of them, I would be less threatening in my role. For example, as one of them, I would ask rational questions and not ask about feelings. In my role, I was very threatening to a group who wants control, where every rational and tangible choice and task must be perfect. Discussing what is not perfect or considering the nonrational was not just threatening to the individuals, but as later became clear, to the organization.

How I used countertransference

When I used my experience with them, there was a shift in the dynamic – from the outsider who has to be controlled, I became an object of curiosity to be examined. In this company, rationality is valued, and emotions and feelings are dismissed or ignored (or in some cases, sent out of the room). This was a tipping point moment, in moving to a different kind of conversation where the irrational could be acknowledged as well as the rational.

By being more human in their leadership roles, they were able to connect differently that week, and in other relationships in the wider organization. They all reported the impact on their personal and professional relationships, and the quality of those relationships, and how this, in turn, enables them to be more effective leaders.

Case study 3: Same person, different roles and organizations

This third case focuses on a senior manager, Bruno, in three different roles in two different nongovernmental organizations (NGOs). The individual remains the same, but the role and organization change. Bruno worked with me as a coach and consultant at different times over a period of five years.

In the first experience of working together, he had been in his management role for about three years. He is ambitious and driven to move up and expand his scope of responsibilities. When I walked into the organization, the reception area was colourful, filled with posters representing the NGO and its mission. However, the atmosphere conveyed something else. I spent quite some time riding up and down in the elevators of the building gaining a sense of the culture, mostly feeling confused, cynical and skeptical. Elevator conversation followed one of three patterns: nonexistent, excessive smiling and forced politeness discussing issues outside the organization, and complaint – when discussing anything from inside the NGO, it was in a resigned way, as if nothing could ever change.

In working with Bruno in this first assignment, the rational part of the conversation was often around his ambitions and goals for his department, his energy and vision to get it done, and the frustration with having the organization not seem willing to adapt and grow at the same rate as he wanted to. It emerged that the organization was in a period of great skepticism and cynicism. Bruno saw many staff as lazy or not willing to work hard enough, and many senior managers as not decisive enough.

About a year later, the NGO went through a significant restructuring. Many people were made redundant, new people were brought in, the posters disappeared from the reception area and a depressed and fearful lull dominated the corridors and elevators. Bruno had been promoted and his scope of responsibility significantly expanded.

As part of the restructuring, many people were forced out of the organization and others chose to leave, including a significant share of Bruno's department. He was perceived by many as ruthless and hard headed. He was unwilling to see himself (only) in this way, and much of our work at that time focused on these dynamics and his role.

The following year, he was offered the role of executive director in a different NGO. In this significantly more senior role, he was no longer in daily contact with peers and superiors; his daily life was mostly with his direct reports and many of his staff felt the need to please him more than challenge him and his views.

After about six months in role, he asked me to work with him and his team. The organization moved office, from a very dark, dungeon like and depressive building and atmosphere to a light, airy suite of offices on the eighth floor, with impressive views and a hopeful feeling.

Interpreting case study 3

In our initial conversations while Bruno was in his first role, I alternated between feeling powerful and competent, and dominated and used. While Bruno did not appear to challenge his senior managers directly, I felt both challenged and also inadequate, as if nothing was ever enough. As we worked together I was gradually able to share with him my own experiences and explore with him in his interactions with me. He was not feeling intellectually challenged at work, so he would relentlessly challenge me to generate a reaction and as a way to find the challenge.

During our second assignment (the period of major change) in the building and the organization as a whole, I found myself feeling tired, and the quiet corridor and elevator murmurs felt more secretive and subversive. The fear of losing jobs was palpable, and much of the murmured conversation was of what was not fair – the jobs which no longer existed, poor communication and a feeling of despair. Using the transactional analysis themes of rescuer, persecutor and victim, my feelings were that most in senior management were seen as persecutors (or potential persecutors). Many staff saw themselves as victims, or colleagues of victims, and any outsider such as coach, therapist or consultant was a potential rescuer – and I often found myself pushed into this role, or used in that way. This was a pattern in many interpersonal discussions I had at that time.

Bruno's interactions with me changed – he was much less likely to challenge me and much more curious to explore what might be happening, using me as a (possible) rescuer to help him see his part in the dynamic of persecutor, and how he could get the same results without contributing to people feeling like victims. In working with him I felt curious, competent and hopeful. While he still liked to dominate and show his power, this was no longer the dominant part of our interpersonal relationship. I left his office feeling like I had delivered value, asked some good questions, and hopeful that relief would follow. This was a complete contrast to earlier times when I frequently left his office exhausted, feeling professionally hopeless and incompetent.

He and I had known each other for several years when he was appointed as head of the second NGO. I was aware of my own responses of how I felt in the first (dark and depressing) building and then in the second (light and hopeful) as I had other clients in both buildings. Bruno explored why the office move was so important to him, what it represented, and what would be possible with the organization in the new building that was impossible in the dark, depressive building. He was able to consider his individual needs (ego, big office, status and power) as well as those of his role (revolution and transformation as the new head, credibility in showing a clear change with a geographical move) and for the organization (literally, going up in the world, visibility, hope). Beyond the status symbol of the nice office, I could help him explore and understand why he and his organization needed to change geographic location in order to bring about the hope, change and growth his vision called for.

How I used countertransference

For Bruno, a "bright" office building had an impact. This showed up in his optimism, positive body language around the office, ability to get the organization to buy in to a bigger future vision, and so on. In this phase of our work, it became clear that my role included meeting his need for head-on challenge. After our interactions, I felt mentally exhausted, challenged and provoked in the way I sometimes feel after interactions with my teenage son. My interpretation was that, like an adolescent growing and adapting to his new world, I became a representation of the parental figure or boundary he needed to push against to meet some of his own ego needs. He would ask me for an impression or observation, and then tell me why I was wrong.

In sharing the metaphor of an adolescent pushing boundaries, Bruno was able to see how his own organization could be compared to an adolescent stage of development, for example, deciding which policies from the host organization should be accepted and which challenged, and the growing pains of significantly increasing staff numbers. The adolescent NGO was becoming more visible in the market place, and facing the advantages and disadvantages of the growth and visibility in the initial stage of our work together, I often shared with Bruno his impact on me – the unconscious part of some of his behaviors, in particular, the need to dominate. My bringing them to his conscious awareness enabled him to reflect on his unconscious behaviors further, developing his awareness of his impact on others.

In looking at both the intrapsychic (Bruno) and organizational levels of analysis (Wells, 1985), our changing interpersonal relationship could be understood as a representation of his own growth and development over time as well as the development in his organization.

Case study 4: An in-depth review of person, role and organization

In this final case study we incorporate all the frameworks introduced earlier.

This case focusses on Stephanie, the HR director of another NGO. She has been with the organization for about three years and has a history of good performance evaluations. She has two bosses, the executive director (ED) Ben and his deputy executive director (DED) Maria. I had worked with the NGO previously, so already had some memories of my own experience in the organization and of meeting both Stephanie and the DED.

Ben hired a strategy consultant (Dan) to work on the organizational task to streamline the delivery model and "identify landmines in doing so" (direct quote from his report). He is known to be direct, extreme and to provoke a strong reaction and hence achieve major change. Soon afterwards, Stephanie asked me to be her coach for a one-year assignment. Dan's interim report contained a significant amount of negative feedback about Stephanie herself, her in her role, and her department. She was looking to hire a coach to work with her to develop as necessary, to fight for her job and her reputation.

Stephanie was clear that she wanted to understand the feedback, overcome any performance or behavioral shortfalls, and be seen (again) as a good and strong performer. While the task was clear enough, I also had a slight feeling that she had been set up to fail. Nonetheless, as an individual, Stephanie was initially defensive, hurt and in a lot of pain. The rational part of her wanted to turn the page and move forward, and the emotional part of her needed to understand what had happened, why it happened, her part in the dynamic, and to move forward from a position of strength.

My experience of the work together

Often, a coaching assignment includes meeting the client with their superior, to agree on coaching objectives and success criteria. Stephanie and I met with the ED and DED. I was paying close attention to the dynamics in the room and to my own and Stephanie's responses.

During the meeting, I could rationally follow the conversation. However, emotionally, I was confused, as if my eyes, ears and stomach were having three different experiences and it was impossible in the moment to reconcile the differences. For example, I heard general words expressing support for Stephanie, but it was difficult for them to answer specific questions about how she needed to develop or what needed to change. They supported the idea of her development but it was hard to get them to agree to an objective assessment of her in her role.

As a way to move forward, I asked how many of the problems would be solved if Stephanie left the NGO and a new HR director was hired immediately – same role, same organization, different person. This was a pivotal question: Was the problem solely located in her? Dan had clearly located the problem in her. Her two bosses were more reluctant to do so, and expressed support to help her develop her strengths and cope in these very difficult times. They also seemed to take their responsibility for what needed to happen at the level of the organization. In particular, when asked, they stated very clearly that her role was not to protect them. As HR director, many "HR issues" were assumed to be Stephanie's responsibility, and in reality, many decisions were made (or not made) by the ED and DED, although the blame fell at Stephanie's feet. She never questioned this, and hence often protected them.

I left their office with a small amount of hope that the organizational issues would be addressed and that Stephanie and I could focus on her, and her in her role, as the focus of our work together. I felt the compassion and support from the bosses, and also an ambivalence and caution about whether this was possible. I felt emotionally and physically exhausted, but less set up to fail. I also really wanted to prove Dan wrong – where my client had unnecessarily protected her bosses in the past, I felt very strongly I wanted to protect her.

Just before midnight, some ten hours later, I received a phone call from Dan (who lives a nine-hour time difference from me). He had spoken to the ED, and called me as a result of that discussion. It was direct, confrontational and felt like a verbal attack. In his version of the meeting, the discussion and commitments reversed; for example, I was told that Stephanie should be fired and that she had almost no credibility in the organization.

About a week later, the DED called me. I shared with her part of the conversation, and before I could share my hypothesis and how I felt I was being used, she exclaimed that Dan had "overstepped his remit in an extreme way" and that it was a grossly exaggerated and misconstrued version of the conversation. Stephanie continued to have the support of her and the ED, so long as she continued to show the humility to develop and accept her part in what had happened.

Stephanie and I worked together throughout the year. She is still in her role, had a good performance evaluation, and is, again, seen as adding value to the organization.

The consultant's capacity to think and reflect

In trying to access Stephanie's unconscious, we often discussed her basic instincts – the flight-or-fight mechanisms from Bion (1961), for example. Dan's report "attacked" her professional identity, such that the unconscious response was more survival than defensive.

After and during my first conversation (by phone) with Stephanie I felt helpless, despondent, like I could not say no and at the same time having no idea if this was a coachable issue or not.

In the meeting with her, the ED and DED, emotionally, I was confused, and could not understand the difference between the words that I was hearing and the emotions I was feeling. Stephanie had been described by the consultant as "tone deaf to organizational dynamics" and in that moment I felt tone deaf, blind and oversensitive, all at the same time.

During my late night phone call with Dan, I first felt incredulous, and then lost all my words and ability to speak. I lost my ability to feel. I then felt useless, incompetent, like I had not understood anything earlier in the day. I felt threatened, bullied and afraid of where the conversation was going. At one moment, there were tears in my eyes. This paralleled his dynamic with my client.

During and after my first call with Stephanie, I was already aware of feeling hopeless, which, after reflection, I attribute to her feeling of hopelessness. Where I felt she had been set up to fail with Dan's report, I also questioned whether I was setting myself up to fail with this assignment.

After reading his report, my assumption at the individual level of analysis was that she was being used as a scapegoat to protect the ED. At the organizational level, I suggest that the HR department was the scapegoat for many of the organizational issues.[1] Dan's report was based on the question "where are the unexploded landmines?" In my discussion with the ED, I tested my hypothesis. The feedback had been hard for me to read as it was so negative.

The night that Dan called me it was about 11:30 p.m. – a very late phone call for me, and an early afternoon phone call for him, which may have been his need to show power and control.

During and after that conversation, I became more aware of what might be happening unconsciously and how he was using me. He needed Stephanie to be seen as incompetent, and in his conversation with me I was a proxy for Stephanie. I was aware of my emotional response, and could make some sense of it and use it to help me in my role but it was difficult. I questioned whether it was me feeling incompetent and useless or whether it was the countertransference from Stephanie and projective identification from his (chosen) task, which, in that moment, seemed to be to get rid of Stephanie such that his project could be deemed successful (as defined in his report).

I started to question whether Dan's anger and extreme emotional reaction were driven by his ambition: He wanted another successful project (at any cost) and he was frustrated the ED would not take drastic action.

Dan knew the ED would not have this conversation with Stephanie, so he tried to have it with me, with the assumption that I would tell Stephanie. His words to me included "this is 'game over' . . . you have to tell her". In the awareness of how he seemed to be using me, I instead suggested this was a conversation the ED needed to have with his staff member, Stephanie. This seemed to infuriate Dan even more – as if I was not accepting his seniority.

I did not agree to do what he told me. I know that the ED never had a conversation with Stephanie telling her "game over".

In the conversation with the DED two weeks later, I was aware of the differences between my countertransference for Stephanie as an individual (my feelings of hope), for her role (what was possible and impossible and the conundrums of ambiguity) and for the organization (how the ED was using the consultant at the organizational level and how I was being used at the individual level).

If we look at this example through the lens of organizational role analysis (the intersection of person, role and organization), I was able to use my emotional responses to try and understand what part of this situation was about Stephanie herself (coaching around listening more, partnering with the organization more than being role driven and so on). I was aware of what was about the role, HR director (HR department as scapegoat, all management issues are because of HR rather than the responsibility of all line managers). Within the organization, there was a change effort, identification of the biggest "landmines" to focus on, and quick wins to be seen to be acting quickly and decisively. With the capacity and willingness to reflect on all three parts of this, I was able to work with Stephanie, in her role, to help the organization.

How I used countertransference

By sharing my emotional responses with Stephanie and continuously reflecting on what might be happening and why, I was able to help her find different perspectives and lenses to explore what might be happening in the organization. And together we were able to find solutions for her individually, for her as HR director and for the organization as a whole.

At the time of writing, Stephanie and I have concluded our coaching assignment. She is seen as less defensive, her role is more clear and she is more confident both in herself and her role. She has the full support of her two bosses. The consultant is no longer working with the organization. Stephanie and the HR department continue to grow, are no longer seen to be set up to fail, and are not, at the time of writing, being used as scapegoats within the NGO.

If you were the consultant in this situation, what question would you ask Stephanie? What would you ask the ED?

What are your experiences of using your own emotional reactions in the sense-making at the individual level or at the organization level? What is different for you – and how do you use this in your work?

Conclusions around working with countertransference in organizations

"People rush to judgement when they don't have time or energy to think".
(Carl Jung)

Essential to working with countertransference in organizations is a capacity and willingness to reflect on your emotional experience. Countertransference can be a great asset to our work in organizations, in the sense-making and understanding "why" things happen and some of the root causes, such that "problems" can be more accurately diagnosed. "Solutions" then have a greater chance of short-term success and longer term sustainability. Countertransference helps us identify some of the root causes, and not merely the symptoms of the problems that staff, clients or other stakeholders may experience.

As we move beyond interpersonal relationships, everything that happens "under the surface" of the iceberg may be more difficult to access. Equipped with a picture of an iceberg, and the sense that you are working with the person, the role and the organization is a solid basis for a successful organizational intervention.

In sharing your experience and hypotheses within the organization, you become a part of the system and must be aware of how this impacts your experience and capacity to reflect. Sharing your ideas, supervision, and working with colleagues who hold you to account for your experiences and help you make sense of them are crucial in working with organizations.

More essential than all the theory and knowledge, however, is your own curiosity, and your willingness and capacity to be aware of your own experience "in the here and now", as it happens, in any interaction with the organization, and at any level in the organization. Can you suspend judgement about when you feel, for example, competent or incompetent, hopeless or hopeful, and instead be curious to understand the feeling and make sense of it in the context of that organization? This includes paying attention to your emotional experience before you walk into the organization, once on the inside, and again when you walk out the door and any ongoing impact of the encounter.

Note

1 Direct quotes from Dan's report include: "by far HR is our biggest problem"; "many managers lack skills and the ability to get on the balcony and play a managerial role"; "line managers need to step up and have more courageous conversations with people".

Bibliography

Bion, W. (1961). *Experiences in Groups and Other Papers*. London, UK: Tavistock.
Gibbard, G. S., Hartman, J. J., & Mann, R. D. (Eds.) (1974). *Analysis of Groups*. San Francisco, CA: Jossey-Bass.

Hinshelwood, R. D. (1994). *Clinical Klein*. London, UK: Free Associations Books.

Hinshelwood, R. D., & Skogstad, W. (1994). *Observing Organizations*. London, UK: Routledge.

Kegan, R., & Lahey, L. L. (2001). *How the Way We Talk Can Change the Way We Work*. San Francisco, CA: Jossey-Bass.

Newton, J., Long, S., & Sievers, B. (Eds.) (2006). *Coaching in Depth: The Organizational Role Analysis Approach*. London, UK: Karnac Books.

Schein, E. H. (2004). *Organizational Culture and Leadership*. San Francisco, CA: Jossey Bass.

Wells, L., Jr. (1985). The group-as-a-whole perspective and its theoretical roots. In A. D. Coleman & M. H. Geller (Eds.), *Group Relations Reader 2* (pp. 110–126). Washington, DC: A. K. Rice Institute.

Part III

Countertransference in reflective practice, research and in case studies co-written with patients in treatment

Chapter 9

Countertransference in reflective practice

An integrative approach to monitor self-awareness in clinical practice

Sofie Bager-Charleson

This chapter is structured around my understanding of countertransference within a framework of reflective practice. Teaching reflective practice and reflexivity on both research and clinical training have prompted me to look for the equivalence of countertransference across modalities. Doing so has both challenged and expanded my original understandings of the concept. It has opened up different understandings of the concept, both across and within modalities.

An interdisciplinary approach to countertransference

Different modalities use different 'lenses' to understand the intricate combination of spoken and unspoken messages within psychotherapeutic practice. Within psychoanalytically inspired work the concepts transference, countertransference and projections are significant means of addressing what happens in the room. Psychotherapy, asserted Racker (1982), involves a fusion between the past and the present for both therapists and clients; and countertransference is a helpful concept to explore the analyst's contribution and responses. Racker (1982) wrote:

> It is . . . this fusion of present and past, the continuous and intimate connection of reality and fantasy, of external and internal, conscious and unconscious, that demands [countertransference] embracing the totality of the analyst's psychological response.
>
> (p. 133)

Racker (1982) distinguished between conscious and unconscious countertransference responses. Racker suggested that 'all transference situations provoke a countertransference situation, which arises out of the analyst's identification of himself with the analysand's (internal objects)' (p. 137). He referred to this in terms of 'complementary countertransference' which is closely linked to projective identification (see Bateman & Holmes, 1995) and can be considered as a reaction to how the client behaves towards the therapist. Racker referred to 'the law of talion' as part of the 'law of the general and individual unconscious' (p. 137). A positive transference situation is likely to be answered automatically by a positive countertransference situation and 'to every negative transference there responds, in one part of the analyst, a negative countertransference'.

Racker (1982) offered a 'simplified example':

> [I]f the patient's neurosis centres on a conflict with his introjected father, he will project the latter upon the analyst and treat him as his father; the analysis will feel treated as such – he will feel treated badly – and he will react internally, in a part of his personality, in accordance with the treatment he receives.
>
> (p. 137)

This is something which we can see echoing in reflective practice within different modalities. *Transactional analysis* refers, for instance, to 'ego-state shifts' and to how we, when going about in our everyday life, tend to respond to each other's means of relating in an almost inevitable way. As a therapist, asserted Stewart (2013), we can 'judge a person's ego-state by noting the ego-states responses' (p. 34) in and outside the room. When 'diagnosing' the client's means of relating in the room, we notice behavioral means of communication, like words, gestures, tones and facial expressions, and also the way the client's phenomenological, lived experiencing comes across in terms of him or her 're-experiencing' certain past events 'as though they were happening in the present' (2013, p. 34). By exploring the client's relationships outside the room, a focus on ego-shifts will help to 'make historical checks to discover whether she [the client] is replaying childhood patterns of copying parent-figures'. With parallels to Racker's (1982) description of 'complementary countertransference' as guided by 'the law of talion' (p. 137) Stewart (2013) used the term *complementary ego-state* to describe how we can evoke responses from the other in an almost see-saw like way:

> [I]f a person manifests a particular ego-state he will inevitably invite a complementary ego-state in the other person. If he shows Child, the chances are good that he will get a response from Parent. If he exhibits his own Parent ego-state he will probably invite Child in response. If he comes from Adult, the likelihood is that he will get a response from Adult.
>
> (2013, p. 34)

This resonates with Freud's original use of the concept of countertransference. The early psychoanalysis aimed for an ongoing, almost permanent level of self-awareness within the therapist. When conscious of our responses, we can make use of and 'more easily make the patient conscious of the projection' (Freud, 1959, p. 138). If the analyst is unaware of these reactions there is a danger that the patient will have to repeat, in his transference experience, the vicious circle brought about by the projection and introjection of 'bad objects' and the 'consequent anxieties and defences' (Freud, 1959, p. 138). Racker (1982) asserted that 'usually excluded from the concept of counter-transference are the concordant identifications'. He described these as 'a sort of reproduction of [the therapist's] own past processes', based on events being 're-experienced' in 'response to stimuli from the patient' (1982, p. 135).

Concordant countertransference can be seen as 'empathic responses, based on the analyst's resonance with his patient' (Bateman & Holmes, 1995), where the 'analyst and the patient share parallel experiences' (Sedgwick, 1994). Concordant countertransference is about 'those psychological contents that arise in the analyst by reason of the empathy achieved with the patient and that really reflect and reproduce the latter's psychological contents' (Racker, 1982, p. 135). Racker described:

> Consider a patient who threatens the analyst with suicide. . . . There sometimes occurs rejection of the concordant identification by the analysis and an intensification of his identification with the threatened object. . . . This anxiety . . . may in turn generate guilt-feelings in the analyst and these can lead to desires for reparation and to intensification of the 'concordant identification'.
>
> (1982, p. 136)

A development of this thinking can be found in Clarkson's (2002) integrative 'five relational' theory. Clarkson (2002) distinguished between 'reactive' and 'proactive' countertransference. She reserved the first category for responses origi-nating in the client: 'Reactive countertransference describes the psychotherapist which are elicited by or induced in the psychoanalyst by the patient' (2002, p. 90). The reactive countertransference resonates with the earlier mentioned concordant countertransference, and involves, as Cashdan (1988) highlighted, the idea of a projective identification as part of the client's 'pathology':

> Using the counter-transference means reaction to one's reaction. This means (1) allowing oneself to emotionally respond to the meta-commu-nications embedded in the projective identification and (2) using this information as means of identifying the patient's pathology. It means that the therapist has to be willing to turn himself into an emotional barom-eter of sorts. The therapist needs to be emotionally responsible for what is taking place within himself as well as intellectually reflective regarding what is taking place in the relationship.
>
> (1988, pp. 101–102)

Proactive countertransference, on the other hand, attends to feelings or projections which can be said to have been introduced by the psychotherapist herself. It also highlights a general level of distancing within the therapeutic community with regard to the concept of a fully analysed therapist without their own blind spots and need for ongoing, transformative learning, which moves idea of countertransference comfortably into reflective practice.

Humanistic theory introduced the useful concept 'congruence' (Rogers, 1961), or 'congruency' (Stewart, 2013), to capture the complexity of self-awareness for the therapist. *Congruence* is the 'therapeutic condition which is usually slowest to develop' (Mearns & Thorne, 2013, p. 99). They described *congruence* as 'the state of being of the counselor when her outward responses to her clients consistently matches the inner feelings and sensations which she has in relation to the client' (2013, p. 84). It is the unpicking of this potential mismatch of intentions and expressions – what psychoanalytic theory refers to as unconscious responses – around which the rest of this chapter revolves.

Collaborative means of generating 'knowledge'

Humanistic theory typically distances itself from the epistemological realist stance which psychoanalytic theory adopts to, for instance, unconscious processes and the deterministic significance which psychoanalysis pays to early childhood events. The Existential Yalom (1980) asserted, for instance, that 'there is compelling reason to assume that "fundamental" (that is, important, basic) and "first" (that is, chronologically first) are identical concepts' (p. 11). Rogers (1951/1999) disagreed with the use of countertransference as a client induced 'misplacement'. He asserted that transference and countertransference in psychoanalytic practice have been used with a psychopathologising, expert-thinking based stance towards the client. Rogers did however use the term *transference attitudes* as 'common forms of response between the client and the therapist'. In fact, Rogers (1951/1999) suggested that 'we may say that transference attitudes exist in varying degrees in a considerable portion of cases handles by client-centred therapists' (p. 200). Rather than referring to unconscious processes, humanistic theory tends to focus on how 'emotionalised attitudes' (Rogers, 1951/1999, p. 100), such as warmth, irritation or other relational responses, are being communicated in ways which evoke embodied responses in the other. The communication is out of awareness for both, as if experiencing a new note in a melody, which causes us to listen differently. It can be a sense of change triggered by a gesture, tone of voice, repeat or odd use of wording.

The concepts transference and countertransference are, as suggested, increasingly used both across and outside therapeutic modalities. In their book about reflective practice in social work, Knott and Scragg (2008) resonated with the value of a broad use of transference and countertransference for social workers in their general engagement with clients:

For example, a person who uses services who was depressed spoke to me in a calm quiet manner, but I felt uncomfortable, I was becoming tense. I realised that I was mirroring his tension, which was incongruent with his speech. Transference, i.e. of his tension, and countertransference, i.e. my becoming tense, are psychoanalytical concepts which can help to understand your interactions.

(2008, p. 74)

We are also finding references to transference and countertransference in research, to understand the researcher's complex, changing and often-messy process of gaining understanding. Holloway (2009) used the countertransference to capture emotionally attuned and 'experience near' research. Brown, too, asserted that researchers' understanding also is influenced by a 'feeling state which seems to be determined by regular projections from family members' (Brown, 2006, p. 187). Countertransference becomes, in other words, a significant way of conceptualising, discussing and monitoring how the relational and emotionally attuned practitioner generates knowledge.

Extending the use of countertransference to include a platform to collaboratively explore mutual enactment means moving away from the original realist assumption of countertransference as being comparable with an archeological find discovered through the therapist's 'digging'. Postmodernism and poststructuralism are giving voice to previously marginalised groups in all fields of work. Psychotherapy has undergone considerable development as feminist, cultural and LGBT related interests are being put to the forefront. This involves a shift from essentialism and individualism to constructionist and relational approaches. As Rosen and Kuehlwein (1999) put it:

Constructivist psychotherapy is under no illusion of making the client see the world as it really is. Rather, constructivism is fully aware that the new worldview is, and can only be, another construction, another fiction – but a useful, less painful one.

(1999, p. 69)

Case study

Hakim and I are meeting for the first time. Hakim is a PhD student in his late 20s. He is well dressed in what looks like an expensive suit. He comes across as charming and intelligent; his narratives are punctuated with humorous, clever remarks. He brings relationships as his presented problem. He tends to give too much to people.

Hakim is born in Egypt, gay and raised in the UK. He has got many friends, although he feels that they often pull away or ignore him when he wants to 'take things further'. A recent event with a university colleague has left him feeling rejected yet unable to let go of the idea of a romantic involvement.

Hakim appears at ease today. He leans back in the chair and says that he's looked forward to therapy. 'I'm ready', he says. 'I know I can make silly choices, and I really do want to change'. He laughs, but holds my eyes long enough to seem serious.

There is an unspoken message in the room, which I wonder about. Is Hakim enacting something towards me, signaling a general sense of willingness to please, which I react to with unease? He talks fondly about his mother, a gentle musician whom Hakim regrets having watched being bullied by his 'stupid and emotionally unavailable' father. Hakim came out as gay when he was 15 years old, in a relationship with a 10-years-older man who left him after their first sexual encounter. Hakim wrote a love letter, which ended up in his father's hands. Hakim had left it by his own bed, and his father found it when he went in to close a window which Hakim had left open. The letter included explicit drawings. This was the first time his father heard anything about Hakim's sexuality. Hakim is visibly disturbed talking about the event.

Towards the end of our session, I notice myself postponing the mentioning of payment. Hakim stands up, remains still in front of me, and says 'thank you' as if I just saved his life. He leaves the room without my mentioning the fee.

I am baffled.

When I bring the event to supervision, we explore Hakim's story about his father as a trigger for my reaction. My supervisor suggests that we look my inability to address the fees as a 'talion' response, or what Sedgwick (1994) referred to as a 'desire to retaliate in re-enactment of the patient's negative internal object' (p. 21).

Activity 1

Divide, if possible, into pairs.
Think about an incident which stands out particularly to you from a session. What happened? How did it leave you feeling? Discuss in pairs, and compare.

Countertransference for double-loop learning

Countertransference can help us to explore and discuss our responses in the way that Schön (1983) addressed as 'double-loop learning' to expand our analytical frame 'beyond the obvious' (Taylor, 2006) and challenge underlying cultural, personal and theoretical assumptions. It helps us to lean into and explore rather than avoid, disown or displace our embodied responses.

Case study

About a year into our therapy, Hakim had changed into a calmer, sometimes almost timid way of relating. I had warmed immediately to Hakim, although I often experienced a mix of tenderness and frustration. I often felt sorry for him. He continued trying to make friends, but seemed to be unable to sustain many of his relationships. He would sometimes struggle with his studies, and got involved in drink and recreational drugs as well as arguments with his university colleagues. He would then spend time apologising, crying even, for 'being so stupid'. It would sadden me to hear how he referred to his friendship in an apologising tone; 'I frustrate them, I know I do', he would say whilst I often got the impression that the friends had been unfair, not Hakim.

'I wonder if you are worried about frustrating me?' I would ask. He would typically smile in return and say something about feeling safe here. Three sessions before our Christmas holiday, however, Hakim arrived late and smelled of alcohol. He had been out drinking all night and looked harrowed.

'I can't help thinking that I've given therapy a chance', said Hakim. I felt paralysed, deskilled and overwhelmingly concerned. I spoke feebly, it felt, about the looming holiday, encouraging Hakim to explore his feelings around our break. After he left, I felt unable to move from my chair. My embodied response was that of having received a physical blow. When exploring the event afterwards, my supervisor helped me to understand how Hakim's sudden, drastic change had tapped into my experiences with my bipolar father. The feelings have been described with reference to having been gutted, hit by a train and other powerful metaphors. In spite of the sense of a 'blow', the reaction I was left feeling seemed understandable in the sense which Racker (1982) referred to in the context of concordant countertransference situations. The holiday, Hakim's lack of trust and my own sensitivity to sudden changes in people became issues which my supervisor helped me to consider; I felt shaken, but the experience made sense and felt useful.

When Hakim arrived the next week, I noticed a newly won confidence. I invited Hakim to explore what had happened, and welcomed his criticism of the way I had addressed him in the previous session. Hakim made links between the session and the way his father used to threaten and humiliate him during childhood. He would describe how his mother had suffered depression, and how worried he had been at those times. He returned to his father, and explained that his father would punish him by hitting him repeatedly with a slipper on the back of Hakim's legs. Before his father would punish him, Hakim would often run up to his room which made his father even more angry. Hakim said that he would feel still inside, almost calm, when he heard his father on the stairs. He would sometimes climb up on a chair so that his father would beat him on the legs, and he said that he would almost feel a relief and a sense that justice was being done.

Comments

When exploring the sessions in supervision, the experience of reconnecting with my own childhood felt, as suggested, at first both familiar and constructive. We explored Hakim's reaction in light of the holiday and what that represented in terms of trust, and we agreed on the value of Hakim's reconnecting with his memories. His self-destructive lifestyle seemed to highlight a self-representation and identification with his father instead as a defense against the growing anxiety of forming new relationships. This identification with the abusive other continued into adulthood, through provoking partners into rejecting or 'abusing' him, and through excessive drink and drug taking. Hakim's strong reaction to our holiday seemed to break some of this pattern; he reacted against me, whom he had started to trust to be on 'his side'; he felt disappointed and had allowed himself both to get upset and to express his feelings to his therapist. I regarded this a promising opening for work aimed to address how both the abuser and the abused had continued living out their interaction by means of Hakim.

Single- and double-loop learning

The early definitions of *countertransference* can be described as a single-loop learning cycle for the therapists. Schön (1983) referred to different contracts with our clients. The single-loop learning contract is based on the practitioners assuming:

- I am presumed to know, and must claim to do so, regardless of my own uncertainty;
- I will keep my distance from the client, and hold onto the expert's role. I will give the client a sense of my expertise, but convey a feeling of warmth and sympathy as a 'sweetener'; and
- I will look for deference and status in the client's response to my professional persona.

The idea about a fully analysed therapist as neutral and sterile as a surgeon is, as suggested earlier, today contrasted by an emphasis on ongoing self-questioning. Freud's deterministic, realist perspective on therapy as an archeological process unravelling hidden truths is being replaced by an emphasis on the phenomenological experience with therapy resting on an aim to seek our client's lived, phenomenological experience – both as a starting point and an ongoing focus for the work. Epistemologically, this puts a kind of search for a collaborative, ever-changing knowledge to the forefront. The philosopher Merleau-Ponty (1999) specialised in the 'phenomenology of perception', and asserted – like all existentialists – that there is no one 'fixed' meaning with life to be 'found'.

Phenomenology ... does not believe that man and the world can be understood on the basis of their state of fact. ... We must not wonder if we really perceive the world. Rather we must say that the world is that which I perceive.

(1999, p. 86)

Not knowing becomes a significant space in therapy. The liminal space between un-knowing and allowing new understandings to take form happens through a mutual trying out of new knowledge about ourselves in the world. This is what Schön (1983) referred to as the basis for double-loop learning. The contract resonates this relational approach to knowledge, with the practitioner assuming that:

- I am presumed to know, but I am not the only one in the situation to have relevant and important knowledge. My uncertainties may be a source of learning for me and for them;
- I will seek out connections to the client's thoughts and feelings, and 'allow his respect for my knowledge to emerge from his discovery of it in the situation'; and
- I will look for the sense of freedom and of real connection to the client, as a consequence of no longer needing to maintain a professional façade.

Hearing deeply

Something happens when two people meet on this deep level. 'Hearing deeply' means, typically within person-centred theory, to 'hear the words, the thoughts, the feeling tones, the personal meaning, even the meaning that is below the conscious intent' of the speaker (Rogers, 1995, p. 8). Rogers referred to this kind of hearing as one of life's 'sparkling moments', where individuals connect with something universal.

There is [a] peculiar satisfaction in really hearing someone. ... [I]t is like listening to the music of the spheres, because in the immediate message of the person, no matter what that might be, there is the universal.

(1995, p. 8)

Double-loop learning is a term used to highlight our critical questioning of what we hold as true and valued; hearing deeply involves listening inwards too – paying attention to being 'real' as Rogers (1961) put it, and observe how we relate and why. It resonates with the capacity that Trotter-Mathison et al. (2010) described as characteristic for a professional helper. They asserted that lay helpers tend to 'be prone to problem identification, advice giving, and boundary issues' (p. 6), and they continued:

[In lay helping] there is a projection of one's own experiences and one's solution to the life of the other. The lay helper often gives answers own and these can have a base in the notion of common sense. There will usually not be a self-consciousness or reflectivity about the helping process.

(2010, p. 56)

The 'experienced professional phase' is, on the other hand, a phase which puts 'establishing authenticity' to the forefront, and where therapists, as Trotter-Mathison et al. (2010) described 'nearly universally recognise the centrality of the therapeutic relationship in contributing to client change [and] become increasingly comfortable with the necessary ambiguity in counselling interactions' (p. 6). We can, in other words, be both part of the solution and the problem.

Whilst humanistic theory attends to the 'sparkling moments' (Rogers, 1995), highlighting listening as a beautiful experience 'like the music of the spheres', psychoanalytic theory has helped us to look at the value of negative feelings in the room. Negative feelings towards clients can be uncomfortable to consider or discuss. In my first placement as a psychoanalytic honorary student, my supervisor and Jungian analyst, Paola Valerio (2002), contributed with valuable reading and learning about how love and hate are inseparable aspects of a relationship; they are a 'fusion of opposites':

I . . . work with patients where strong countertransference feelings ranging from irritation to actual repulsion and hatred of patients, were judiciously disclosed and worked with in the consulting room. Hate is more commonly written about in relation to work with severely disturbed or borderline patients, but in my experience it is a more frequent occurrence that is usually acknowledged in work with all patients, if the analyst is open to it.

(2002, p. 264)

Valerio (2002) emphasised an important point often made in psychoanalytic literature, namely that negative and positive feelings are there; the question is not whether or not they exist, but whether the therapist 'is open to it':

When love and hate are treated as mutually exclusive the tendency is to idealise the one and demonise the other. [But] as Winnicott . . . noted (rather radically for his time), the mother hates her infants from the word go, for all sorts of good reasons. Primitive feelings of love and hate are inevitably stirred up in this analytic vessel.

(p. 264)

I have grown to regard this thinking as overlapping with what reflective practice considers in terms of collaborate, attuned work; how we feel, think and respond as practitioners is significant to explore from all angles. The therapist's contribution becomes, as Schön and Rein (1994) suggested, an ongoing concern:

Participants in [frame-reflective] must be able to put themselves in the shoes of other actors [and] they must have the complementary ability to consider how their own frames may contribute to the problematic situations.

(pp. 29, 187)

Metacultural frames

Double-loop learning conveys an emancipatory angle, with an aim to expand the analytical frame beyond 'the obvious' in order to explicitly identify and challenge underlying cultural, personal and theoretical assumptions 'to free you from taken-for-granted assumptions and oppressive forces', as Taylor (2005, p. 15) put it. This involves critically considering our work 'meta-cultural frames', frames conditioned by the particular society and cultural understanding of our time. Gardner et al. (2008) wrote:

Being 'critical' adds an expectation of exploring practice in the context of the social system in which it operates, looking, for example, at the influence of social expectations about such issues as gender or age, class or ethnicity. It encourages us to think about where our actions might lead in the long run.

(p. 145)

I trained first as a psychodynamic couples therapist, and have kept the relational focus since then. Although my training evidence traces from sharp divides between modalities, studying postmodern theory on psychotherapy influenced my practice towards an interdisciplinary interest in the therapeutic relationship as characterised by reflective practice and reflexivity.

Schön (1983, 1994) drew our attention to the 'comfort' which professionals normally draw from our professional frameworks. Professional frameworks give us a sense of belonging; we often identify ourselves with reference. Schön's theory on reflective practice explores two different ways of monitoring quality. Argyris and Schön (1978, pp. 2–3) distinguished this, as suggested, in terms of single-loop (Figure 9.1) and double-loop learning. We can, on the one hand, focus on the strategy itself. If something goes wrong, we can look for another strategy that will address and work within already chosen goals and values. Hawkins and Shohet (2005) wrote:

'Single-loop learning is like a thermostat', write Schön and Argyris (1978); it revolves around whether it is too hot or too cold and turns the heat on or off. The thermostat receives information and takes corrective action. Single-loop learning is 'completed within a single coherent frame of references'. It addresses explicit objectives and strategies.

(2005, p. 79)

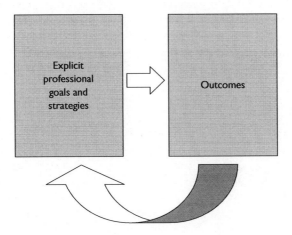

Figure 9.1 Single-loop learning

A significant problem with single-loop learning is the suggested tendency to consider ourselves as adhering to an 'espoused' or officially committed-to theory whilst actually acting on a different theory-in-action. In fact, in their research, Schön and Argyris (1978) found that people regularly failed to implement their espoused theory:

> When someone is asked how he would behave under certain circum-stances, the answer he usually gives is his espoused theory of action for that situation. This is the theory of action to which he gives allegiance, and which, upon request, he communicates to others. However, the theory that actually governs his actions is this theory-in-use.
>
> (1978, pp. 6–7)

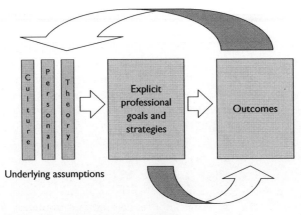

Figure 9.2 Underlying assumptions

Double-loop learning (Figure 9.2) invites, as suggested, the practitioner to consider underlying assumption behind their expressed goals and strategies. It encourages us to adopt a critical view on how underlying cultural, personal and/or theoretical beliefs and assumption may affect our practice.

Case study

The work with Hakim resumed after the holiday, in much the same vein during the coming year. Hakim was often positive about the therapy. He said he felt more confident. During one weekend, I received a text from Hakim. This was unusual; I had only received texts in connection with practicalities. The text was difficult to read. I replied back, explaining that I might have misunderstood him, but understood it as a welcome confirmation of our next session date. It was not for me, he explained. Had I not seen that? I admitted not being able to read his text. 'I like to freely associate', he replied.

During our next session, Hakim seemed to be in a more excited state than before. In the middle of the session, he reached into his bag for a hand cream which he applied to his well-manicured hands. There was a scent of perfume left, after he had gone.

The following session, he arrived even better dressed than before. During the middle of our session he grew quiet, as if distracted by something. He looked sultry. 'I'm bored', he said. There was an unusual sense of intimacy in the room, verging on excitement. I explored the event afterwards in terms of erotic countertransference at first, but felt it seemed as if he had expressed a deep sense of trust our relationship after sending his stray text; there was a sense of regression in the room, as if he had become younger.

Over the next couple of weeks, things started to change around me. I was offered a promotion at one of the training institutes where I worked, and reacted to this with an intense feeling of fear for letting my other colleagues down by accepting the opportunity. When I finally accepted the offer, it was almost too late; I had behaved in ways which had surprised both myself and others. My supervisor observed a change; she wondered if I felt stressed. Feeling invited to lean into and listen to my embodied responses rather than avoiding them, I noticed over the next couple of days an almost intolerable tension, I was clenching my fists and jaw as if a scream would escape my lips at any time. I experienced an almost electric sense of danger, as if an alarm was ringing, or vibrating from the roots of my hair down the legs which almost made my toes tingle. My breathing was shallow, and it felt as if all the dangers of the world were gathered behind my forehead.

Leaning into and acknowledging the experience

When exploring this reaction in supervision, unwanted and unprepared for aspects came up from my past. The relationship with Hakim had developed into something which I could explore in context of another, less attended to childhood experience, linked to early bonding experiences. Hakim's positive remarks about therapy had, I noticed with hindsight, left me 'paralysed' without noticing it. I revisited a familiar dread of being too much, trying to be too good, and subjecting myself to envy. Afraid of acting out in the session, I felt I had frozen, and displaced some of the responses outside of the room, for instance into my other teaching work. It was when my supervisor mentioned my often feeling 'sorry for' Hakim that something fell into place. Feeling sorry for Hakim for being gay had been at the forefront for most of my work, without my noticing it. 'Feeling sorry for' was at the same time something which I intimately connected with my mother. The guilt for having 'trapped' her into an unhappy marriage by being born into an ill-considered teenage romance was being revisited with its full force of hopelessness, helplessness and self-loathing.

Group supervision

Reflective practice involves, as suggested, ongoing double-loop learning. During the next couple of weeks, I started to look in new and different places to understand my work with Hakim. The countertransference situation had, as Racker (1982) described, found its way into unconscious areas for me; it also gradually threw light on the so far hidden dynamics behind the first unpaid session, which had loomed as an unresolved riddle. I had failed to address the issue with Hakim, and that seemed significant for my understanding of our work. The 'feeling sorry for' seemed significant, and I began to widen my input from colleagues. The 'feeling sorry for' was immediately being picked up on by a member in our peer supervision group representing different modalities. Whilst 'feeling sorry for' made sense to me to explore from an object-relational perspective on a personal level, the colleague who specialised on work within the LGBT community from a systemic therapy approach quickly noticed my gaps in knowledge. Pursuing Hakim's free associative texts from an object relations angle, and as means of him reaching out to others to contain his thoughts and help him to tolerate thinking for himself (Bion, 1961), made sense to a certain degree. My colleague also pointed me, however, towards social constructionist theory to consider Hakim's narratives in context of culture, gender and sexuality. Mair's (2010) article about queer theory from a cross-cultural perspective felt particularly valid. He described how sexual-minority individuals involved in creating a unified narrative-of-self often are undermined by the incompatibility of competing, intersecting narratives. The potential limitations of language to adequately narrate lived experience felt crucial to explore to move our work forward. My new reading also involved curiosity into postcolonial psychoanalysis, with its political analysis of the role of the psyche; it explores the 'psychic life of colonial power' (Clarke, 2003), for instance in context of institutionalised and systematic racism.

Comments

Countertransference triggers embodied responses which invite us, as practitioners, to consider different and – ideally, to our espoused theory – contrasting angles, both with our personal history and with our values and beliefs about society in mind. As therapists, our first check-in point is with our clients. When something shifts in the room, as in the case of countertransference when sudden embodied and emotional responses come to the forefront, our attention moves typically to what might this have felt like for the client. How might that feeling, reaction, response 'sit' in the client's relational history? Might you have enacted in response to a relational blueprint addressed earlier by the client who felt 'too much' for his depressed mother – or who, like Hakim, had internalised a sense of self who deservedly was punished?

In the case study, my own relational past became a 'hook' for both of Hakim's projections to latch onto. Racker (1982) and Sedgwick (1994) have both asserted that all therapists' experience projections but that it is our personal 'hooks' that decide whether a projection will latch on. Feeling sorry (and guilty, and too much for the other) represented on the one hand ambivalent attachment from my own past, but – as highlighted to me by the systemic colleague in the peer group – it had been displaced onto an ill-informed prejudice about Hakim as a gay male. The peer supervision triggered a new perspective which moved from focusing on Hakim's mother–child dyad and oedipal disturbances, to considering his narrative knowing (Taylor, 2006; Mair, 2010) and development of self within cross-cultural and LGBT-related contexts – with his own unique biography in mind.

ACCTT SMART

In this chapter, I have suggested countertransference as a significant aspect of reflective practice. The therapist 'must construct an understanding of the situation as he finds it', asserted Schön (1983), and will each time need to 'approach the practice problem as a unique case'. Schön regarded this as 'the conditions for reflection-in-action' and continues:

> I propose that by attending to the practitioner's reflection-in-action . . . it is possible to discover a fundamental structure of professional inquiry, which underlies the many varieties of design or therapy advocated by the contending schools of practice.
>
> (1983, p. 130)

Countertransference encourages us to lean into our embodied responses and consider them with intense curiosity rather than avoiding, enacting or displacing the evoked emotions. It becomes, as suggested, significant aspects of the reflective practice jigsaw puzzle. It is easy to underestimate the discomfort, upset and sometimes despair that this level of not-knowing actually involves on an embodied and emotional level; and reflective practice relied in this sense on a significant amount of self-care. One important part of the self-care is to share the experience. During my teaching, I have tried to develop some visual, more tangible models to relate and compare experiences around. The ACCTT SMART (Figure 9.3) model is intended as an aid to conceptualise and discuss this process. ACCTT SMART stands for transformational learning, and the boxes below highlight how work with a couple (Andy and Janet) began with a focus on the male client's defences, but moved towards a more holistic perspective with my countertransference and the female client's childhood patterns in mind. My own defence from seeing the woman as vulnerable resonates with some biographic aspects referred to earlier in this chapter.

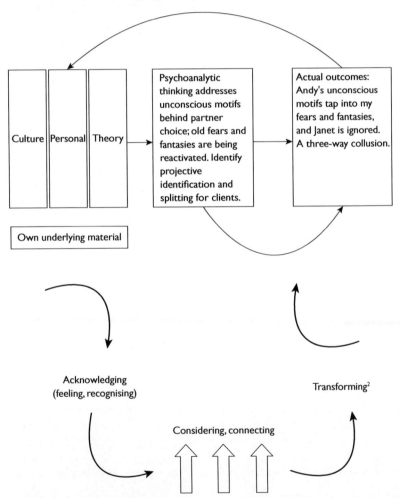

Figure 9.3 ACCTT SMART model for transformational learning. Example from a couple therapy session

- Personal therapy
- Supervision
- Clinical experience and client contact
- Reflective writing
- Training, research and general continuous professional development (CPD)
- Resting, relaxing
- Engaging in creative activities

The engine that drives us

ACCTT always starts in a problem, and can be helpful to conceptualise the 'engine that drives' us with a transformative learning structure in mind. The ACCTT model builds on many different approaches to learning as conceptualised by for instance Kolb's (1984) and Gibbs' (1988) models for experiential learning. It also builds on Biggs and Collis' (1982) SOLO taxonomy, which stands for structure of reflective learning outcomes, and the way Atherton (2005), Roffey-Barentsen and Malthouse (2009) and Moon (2004) have developed this thinking with practitioners' emotional responses in mind. Countertransference is a significant part of this process; often the first trigger through a surprising embodied, emotional response. ACCTT stands for:

> **Acknowledging** a problem to listen to the 'rattling noise' of your engine. What do you feel after the event? List what comes to your mind when connecting with your bodily responses. Feeling drained, hollow, angry, shamed or agitated may be some of the responses. How do you feel in your shoulders, or in the area behind your eyes or in your jaws? How do you feel and behave with others right now; what is happening in your family, at work and in other places of your life? This stage of transformative learning revolves around 'leaning into' your responses, to stay and explore rather than avoid, escape or maybe displace, enact them.

> **Considering** the situation on a 'unistructural' level involves exploring the 'rattling' sound in context of your own 'engine': How does the event 'sit' in the context of your own history? Have you ever felt like this before? When? What does this event share with the previous event; what might it remind you of, in the context of your own history?

> This will typically require an environment where it feels safe to 'sit with' what is going on, maybe to associate freely and brainstorm. We need someone whom we feel is on our side, at this stage, a critical friend who can see where you are coming from, and will respect how you feel – but also will help you to bring in new and different perspectives.

> **Connecting** on a 'multistructural' level involves a phase where you explore your 'engine' with its intricate 'parts' in the context of alternatives – or to continue on the metaphor; in the context of other 'types of engines'.

This includes trying to conceptualise your strong response to your client on at least three levels:

- How can your reaction be explained and discussed within your own modality, drawing from for instance the distinction between complementary and concordant countertransference?
- How might that explanation be critiqued, maybe constructively expanded, viewed from other modalities?
- How might your responses and strategies be viewed whilst acknowledging tensions arising from different social positions, for instance, in relation to class, gender and culture?

The first two aspects can be considered with Schön's (1983) suggestion about an often-occurring gap between our espoused theory and an actual theory in action. How might that come into play in your practice, when put under pressure? What might you need to help you to decrease that gap? More personal support? More professional support? More training?

The third aspect revolves around 'cultural countertransference' (Eleftheriadou, 2010, 2013) which can be difficult to explore since 'the last one to see the water is the fish', as the old proverb suggests. Alvesson and Skoldeberg (2000) suggested adopting a reflexive 'ironic deconstruction' where you 'defamiliarise' yourself as a way of engaging with another perspective for long enough to see your old one from a new perspective. Consider for instance if your client had been of the opposite sex? From a different culture? Or look at today's therapeutic practice as if from a distant future. It is easy to with hindsight see errors, but psychotherapy often unwittingly becomes part of a bigger, social system. The Freudian labelling of women as having hysteria and the NHS aversion treatment in the 50s for gay men are some examples of this. What role might we, as therapists, play today in preserving gender, class or culturally specific roles and expectations?

Transforming the experience into practice, first stage. This involves putting the new learning into practice in the context of your modality. It does not necessarily mean 'doing' new things, but is likely to affect the way that you listen to your client(s) with some new learning in mind. You may 'hear' about problems with both your own resistance in mind and in the context of what our modality informs you in terms of, for instance, psychoanalytical concepts of countertransference and transference.

Transforming on an extended abstract level. At this stage, connections are made not only within the given subject area, but also beyond it. You will generalise about the problem, compare it to other situations, and transfer principles and ideas underlying this specific instance onto other contexts. The previous connection and early transformative learning stage are likely to have brought some new learning from other approaches too, for instance in terms of humanistic or systemic, social constructionist approaches. This is a stage when a new sense of significance of the parts in relation to the whole may emerge. This can be an extrovert phase, when you read, consider training, discuss with others and compare different theories and ways of looking at the problem. The original problem has now triggered a chain of new insights, which hopefully will affect the way you approach your role as therapist with new curiosity.

SMART

Reflective practice focuses, as suggested, on underlying values and beliefs of the practitioner and encourages us to ongoing personal development. Reflective practice theory has been criticised as being 'both too nebulous and too difficult to quantify and evaluate' (Youngson & Hughes, 2009, p. 14). The ACCTT SMART model encourages an element of 'measuring' your progress, to make it more accessible for both yourself and others to monitor, for instance with supervisors, managers, employers and colleagues. The SMART aspect of the model is inspired by Roffey-Barentsen and Malthouse (2009) and their adaption of the model originating from Drucker (1954). It refers to an action plan for 'measurable' goals and stands for:

Specific

Measurable

Achievable

Relevant

Time-bound

Activity 2

Return to a 'crisis' in your work with one of your clients. Does that still feel significant, or have other memories been triggered? This is a two-staged exercise involving free, unstructured writing followed by reflective writing structured by the ACCTT SMART stages.

Stage 1. Free writing

Begin with a moment where you sensed, felt or realised that something was 'wrong'. You decide the meaning of 'wrong'; perhaps your client told or show you something had happened, or maybe you reacted

(continued)

(continued)

through your own dreams, sadness, hyperactivity, overeating or other means of enactment? Start writing with the following sentence:

I remember feeling . . .

Trace your responses to the situation; let the words come as they please – there are no right ways of writing this. If you find it difficult to think of what to write next, simply write 'word, word, word . . .' until a new thought and word come up.

Let your story evolve freely, and write for 10 minutes.

Stage 2. Reflective writing

Return to your story with the ACCTT SMART questions in mind. Your free writing might have captured the first two areas, i.e., what it felt like, and how that experience was for you.

To continue putting the critical incident in context of 'the engine that drives you' as a therapist, consider your client's and your own personal responses in the context of your modalities, for instance with different forms of countertransference in mind. Make a SMART plan over what you would have benefitted from learning more about in order to transform your responses into useful practice. Consider the problem within the context of other modalities, and with an interest in potentially unexplored sociocultural or gender-related angles.

Be specific: What do feel and think is the problem? Make it measurable: What do you need more of – supervision, personal therapy, further training? How might that be achievable, time- or energy-wise? How will that improve things for you and your practice? How will, for instance, the new training be relevant? Make it time-bound: When are you doing what?

Stage 3. Discuss in pairs

Explain to the same partner you originally discussed your client session with (Activity 1) about your original client problem, your personal involvement in the problem and how the event can be conceptualised in context of your modality. Present your SMART themes to each other.

Bibliography

Alvesson, M., & Skoldeberg, K. (2000). *Reflexive Methodology*. London, UK: Sage.

Argyris, C., & Schön, D. (1974). *Theory in Practice: Increasing Professional Effectiveness.* San Francisco, CA: Jossey-Bass.

Atherton, J. S. (2009). *Learning and teaching: SOLO taxonomy*. Retrieved from www. learningandteaching.info/learning/solo.htm

Bateman, A., & Holmes, J. (1995). *Introduction to Psychoanalysis: Contemporary Theory and Practice*. Hove, UK: Brunner Routledge.

Biggs, J., & Collis, K. (1982). *Evaluating the Quality of Learning: The SOLO Taxonomy*. New York, NY: Guildford Press.

Bion, W. (1962). *Learning from Experience*. London, UK: Karnac Books.

Brown, J. (2006). Reflexivity in the research process: Psychoanalytic observations. *International Journal of Social Research Methodology*, 9(3), 181–197.

Cashdan, S. (1988). *Object Relation Therapy: Using the Relationship*. Ontario, Canada: Penguin.

Clarke, S. (2003). *Social Theory, Psychoanalysis and Racism*. New York, NY: Palgrave.

Clarkson, P. (2002). *The Therapeutic Relationship*. London, UK: Whurr.

Drucker, P. (1954/2007). *The Practice of Management* (Rev. ed.). New York, NY: Butterworth-Heinemann.

Eleftheriadou, Z. (2010). *Psychotherapy and Culture: Weaving Inner and Outer Worlds*. London, UK: Karnac Books.

Eleftheriadou, Z. (2013). *Incorporating cross-cultural issues in psychotherapy: A relational framework* (Doctoral dissertation). Metanoia Institute & Middlesex University, London, UK. Retrieved from http://eprints.mdx.ac.uk/12628/1/ZEleftheriadou_thesis_EMBARGO.pdf

Freud, S. (1959). *An Outline of Psycho-Analysis*. London, UK: The Hogarth Press.

Gibbs, G. (1988). *Learning by Doing: A Guide to Teaching and Learning Methods*. Oxford, UK: Oxford Polytechnic, Further Education Unit.

Hawkins, P., & Shohet, R. (2005). *Supervision in the Helping Professions* (3rd ed.). Buckingham, UK: Open University Press.

Hollway, W. (2009) Applying the 'experience-near' principle to research: Psychoanalytically informed methods. *Journal of Social Work Practice*, 23(4), 461–474.

Kolb, D. (1984). *Experiential Learning*. Englewood, UK: Prentice Hall, Middlesex University.

Knott, C., & Scraggs, T. (2008). *Reflective Practice in Social Work*. Exeter, UK: Learning Matters.

Mair, D. (2010). Fractured narratives, fractured identities: Cross-cultural challenges to essentialist narratives of gender and sexuality. *Psychology and Sexuality*, 1(2), 156–169.

Mearns, D., & Thorne, B. (1999). *Person-Centred Counselling in Action*. London, UK: Sage.

Mearns, D., & Thorne, B. (2013). *Person-Centred Counselling in Action* (2nd ed.). London, UK: Sage.

Merleau-Ponty, M. (1999). What is phenomenology? In M. Friedman (Ed.), *The World of Existentialism: A Critical Reader* (pp. 83–87). New York, NY: Humanity Press.

Moon, J. (2004). *A Handbook of Reflective and Experiential Learning*. London, UK: Routledge.

O'Leary, J. (2011). Growing up to be a good psychotherapist, or physician – Know thyself! In R. H. Klein, H. S. Bernard & V. L. Schermer (Eds.), *On Becoming a Psychotherapist: The Personal and Professional Journey*. Oxford, UK: Oxford University Press.

Racker, H. (1982). *Transference and Counter Transference*. London, UK: Karnac Books.

Racker, H. (1988). The meanings and uses of countertransference. In B. Wolstein (Ed.), *Essential Papers on Countertransference* (pp. 158–201). New York, NY: New York University Press.

Roffey-Barentsen, J., & Malthouse, R. (2009). *Reflective Practice in the Lifelong Learning Sector*. Exeter, UK: Learning Matters.

Rogers, C. (1951/1999). *Client-Centred Therapy*. London, UK: Constable.

Rogers, C. (1961). *A Therapist's View of Psychotherapy*. London, UK: Constable.

Rogers, C. (1995). *A Way of Being*. New York, NY: Houghton Mifflin.

Rosen, H., & Kuehlwein, K. T. (Eds.) (1999). *Constructing Realities*. San Francisco, CA: Jossey-Bass.

Schön, D. A. (1983). *The Reflective Practitioner: How Professionals Think in Action*. New York, NY: Basic Books.

Schön, D. A., & Rein, M. (1994). *Frame Reflection: Toward the Resolution of Intractable Policy Controversies*. New York, NY: Basic Books.

Sedgwick, D. (1994). *The Wounded Healer: Countertransference from a Jungian Perspective*. London, UK: Routledge.

Skovholt, T., & Trotter-Mathiason, M. (2010). *The Resilient Practitioner: Burnout Prevention and Self-care Strategies for Counselors, Therapists, Teachers, and Health Professionals*. New York, NY: Routledge.

Stewart, I. (2013). *Transactional Analysis Counselling in Action*. London, UK: Sage.

Taylor, B. (2005). *Reflective Practice: A Guide for Nurses and Midwifes* (2nd ed.). Berkshire, UK: Open University Press.

Taylor, C. P. (2006). Practising reflexivity: Narrative, reflection and the moral order. In S. White, J. Fook & F. Gardner (Eds.), *Critical Reflection in Health and Social Care*. Berkshire, UK: Open University Press.

Trotter-Mathison, M., Koch, J., Sanger, S., & Skovholt, T. (2010). *Voices from the Field: Defining Moments in Counseling and Therapist Development*. New York, NY: Routledge.

Valerio, P. F. (2002). Love and hate: A fusion of opposites – A window to the soul. In D. Mann (Ed.), *Love and Hate: Psychoanalytic Perspectives* (pp. 253–266). London, UK: Routledge.

Webber, M. (2008). *Evidence-Based Policy and Practice in Mental Health Social Work*. Exeter, UK: Learning Matters.

Yalom, I. (1980). *Existential Psychotherapy*. New York, NY: Basic Books.

Youngson, S. (2009). Personal development in clinical psychology. In J. Hughes & S. Youngson (Eds.), *Clinical Psychology*. London, UK: Wiley-Blackwell.

Chapter 10

Countertransference in research

An intersubjective reflexive approach

Sofie Bager-Charleson

The way we 'know' in therapy

Counsellors and psychotherapists rely heavily on their emotional and embodied responses when generating 'data' in clinical practice. A reflective, 'self-critical and ethical clinical practice' will typically, as Stedmon and Dallos (2008) asserted, involve relying on feelings, 'musing, contemplating, daydreaming, wondering, doubting, guessing, and intuiting' (p. 3) as means of generating knowledge. Bondi (2013) resonates with this thinking and suggests that therapy 'entails working with such things as the often formless, fragmentary, articulable thoughts, feelings and vague inklings' (p. 4). What happens with this attention to emotional entanglement and embodied responses when we so research? Research is an essential component of the counselling and psychotherapy core curriculum. We need, for instance, to evaluate research literature and are often required to conduct research to monitor and support our practice. References are, however, frequently made to a 'gap' between clinical practice and therapy research. Tasca et al. (2015) referred to a 'practice–research divide, which is widely acknowledged as a problem in psychotherapy' (p. 2). Castonguay et al. (2010) chimed that '[i]t is well established that the practice of many full-time psychotherapists is rarely or nonsubstantially influenced by research' (p. 346).

Bondi (2013) asserted that therapists' 'accounts are at risk of being forgotten or drowned out in a re-presentation of [therapeutic] practices' (p. 1). Psychotherapy offers 'a very particular kind of relationship and a very particular kind of space in which we hope that new meanings can be made and new stories told, stories that may make life more liveable through an enrichment of meaning', concludes Bondi (2013, p. 4). To capture this reality in research, Hollway (2009) and Bondi and Fewell (2016) wrote about the importance of 'experience near' research about 'actual people' instead of aiming for a distancing, neutral research role. Hollway (2009) asserted that

> the dominant methods of research in health and social care have taken a quantitative and reductive turn, modelled on medical science and obsession with randomised controlled trials. . . . Actual people are nowhere to be found in this kind of research.

(p. 462)

This echoes with Bondi's (2013) critique of 'individualistic health treatments and narrowly construed psychological interventions [with] a gap between the flow of experience and our narrations of experience' (p. 1).

They both use the concept 'experience-near' research, and refer to a psychoanalytic 'third space', which are essential when focusing

> on the experiences of subjects who suffer and who care, and on psychological resilience and damage, in the particularities of the settings, past, present and anticipated future, as people engage with and make meaning out of their situations and actions. This is what I mean by **experience-near research.**
>
> (Hollway, 2009, p. 462, emphasis added)

This chapter is guided by the critique regarding a 'gap' between research and psychotherapists. It resonates with the importance of research-supported practice, but also suggests that therapeutic practice has got much to offer research. This chapter has been written with an epistemic congruence between psychotherapeutic practice and research in mind.

Intersubjective research

Whilst learning how to creatively and effectively use oneself with relational, emotional or embodied responses as part of gaining knowledge is an important aspect of our clinical practice, the area of emotions is surprisingly neglected when we are expected to 'do research'. There is relatively little written about the therapists' relational, embodied and emotional attunement when it comes to generating knowledge in research. Orange (1996, 2009), Bick (1997), Etherington (2004), Todres (2007), Clarke and Hodgett (2009), Anderson and Braud (2011), Josselson (2011), Willig (2012), Hollway (2000, 2009, 2011) and Finlay (2016) are helpful exceptions.

Finlay and Gough's (2003) way of highlighting relationships and the positioning of the researcher in terms of different reflexive 'variants' provide us with a framework. Finlay and Gough (2003) referred to reflexive 'introspection', 'intersubjectivity' and as 'mutual collaboration' or 'social critique'. Thinking in terms of how the researcher positions herself reflexively and relationally, resembles the way therapists think about how knowledge is being generated in the practice. This chapter revolves around an *intersubjective* approach, focusing on how we may draw from countertransference in our research. The 'free association' (Hollway & Jefferson, 2000) interview and the 'infant-observation' (Bicks 1997, Datler, Laxae & Trunkenpolz, 2012) model are used as examples of reflexive approaches where transference and countertransference are becoming significant means to generate 'data' and new 'knowledge' in research.

Intersubjective research in context

The intersubjective variant of reflexive research is complemented by research approaches which focus on relationships with power dynamics to understand how meaning-making processes take shape, for instance from the perspective of systemic and social constructionist approaches to the research relationship. Power structures are put to the forefront, with questions about who is being heard in the research and why. Reflexivity on introspection is, on the other hand, often illustrated with examples by therapist-researchers within humanistic frameworks, for instance with reference to heuristic and autoethnographic approaches to research.

A common theme for all reflexive approaches is that subjectivity is regarded as an asset: The way we learn about how the researchers and their participants engage will help us learn more about intra- and interpersonal issues in our practice – and in life. Researchers' and research participants' idiosyncratic and unpredictable reactions and experiences are, in this sense, welcomed and valuable aspects of the findings. Social background, gender, nationality and prior emotional experiences are likely to impact the research in terms of creating 'lenses' for our world view, but attending to how that happens will also add to the findings. This resonates, in turn, with how therapists bring and hope to use their reactions and themselves as part of the process to a rich, new understanding about what it is like to live in the world we live in.

Countertransference in research

Introspective, intersubjective and collaborative, socio-politically informed 'variants' to reflexivity are interlinked and related as suggested earlier in my chapter about countertransference and reflective practice. Typically, for what Finaly referred to as a form of reflexivity based 'on intersubjective reflection', researchers 'explore the mutual meanings involved in the research relationship' – the self in relation to others becomes 'both focus and object of focus' (Finlay & Gough, 2003, p. 6).

The focus on self in relation to other is not dissimilar from, for example, an autoethnographic, heuristic or narrative approach, but an emphasis of transference, countertransference and unconscious processes typically positions this approach within a psychosocial research approach. The psychosocial research can, as Clarke and Hodgett (2009) explained, be seen as a cluster of methodologies [which] 'considers the unconscious communications, dynamics and defences that exist in the research environment' (p. 2). The way we understand 'reality' with our past in mind 'plays a significant part in the generation of research data and the construction of the research activity' (2009, p. 2).

The psychosocial research brings projection, transference and countertransference to the forefront, so that, as Hollway and Jefferson (2000) addressed, an 'unconscious intersubjective dynamic' (p. 93) affects how 'we are influenced by our emotional responses'. Hollway and Jefferson (2002) continued:

This means that both will be subject to projections and introjections of ideas and feelings coming from the other person. It also means that the impressions that we have about each other are derived simply from the 'real' relationship, but that what we say and do in the interaction will be mediated by internal fantasies which derive from our histories of significant relationships. Such histories are often accessible only through our feelings and not through our conscious awareness.

(p. 45)

Hollway and Jefferson's (2000) theory on the 'subject' suggests that we incorporate anxiety and defensive functions in our research:

[P]sychosocial research adopts a theoretical starting point [to] construe both researcher and researched as anxious defended subjects, whose mental boundaries are porous where unconscious material is concerned.

(p. 43)

Countertransference

The concept of countertransference is helpful to understand situations when something in the researcher is being stirred in the context of the research relationship. Whilst originally understood as something which the client 'put' upon the therapist, countertransference is – as suggested in other places in this book – now often used to conceptualise how the therapist's prior experiences impact the therapeutic relationships with the therapist's own history in mind. Projections can act both as a resource (through for instance identification, recognition and containment) and an obstacle, and trigger defences and misunderstandings in the interview. The following extract is an example of how an unconscious intersubjectivity enters the research relationship in terms of a mother–daughter dynamic. Hollway and Jefferson (2000) wrote:

Jane and I were both white . . . our class difference was stark . . . I was probably close to the age of Jane's mother. I think it was this structural feature of our identity which precipitated the unconscious dynamics of which I got a glimpse in my unease about leaving Jane at the end of the second interview, [and when] Jane trailed off, I felt responsible for keeping the interview going.

(p. 48)

Hollway and Jefferson are recognising and bringing their own emotional response into the research. Psychoanalytic researchers who go into 'the field', as Price and Cooper (2011, p. 64) put it, are expecting to feel 'exposed to primitive and unprocessed psychic material'. As researchers, we 'will also inevitably identify with research subjects and their ordinary defensive functioning', continued Price and Cooper (2011). They added:

> Members influence each other intersubjectively and the observer too has no privileged uncontaminated position in the field. The researcher becomes a transference object for those inhabiting the field, as do they for her . . . as she becomes entangled in transference countertransference dynamics and enactments.
>
> (p. 64)

Atkinson (2011) used Hollway and Jefferson's 'free association narrative interview' as part of her research about therapy for clients considering abortion. She reflected over how the 'overall context of the free association narrative interview (Hollway & Jefferson, 2000) [suggested that] I did not introduce the interview with a question or set of questions, but merely invited Lucy to talk about her post-abortion experience' (Atkinson, 2011, p. 65).

Exploring the interview afterwards highlighted how intimately her own narratives had been woven into the narratives by her research participant:

> [T]he end product is . . . a mutual construction and one that is in some respects, as much about me, as about Lucy. . . . [W]hen Lucy said she wanted to continue her pregnancy because in her own words 'what I would do for that baby that I didn't get', I interpreted this as relating to her internalised fragile baby self that had never felt properly nurtured, and responded, 'So the baby was really you: a tiny, vulnerable, needy part of you. . . ' – again, using my analytic background to think about projective processes and how we use projection to deal with unprocessed internalised trauma . . . Lucy was continuing to repeat the same words whilst I spoke, and my coming in quickly with asking about the teaching she had received around abortion . . . shows that within the scope of the free association narrative interview, there is considerable leeway for influencing the way in which the story unfolds.
>
> (Atkinson, 2011, p. 65)

The infant-observation model in different settings

The psychoanalytically informed infant observation model is, as Shuttleworth (2012, p. 171) put it 'an ethnographic research method' which is being applied in new areas, for instance the health sector and in nursing homes. Shuttleworth stated:

In recent years, infant observation has come to be seen not only as part of clinical training, but as an ethnographic research method that gives access to the psychological development of the infant within ordinary family life. . . . It has also been used as a research method in new areas of study . . . as a wider social research project.

(Shuttleworth, 2012, p. 171)

The infant-observation model (Clark & Hoggett, 2009; Hollway, 2011; Hollway & Jefferson, 2000; Urwin & Sterberg, 2012) is another example of research with an intersubjective emphasis. Infant observation refers to a method developed by Esther Bick at the Tavistock Child Psychotherapy course in 1948 to typically observe a new baby in a home where parents were willing to allow an observer to visit them regularly over two years. Stewart (in Bager-Charleson, 2014) used the infant-observation model when exploring the relationship between mother and child in prison:

Over the last two years, observation became my work. The essential supervisions took the form of work discussion. I found observing enormously difficult. Observing involved a carefully monitored understanding of the unique unit within the general prison setting and an attempt at understanding the impact of the work on me . . . . The prison visiting room is a highly emotional place. The women wait for their visits in a small room to the side of the large visitors' room. The women refer to this area as 'cunt's corner'. If the visitor does not arrive as planned, the women still must wait in this corner watching the other visits until the visiting hour is over. . . . The effect on me in general was to leave prison feeling absolutely scooped out and raw. Noise hurt. . . . Action felt impossible alone. This was hard to balance with the very strong feelings of love and concern that I developed for many of the mothers and babies. In order to observe clearly I had to accept that I could do nothing more than that. Supervision was essential. Supervision evolved, taking on the quality of a work discussion. The setting was always part of the experience.

(Stewart, in Bager-Charleson, 2014, pp. 82–83)

In their book about infant observation as an applicable model in different areas of research, Urwin and Stemberg (2012) concluded firstly that 'the student tries to take an unobtrusive, noninterfering position, concentrating on the infant and taking in as much as possible of what is happening. . . . No notes are taken at the time' (p. 6).

The psychoanalytic infant-observation method suggests that 'emotions, qua emotions, have to be felt in some way, even in a very mild identificatory way, to be faithfully recorded by an observer' (Price & Cooper, 2012, p. 57). Like in therapeutic practice, a significant aspect of the observation model is its use of others to explore the border between what role the conscious and the unconscious might have played for the researcher's mean of generating new 'knowledge'.

Like in regular infant observation, the input from 'seminar groups' play a significant role. Urwin and Stemberg (2012) described how 'students are encouraged to make their actual observations as free from theoretical preconceptions as possible, and the descriptions of what they have seen often have a spontaneity, even rawness, that may reflect the impact of the observation experience' (p. 6).

Not dissimilar to autoethnographic research, the psychoanalytical model for infant observation will draw from the researcher's personal experiences to learn about the experience of others. The observation model has become increasingly used in other contexts to build in this rich dynamic. The example below is from a nursing home, where the observer follows patients who are deteriorating for, as the staff has suggested, 'no obvious reason'. The observer visits the home weekly and repeatedly records episodes from Mr Hartz's day-to-day life. The following extract illustrates some of Mr Hartz's life. Datler et al. wrote:

> Mr Hartz is a tall, slender 75-year-old man who suffers from dementia and, for that reason, now lives in a nursing home. During the day he enjoys going for walks through the corridors of the dementia unit, but is otherwise barely able to eat or drink without assistance. His ability to communicate with others is steadily diminishing. . . . Mr Hartz is visited by his wife. The observed, Ms Ursula Bog, who visits on a weekly basis, repeatedly records episodes of tender contact between the . . . 12th observation, for example, illustrates such tenderness.
>
> (2012, p. 160)

Observation notes 1:

Mr Hartz carefully reaches out towards his wife's hand. He lifts her left hand slightly upward and places it on the table. Mrs Hartz is still talking to the lady, while her husband turns her hand to and fro, again and again. She then slowly reaches for his and holds it gently in hers. Both of them also put their other hands on the surface of the table and stroke each other's hand, etc.

Observation notes 2:

Mr Hartz approaches me. He comes up very close in front of me, staring down my cleavage. As he does so, he smiles. He remains standing like this for some time without moving at all, looking at me. The short distance between us eventually makes me uncomfortable, and I take a step back. He comes a step forward, and again stands directly in front of me. Only after Nurse Martha has returned does he retreat from me, and goes to stand by the window.

(log, cited in Datler et al., 2012, p. 164)

Comments

There were several observation sessions, but the above illustrates the range of experiences which the observer brought to her seminars. Datler et al. (2012) reflected:

> In the observers' accounts, there was not a single scene in which nurses or relatives showed any kind of deep interest in Mr Hartz' sexual feelings, desires or fantasies, or of understanding how painful it must have been for him to no longer experience himself as attractive, desirable and potent. After analysing all the reports, the research team concluded that this reflected a common characteristic in the day-to-day experience of all nursing home residents.
>
> (p. 167)

Group supervisions or research seminars play a significant role in throwing light on and adding new perspectives to the researcher's understanding. The seminars will aim to help the researcher to tease out meanings which remain on an enacted, yet out of awareness, level, particularly when there have been strong emotions involved and the researcher may have acted on a 'wish to protect themselves from more intense encounters with the painful emotions', as Price and Cooper (2012) put it:

> Researchers are exposed to primitive and unprocessed psychic 'material' and will also inevitably identify with research subjects and their ordinary defensive functioning in the field. They will need the help of others who are not so emotionally involved with the material in order to rediscover reflective thinking capacity in relation to unprocessed . . . data. This is the function of individual, and especially group, psychoanalytic research supervision.
>
> (p. 64)

Anxiety provoking and defensive reaction are becoming part of the research 'knowledge', so that cognitive and affective reactions of the researchers will be added rather than subtracted from the material gauges from research participants in the specific context. If the observer might have acted on a 'wish to protect themselves from more intense encounters with the painful emotions', asserted Price and Cooper (2012, p. 167); perhaps the research is highlighting something which goes on for the staff as well.

Daniels (2012) stressed the value of supervision to allow emotional material to elicit. In her research about role-play for victim empathy with imprisoned sex offenders, Daniels described how although supervision was a natural part of her clinical practice, she had felt unprepared for similar needs as a researcher:

As a conscientious clinician, I know how to be non-judgmental, empathic and supportive to offenders in helping them to disclose information and work through the difficult aspects of their lives. However, I am also human, experiencing conflicting emotions that I will take to supervision in order to make sense of it by exploring the countertransference. . . . Strangely, I did not do this after the interviews because I was in a new role of researcher and did not equate this with being a clinician and needing to seek personal support.

(2012, p. 62)

After interviewing the ex-offenders, Daniels (2012) transcribed her interviews. However, during the reading she noticed how she became increasingly affected by the readings. She began to put off reading certain transcripts, as described in the extract below:

Although I have many years clinical experience working with this client group, I was not prepared in my role as researcher for the disturbing and vulnerable feelings that were evoked in me when I analysed the data. . . . My first interview involves a man who had abused his daughter from the age of twelve years, continuing through her leaving home and going to university. . . . I struggled at the parts where he said it was like 'having a love affair' . . . reading his account line by line, immersing myself in his experience, left me on an emotional roller coaster. . . . I avoided the analysis . . . and would make excuses and do something else. . . . I would look at my own children, especially my sixteen year old daughter, and think about how this could happen. . . . I knew I had to find specific supervision. . . . I also wanted someone who was a trained therapist, as I realised this material was no doubt triggering my own issues, and in order to be clear about what belonged to me and what belonged to the offender, I wanted a professional who could help me explore my own personal material. . . . It was this latter area that made me realise the importance of reflexivity.

(p. 69)

As often in the case of countertransference, the links are complicated and by no means obvious. Daniels (2012) was used to working in prisons and experienced in working with sex offenders. She describes how personal the link was for her, and how important it was to be able to explore the connection with a mind open for surprises:

[The supervisor was] a counsellor who had worked in . . . prison and had trained in sex-offender treatment work. [In a session] my anger and tears about the injustice of this twelve-year-old had indeed resonated with me. It was about me as a young child feeling a victim, not in a sexual sense, but more in that my father died when I was five years old and the feelings of loss of power I had, and that my mother struggled to cope. It was very insightful gaining this knowledge, and feeling I was also regaining control, the separation between myself and the twelve-year-old victim helped me to process my information and then the interview.

(p. 71)

As in regular therapeutic practice, Daniels (2002) highlighted the value of supervision which attends to emotional and embodied responses to learn what is going on. Daniels concluded by revealing how a clinical supervisor became invaluable to help her 'to be clear about what belonged to me and what belonged to the offender' (p. 72).

In a recent piece of research (Bager-Charleson & Kasap, in press) I experienced a similar need for clinical supervision. To me, free and creative writing became invaluable to 'side step the gate of reason' as Freud put it (Freud, 1953). I am including some of the research journal stemming from this writing process:

Research journal (Bager-Charleson & Kasap, in press): Tussling with 'svammel'

My initial feeling when looking at the transcripts is one of discomfort. The accounts seem 'messy'; mumbling, difficult to follow, and the Swedish phrase 'svammel' springs to mind. *Svammel* means that something is unclear, nonsensical; just a lot of noise. I am trying to hold onto that feeling, wondering where it comes from? We have kept the transcripts as close to real speak as possible. I read:

'so, that's that was ummm, kind of difficult, ummm . . . I suppose also umm . . .'

It feels like the therapist might be suffocating, gagging for words. Is this the lived experience of multilinguals? The brain keeps sending words which cannot be delivered? Is it me, or is it the participants; where does the 'mist' come from? Why do I react so strongly to the mist? [. . .]

I am the daughter of a bipolar parent. For me, moving between explanations can be both unnerving and comforting through the sense of familiarity it evokes. In therapeutic practice, we need to 'own' this rather than hiding behind clients, assuming that we are experts. Sedgwick suggested that 'analysts need not try to eliminate their pathology, but know it and utilize it'; to avoid enacting it, he addresses a 'fluid awareness of new and old shadows, as well as a concern not to rationalize or project this upon the client' (1999, p. 112). This is true for research, too. Staying with the unknown is invariably unsettling – on many levels – and I am greatly helped by my supervisor to consider knowing in the context of my family script.

McLeod (1999) suggested that 'counsellors engaged in clinical activity necessarily focus mainly on the issue presented by individual clients, and find it difficult to apply findings or conclusions derived from research on groups or populations' (p. 6). This may or may not be so, but it is clear that therapists are trained for an ethical, collaborative relationship which many aim to transfer onto their relationships in research. It often echoes with what Robson (2002) asserted in terms of real-life research being a nonexploitative relationship. Drawing data about peoples' unique, personal experiences comes with a responsibility. Robson (2002, p. 11) asserted that 'the research relationship [must be] between equals . . . the client organization is not being "used" merely to develop academic theory or careers nor is the academic community being "used" (brains being picked). There is a genuine exchange. . . negotiated' (p. 11).

Activity 1

If possible, divide into pairs:

Reserve ten minutes to think about an area in your clinical practice which you would like to explore further through research. What are your thoughts about research? Share experiences, whilst taking notes about your thoughts and experiences about overlaps and differences, potential clashes between research and your way of building your 'knowing' in clinical practice.

Ethical concerns

Consent, choice and decision are ambiguous terms in this kind of research. Hollway and Jefferson (2000) referred to the traditional consent forms as a form of 'doorsteps decisions' (p. 88). It is likely to be informed by first impressions and fantasies, rather than a rational, considered decision: 'The decision to consent . . . cannot be reduced to a conscious, cognitive process but is a continuing emotional awareness' (2000, p. 88).

Consent becomes a subject for ongoing negotiations. Hollway and Jefferson (2000) suggested a before-and-after consent, with debriefing: 'Typically, the guidelines construe the issue of consent as "before" and "after" the research intervention; "After" . . . involves "debriefing" to deal with ethical issues' (p. 89).

Josselson (2011) concluded that 'to obtain rich and meaningful material in interviews, we enter a relationship of trust, respect, and empathy with our participant' (p. 49). This kind of closeness and collaborative nature of the research is riddled with ethical concerns; we move, suggests Josselson (2011), between an I–thou relationship and an I–it one when we position our interviews in the context of colleagues, books and articles. This move from closeness to distance can come as a surprise. Josselson (2011) stressed that 'we retain a responsibility to protect those who inform us, even as we return to our colleagues to relate our own narrative of what we believe we have learned' (p. 34). Like Hollway and Jefferson (2000), Josselson (2011) referred to informed consent as an ongoing process:

> Participants do not actually know at the outset what they will tell us. . . . If we interview well we may often evoke disclosures that the participants were not prepared to reveal when they began to speak. Therefore, we need to ask them again if they consent to our using what they have revealed – after they have revealed it. . . . The concept of 'informed consent' is a bit oxymoronic, given that participants can, at the outset, have only the vaguest idea of what they might be consenting to. . . . I suggested that we need to request informed consent both at the beginning and at the end of the interview.
>
> (p. 47)

The research relationship becomes in this way a conduit for transformative learning for both researcher and participants and requires discussions about expectations and experiences of research. Josselson (2011) asserted that

> we need to say who we are as interpreters who bring our own subjectivity to the topic or people we are writing about. Interpretive authority cannot be implicit, anonymous, or veiled. We have to come out from behind the curtain and say how we are claiming our authority.
>
> (p. 49)

Etherington (2004) compared reflexive research with the skills which we develop in our therapeutic practice. Psychotherapy students are often surprised over how useful their counselling skills are for reflexive research, suggested Etherington (2004), and that

> they [the students] are often pleasantly surprised to discover that reflexive research training uses and values all that they bring with them and come to value. . . . It could be argued that as counsellors/therapists we do not need to adopt a new role of 'researcher' because every encounter with our clients is itself a re-search activity.
>
> (p. 210)

There are, as suggested, needless to say significant differences between the research and the therapeutic relationship. One major difference is, as Etherington (2004, p. 210) put it, that 'as a counsellor people seek me out, as a researcher I seek them'. This has an inevitable impact on the dynamic of the relationship. Etherington (2004) continued:

> As a therapist my purpose is to assist my clients' re-search . . . and in my role as researcher the positions are reversed: they are there to assist me in discovering something about a topic or concept that I am curious about.
>
> (p. 210)

Therapists' embodied responses to research

The distinctions between research and clinical practice are important to keep in mind. However, the overlapping aspects in the way that a relational, emotionally attuned practitioner hopes to gain knowledge are often both underestimated and undervalued.

In a recent narrative inquiry (Bager-Charleson & DuPlock, in press) into accredited therapists' narrated experience of doing research, we drew from a large sample of 50 doctoral dissertations; a smaller sample of research journals, personal notes, poems, creative writing or other forms of communicating created by 20 doctoral students in the course of their research journeys; and taped interviews with 5 graduates. Many of the therapist-researchers said they were unprepared for what research would 'feel like':

Sofie/Interviewer (S):	What comes up to you, what do you associate to when I ask 'What have you felt during your research?'. What's been your embodied experience?
Therapist-Researcher (TR):	Really difficult actually. . . . The end result was very nicely polished and well presented, but I don't think it really captured what went on and how that journey to the data analysis from the interviews, how it really played itself out, and how difficult it became. . . . I'd underestimated it, I don't think I gave it that much thought until I came to do it. Up till that point it was all about, you know, trying to get participants, trying to do my literature review. You know, sort of show how clever I was, and all my whizzy little ideas. I think I underestimated what it was going to be like to do the interviews, to do the data analysis. I mean, you say you're going to just follow the data but it didn't work out that way. . . . **It's hard to get away from that, you're desperately trying to find themes and codes and things but actually this is somebody's life.**

(Bager-Charleson & DuPlock, 2017, p. 7, emphasis added)

Again, like in the previous example, supervision as a place to explore emotions is crucial for the researcher. Many therapist-researchers stressed the significance of inspiration, support and containment. One therapist-researcher described:

What was really critical was having that mentor and be able to write down a kind of pre flow of kind of jibberish which didn't make any sense but her [the supervisors] willingness to read it and stay with me through the process. . . . I took my strength . . . from her you know to hear her voice in my head.

(Therapist-Researcher)

Many of the therapist-researchers suggested that research has been neglected in their clinical training, which has left them even more unprepared:

Therapist-Researcher:	I think it's a shame really that more therapists don't consider it earlier on in their training, because I don't think I had thought about it until I had met other people who had gone into that field. I don't know whether it's worth having a module on research in our therapy training; how do you influence a field of therapy?
Sofie/Interviewer:	If we had such a module, would you have chosen to both talk about the theory but also talk about what it feels like?
Therapist-Researcher:	Yeah I think it should, and not just the theory aspect, but also the more . . . existential crisis you're going to go through. Or what it is like in a real felt way as a therapist to enter into the world of research, to understand it before you enter the door. It's not just your hopes and ambitions, but in much like therapy you will impact people, and you yourself will be impacted as well. **Therapists have a lot to add to the field of research, but many don't make it.**

(Bager-Charleson & Du Plock 2017, p. 8, emphasis added)

Some therapist-researchers spoke about a 'glass ceiling', describing counsellors often engaging in a 'race to the bottom to stay on the ground [to] help the marginalised'. Our participants referred to feeling selfish and self-promoting when 'trying to be' a researcher; many of them chose to keep quiet about it at their work place. One therapist-researcher described it thusly:

> It is in my DNA to help those who are marginalized and in a way my own kind of experiences of barriers . . . of hitting a ceiling that I can only as a woman, who identifies as being black that I would only go so far, and that, and the whole world of research and being with all these well-spoken, articulate, bright people.

Another therapist-researcher said, 'For me there were these particular archetypes of being a woman in my family; nurturing, giving, sacrificial. I had always felt like I was a secret pioneer. . . . But who was I to think that I would be a researcher?' (Bager-Charleson & Du Plock, 2017, p. 7).

Comments

Our study suggested that there was an absence of 'research identity' for counsellors. The emphasis on 'being there' for 'the marginalised' appeared to clash with expectations of being a researcher as self-promoting and sometimes exploitative. 'Who was I to think that I would be a researcher?', as one therapist-researcher put it. Some referred to how this clashed with the expectations of them as women. Others came from working class backgrounds, where again 'sitting reading all day' was a luxury. This heightened the sense of 'shame' when things did not work according to plan; one therapist-researcher described suffering from palpitations during the whole data analysis phase: 'I didn't tell anyone; they'd just say, "How can you get ill from just reading a book?" '.

Interviewing and other collaborative means of generating knowledge appeared to come relatively easy to most therapist-researchers. Data analysis appeared however to bring up particularly strong feelings, sometimes of a countertransference level, where the childhood of the researchers comes into play. The need to do justice to the material can be experienced as a burden, and a number of researchers wrote about their fear that they might not be equal to the task. Some therapist-researchers explored their strong reactions in the context of their own biography:

> Research activated some of my own inner psychological scripting . . . the shame of public opprobrium are the most powerful scripts that operate my inner world of thinking.
>
> (Therapist-Researcher)

> I found myself with two paradigm set against each other, which recreated my adolescent struggle with my father.
>
> (Therapist-Researcher)

Another therapist-researcher described:

> It's been horrific, I've agonised so much, feeling like a fraud, so stupid. . . . I've been feeling desperate, all the time thinking that I am doing this right with themes and codes and tables.
>
> (Therapist-Researcher)

The fear of misinterpreting and misrepresenting people appears to be as strong in research as in clinical practice for most therapists. Ultimately, we (Bager-Charleson & DuPlock, 2017) found this to be a reoccurring point, made by our participants from all strands of contributions.

Concluding remarks: Research, countertransference and reflexivity

In research about people, meanings are, as Finlay and Gough (2003) suggested, 'always disputable depending on who is speaking to whom and the power relations either held or perceived to be held within these interactions' (p. 164). As highlighted in the context of different examples in this chapter, there is always an element of 'inconcludability' in therapy-related research. Parker et al. (1994) described this well:

> There will always be a gap between the meanings that appear in a research setting and the account written in the report. . . . An account can always be supplemented further. . . . While a positivist will see inconcludability as a fatal problem, qualitative researchers who follow the change in meanings in the course of research will both understand and welcome the opportunity for others to supplement their account.
>
> (p. 13)

In this chapter we looked at examples of how the researcher's use of self can overlap the way we generate knowledge and gain understandings as practitioners, drawing from relational, emotionally attuned means of generating new understandings. Infant observations and free-association narrative interviews are some of the examples of research approaches where intersubjectivity and emotions are invited as both useful and inevitable aspects of the search.

Activity 2

1   How do you feel that your clinical training has prepared you for research?
2   Doing a literature review:

Literature review is an important part of research. Literature reviews are typically based on computer searches. Practice on an accessible search engine, such as Google, in case you do not have access to any online library. Identify your interests, for instance, *countertransference in psychotherapy*.
   Type in your search words.
   Make a list of the first 20 research papers or references that come up:

- How has the research been conducted?
- What are the methods referred to in the abstract or under the methodology section?
- Who has been included in the research?
- What were the findings?

- What do you think and feel about the research; how does it cover or differ from your interest area?
- What would you like to do differently?

Discuss and compare, if possible, in pairs.

For further reading about doing a literature review, go to:

Du Plock, S. (2014). Doing your literature review. In S. Bager-Charleson (Ed.), *Doing Practice-based Research in Therapy*. London, UK: Sage.

Bibliography

Anderson, R., & Braud, W. (2011). *Transforming Self and Others Through Research*. New York, NY: SUNY Press.

Atkinson, A. (2011). *The long-term post-abortion experience* (Doctoral dissertation). Middlesex University and Metanoia Institute, London, UK.

Bager-Charleson, S. (2014). *Doing Practice-Based Research in Therapy: A Reflexive Approach*. London, UK: Sage.

Bager-Charleson, S., & DuPlock, S. (2017, in press). *Therapists' Use of Self in Research: A Narrative Inquiry into Psychotherapists' Embodied Situatedness and Emotional Entanglement During Data Analysis*. London, UK: Metanoia Institute.

Bick, E. (1964). Notes on infant observation in psychoanalytic training. *International Journal of Psychoanalysis*, 45, 558–566.

Bondi, L. (2013). Research and therapy: Generating meaning and feeling gaps. *Qualitative Inquiry*, 19(1), 9–19.

Bondi, L., & Fewell, J. (2016). *Practitioner Research in Counselling and Psychotherapy: The Power of Examples*. London, UK: Palgrave Macmillan.

Briggs, S. (1997). *Growth and Risk in Infancy*. London, UK: Jessica Kingsley.

Castonguay, L. G., Nelson, D. L., Boutselis, M. A., Chiswick, N. R., Damer, D. D., Hemmelstein, N. A., Jackson, J. S., . . . Borkovec, T. D. (2010). Psychotherapists, researchers, or both? A qualitative analysis of experiences in a practice research network. *Psychotherapy: Theory, Research, Practice, Training*, 47(3), 345–354.

Clarke, S., & Hodgett, P. (Eds.) (2009). *Researching Beneath the Surface: Psycho-Social Research Methods in Practice*. London, UK: Karnac Books.

Daniels, M. (2012). *Using role play as a therapeutic tool in offending-behaviour programmes in Her Majesty's prison service* (Doctoral dissertation). Middlesex University and Metanoia Institute, London, UK.

Datler, W., Laxae, R., & Trunkenpolz, K. (2012). Observing in nursing homes: The use of single case studies and organisational observation as a research tool. In C. Urwin & J. Sternberg (Eds.), *Infant Observation and Research: Emotional Processes in Everyday Lives*. New York, NY: Routledge.

Etherington, K. (2004). *Becoming a Reflexive Researcher: Using Our Selves in Research*. London, UK: Jessica Kingsley.

Finlay, L. (2016). Being a therapist-researcher: Doing relational-reflexive research. *The Psychotherapist*, *62*, 6–8.

Finlay, L., & Gough, B. (2003). *Reflexivity: A Practical Guide*. London, UK: Blackwell.

Freud, S. (1953/1985). *The Interpretation of Dreams* (Trans. J. Stratchey). London, UK: Penguin Books.

Hollway, W. (2009). Applying the 'experience-near' principle to research: Psychoanalytically informed methods. *Journal of Social Work Practice*, *23*(4), 461–474.

Hollway, W. (2011). In between external and internal worlds: Imagination in transitional space. *UK Methodological Innovations*, *6*(3), 50–60. Retrieved from www.pbs.plym.ac.uk/mi/pdf/8-02-12/MIO63Paper23.pdf

Hollway, W. (2016). Emotional experience plus reflection: Countertransference and reflexivity in research. *The Psychotherapist*, *62*, 19–21.

Hollway, W., & Jefferson, T. (2000). *Doing Qualitative Research Differently*. London UK: Sage.

Josselson, R. (2011). *'Bet you think this song is about you': Whose narrative is it in narrative research*? Retrieved from Journals.hil.unb.ca/index.php/NW/article/download/18472/19971

Josselson, R. (2016). Reflexivity and ethics in qualitative research. *The Psychotherapist*, *62*, 22–25.

McLeod, J. (1999). *Practitioner Research in Counselling*. London, UK: Sage.

Orange, D. M. (1996). *Emotional Understanding: Studies in Psychoanalytic Epistemology*. New York, NY: Guildford Press.

Orange, D. M. (2009). *Thinking for Clinicians: Philosophical Resources for Contemporary Psychoanalysis and the Humanistic Psychotherapies*. Abington, UK: Routledge.

Parker, I., Banister, P., Burman, E., Taylor, M., & Tindall, C. (1994). *Qualitative Methods in Psychology*. Buckingham, UK: Open University.

Price, H., & Cooper, A. (2012). *In the Field: Psychoanalytic Observation and Epistemological Realism*. New York, NY: Routledge.

Robson, C. (2002). *Real World Research* (2nd ed.). Oxford, UK: Blackwell.

Shuttleworth, J. (2012). Infant observation, ethnography and anthropology. In C. Urwin & J. Sternberg (Eds.), *Infant Observation and Research: Emotional Processes in Everyday Lives*. New York, NY: Routledge.

Stedman, J., & Dallos, R. (2009). *Reflective Practice in Psychotherapy and Counselling*. Maidenhead, UK: Open University Press.

Tasca, G., Sylvestre, J., Balfour, L., Chyurlia, L., Evans, J., Fortin-Langelier, B., Francis, K., . . . Wilson, B. (2015). What clinicians want: Findings from a psychotherapy practice research network survey. *Psychotherapy*, *52*(1), 1–11.

Tordes, L. (2007). *Embodies Enquiry: Phenomenological Touchstones for Research, Psychotherapy and Spirituality*. London, UK: Palgrave Macmillan.

Urwin, C., & Sternberg, J. (2012). *Infant Observation and Research: Emotional Processes in Everyday Lives*. New York, NY: Routledge.

Willig, C. (2012). *Qualitative Interpretation and Analysis in Psychology*. Maidenhead, UK: Open University Press.

Chapter 11

'The recovered therapist'

Working with body image disturbance and eating disorders – Researching the countertransference

Linda Verbeek

Introduction

It is common for female therapists who have recovered from body image disturbance or an eating disorder to be drawn into working with others struggling with these problems. In Jungian terms, this may be described as the archetypal energy of the 'wounded healer', whereby the therapist's 'own experience of being wounded is what helps her face the suffering client in simple relatedness' (Larisey, 2012, para. 3). By having personal insight into the healing process from body image distress and eating pathology, the recovered therapist may have a lot to offer her clients, such as understanding, hope and motivation that recovery is possible, and encouraging trust in those who desperately fear change (Bowlby, Anderson, Hall & Willingham, 2012; Costin & Johnson, 2002). In this regard, Adams (2014) suggested that the issue is less about therapists having struggled at times in their lives, but rather how they have transformed their trauma and distress into something meaningful for themselves through working as therapists.

It is well established that working with this client group often tends to evoke various embodied and emotional countertransference feelings in the therapist, particularly in relation to body image, food, shape and weight (Delucia-Waack, 1999; Costin, 2009). This is likely to occur even if the therapist has not directly experienced these issues themselves, but will predictably be more evocative in those with a history of body image concerns and eating problems, with the possibility of relapse as a risk factor. Therefore, it is essential that therapists should have appropriate support in place; and engage in their own process of self-reflection to develop reflexivity and awareness of their embodied and emotional responses.

This chapter draws upon the findings of my doctoral research (Verbeek, 2016) which explored the subjective embodied and emotional countertransference experiences of a sample of nine recovered female therapists in their work with clients suffering from body image disturbance and eating disorders. This research also highlights the management of typical countertransference responses with this client group, and the importance of personal and professional self-support strategies for recovered therapists to maintain well-being, and to prevent burnout or relapse.

Treatment of eating disorders and body image disturbance

Sociocultural view of female body image problems

The current literature on body image shows that body image problems occur more often in females than males, regardless of age (Murnen, 2012). A possible sociocultural explanation for this gender difference in Western society is due to the acceptance and internalisation by women of the complex cultural schema, that beauty, appearance and the slender ideal are essential requirements to achieving happiness, success and desirability. This internalised belief system about appearance creates a core basis of self-evaluation, with an individual's self-worth becoming equated with their 'self-perceived' attractiveness (Levine & Smolak, 2004; Tiggemann, 2004). Consequently, this often leads to dieting and other unhealthy attempts to pursue the slender, youthful ideal, eventually leading to body image problems and disordered eating symptoms (Tiggemann, 2012).

Many women may therefore admit to feeling unhappy with their bodies, particularly in relation to body size, weight and a desire to be thinner, to the extent that 'weight has been aptly described as a "normative discontent" for women' (Tiggemann, 2012, p. 12). Feminist literature stresses that this normative body dissatisfaction seen in many women is a systemic social phenomenon rather than a function of individual pathology (McKinley, 2012). Thus, women (both therapists and clients) have a shared culture as they are exposed to the same sociocultural messages and pressures about weight and physical appearance (Costin, 2009), unachievable standards of perfection and slimness (Ruskay-Rabinor, 1995) and the socially constructed notions about female attractiveness and goodness (Burka, 1996).

Recovery: A multidimensional view

The current literature indicates that recovery from body image disturbance and eating disorders encompasses more than merely the cessation of compulsive behaviours, disordered eating and restoration of weight. Recovery must include multidimensional factors of change such as psychological, emotional, social and biological aspects to reduce the potential for relapse (Bloomgarden, Gerstein & Moss, 2003; Johnston, Smethurst & Gowers, 2005; Noordenbos & Seubring, 2006). This has implications for recovered therapists working with eating and body image problems as, to limit the risk of their own relapse, they should ensure that they continually manage all these dimensions of their personal recovery in an ongoing manner.

A rather contentious issue exists in the literature about how to know *when* a therapist is 'recovered enough' to see clients with eating disorders and body image issues in a way that provides good clinical care for the client, and is ethically safe for the therapist. There are minimal guidelines offered about this, aside from a recommendation by Costin (2009) that therapists should be recovered from eating disorder symptoms for at least 2 years before starting to work with eating disorder clients; and a suggestion by Sovak (2011) that recovered therapists who are less experienced, should consider first accessing safe supportive supervision before seeing eating disorder clients.

Bloomgarden et al. (2003) also suggested that guidelines should not be too rigid or quantitative regarding what is considered as being 'recovered enough', as this may cause recovered therapists to feel monitored, shamed and afraid of disclosing their history of body image problems. Instead, a judgement of the therapist's personal readiness about working with this client group should rather be carefully considered in supervision and personal therapy. These guidelines seek to reduce the recovered therapist's overidentification and entanglement with their client's struggles to avoid causing harm to the therapist and the client; however, despite lengthy clinical experience and recovery periods, personal body issues may still resurface. In this instance, it is recommended that if a therapist experiences a relapse due to personal material resurfacing, they should ideally reduce or put their client work temporarily on hold while they get support to 'get back on track'.

Therapist countertransference responses

It is widely acknowledged that clinical work with eating disorder clients may evoke powerful countertransference responses in the therapist, whether they have a history of these issues or not. For instance, Delucia-Waack (1999) suggested this may include overidentifying with the client's problems; taking too much responsibility for the client or engaging in a power struggle; becoming intrusive or avoidant about a client's secrecy issues; feeling helpless, ineffective and inadequate; and avoidance of affect. Similarly, Kearns (2005) described some common countertransference reactions with eating disorder clients as ranging from feelings of redundancy, guilt, disorganisation and anger to feeling drained both emotionally and physically, and dreading certain client sessions. The impact of these responses may have a significant impact on the work, and if left unattended, may potentially damage the therapeutic relationship and treatment outcomes.

When a therapist has experienced similar body image concerns and/or eating problems to their clients, it is common to experience a heightened awareness of their personal shame triggers if they identify with their clients; they may become more aware of their body imperfections, dread gaining weight, and be conscious of their own eating patterns and exercise routines (Ruskay-Rabinor, 1995). This emphasises how important it is for therapists to be aware of the complex dynamics of their emergent countertransference responses to avoid unintentionally shaming their clients, or becoming overwhelmed by their own shame (Shure & Weinstock, 2009).

Study on the experiences of recovered therapists working with body image disturbance and eating disorders

Research has consistently shown that approximately 30% of professionals working in the eating disorder field share an eating disorder history, and recovered professionals may have a lot of compassion or a great desire to help others dealing with these painful issues as they personally have an acute aware-ness of what it is like to suffer in that way (Barbarich, 2002; Bloomgarden et al., 2003). The literature on the experiences of recovered female therapists is still fairly limited, but the emphasis has now moved away from question-ing the suitability of recovered professionals working with eating disorders (Johnston, Smethhurst & Gowers, 2005) towards understanding the particu-lar support needs of these therapists, along with highlighting the professional responsibility of therapists to manage their own physical and psychologi-cal wellbeing to practice in a safe, ethical manner with their clients (Sovak, 2011). In these studies, the predominant focus has however been on profes-sionals working primarily with eating disorders; therefore, the purpose of my research study (Verbeek, 2016) was to expand on this concept by investigat-ing the experiences of recovered female therapists working with issues of body image disturbance and dysmorphia, *as well* as eating disorders. The study also looked at how the therapist's subjective experiences and countertransference responses are managed therapeutically, and explored how recovered therapists may support themselves personally and professionally.

Methodology

The sample included nine female therapists (including psychologists and psychotherapists) between the ages of 35 and 65 years. The participants all identified having a personal history of body image problems, which included recovery from mild to moderate body image disturbance (shown by body dissatisfaction rather than the severe distortion as seen in body dysmorphic disorder), and/or an eating disorder, including anorexia nervosa, bulimia ner-vosa, and binge-eating disorder as defined in the DSM-5 (American Psychiatric Association, 2013). None of the participants were currently struggling with an eating disorder, however some identified still having body image concerns.

The participants all had experience seeing clients with eating disorders and/ or moderate to severe body image disturbance and body dysmorphic disorder, and they all worked from a relational perspective with their clients, so were conscious of the relational space and transference dynamics that may emerge in their work, which facilitated the emergence of richer material in the inter-views. The data was collected using semistructured individual interviews, and these were carefully transcribed, and any identifying personal details removed before moving onto data analysis. The methodology I used was interpretative phenomenological analysis (IPA), an idiographic approach which is concerned with 'examining how a participant makes sense of, or sees meaning in, their experience' (Smith, Flowers & Larkin, 2009, p. 187).

Research findings

Experiences of recovered therapists

There were several common experiences which the participants shared in their client work:

I. EMPATHIC RESONANCE

All the therapists in the study spoke about feeling a deep empathic resonance with their clients' suffering; therefore, their personal experience of having body image issues and/or an eating disorder appears to have deepened their capacity to empathise with their clients on a meta-level, by understanding emotionally and cognitively what that struggle is about. Candice shared, 'I can identify with how painful it is sometimes with the clients I'm working with', and she could empathise with a client who said that 'they felt like the biggest in the room, which I know what that feels like'. However, there appeared to be both positive and negative consequences of having this high degree of empathy. For example, some of the positive consequences included feeling hopeful about their client's recovery; having an understanding about the reluctance and resistance of their clients to change; as well as being sensitive to how painful and challenging it may be for some individuals to start addressing their body problems in therapy. Some of the negative consequences of this empathic resonance included having a heightened awareness of their own bodies, overidentifying with their client's experiences, fears about being judged and their personal body issues being exposed, and at times feeling ineffective.

II. WORRY ABOUT JUDGEMENT

Some participants worried that their clients were judging them on their appearance, and making assumptions about their trustworthiness, stability, credibility and worth. This feeling was heightened for some when their size and shape fluctuated (due to illness or pregnancy), or at times of stress when they were struggling with managing their eating habits and weight. Participants worried about their history of eating or body image problems, or any current struggles, being exposed or 'obvious' to their clients and other professionals, which resulted in them wanting to hide their history from others. This demonstrates the shame many therapists may feel about having their own personal struggles, causing a desire to hide behind a professional mask.

For instance, Alice shared that her default position is 'to think that the female client opposite me is going to criticise me in her mind about the way I look. And I have to be very, very careful about that'.

Unfortunately, these concerns of the participants are somewhat realistic as eating disorder clients typically do relate to others by comparing their bodies, and therefore often tend to scrutinise their therapists' body shape, size and appearance. This does not suggest by any means that therapists need to try to change their bodies to improve their therapeutic relationship with a resistant client. Rather, a key issue highlighted here is the importance of therapists being mindful of the explicit and implicit factors which may impact the therapeutic work in which physical appearances play a significant role. Therefore, this presents a challenge to recovered therapists of being able to manage their own feelings and behaviours without becoming self-destructive towards themselves. In this regard, Costin (2009) suggested that ideally, female therapists working with body issues should work on demonstrating self-acceptance, care and love for their own bodies, and aim to be positive, healthy role models to their clients.

III. ASSUMPTIONS ABOUT THE THERAPIST

A therapist's particular physical characteristics, shape, size and weight, will inevitably impact clients with eating and body image problems in varied ways, and is likely to play a part in the unconscious dynamics of the therapeutic process (Burka, 1996). Clients may make powerful assumptions about the therapist's relationship with food, self-control and well-being (Sheehy, 2009) which may be used as perceived evidence of the therapist's attitudes, morality, mental and physical health, to create an awareness of who the therapist is and how they should try to relate to them, as well as the therapist's capacity to understand and help them (Liebermann, 2000; Lowell & Meader, 2005; Rance, Clarke & Moller, 2014).

Several participants in the study had experienced their clients making assumptions that they were unaffected by body image problems because they were at a healthy weight. Some clients perceived this as evidence that their therapist wouldn't be able to relate to having horrible feelings about one's body: 'In the room, the dynamic between us transferentially, I felt very much that I was on the receiving end of a lot of projection: you're okay, I'm not okay, you can't possibly understand' (Leigh). Other therapists who were quite slim or petite, experienced similar assumptions from their overweight and obese clients who believed that they couldn't understand their body struggles. For instance, Megan's client told her, 'How can you relate to my problem? You know, you're clearly not obese'. These therapists had also experienced some competitiveness and jealousy in the therapy room with their anorexic clients scrutinising the therapist's body, and asking personal questions about the therapists' exercise routine, diet and weight. This projection onto the therapist of being a 'perfect person', untroubled and unburdened by the usual challenges and restrictions of being an ordinary human being (Adams, 2014), may subsequently reinforce the client's feelings of isolation and alienation in their relationships with themselves and others (Kearns, 2005).

IV. OVERIDENTIFICATION WITH THE STRUGGLE

Recovered therapists are likely to connect at some level with their client's stories due to having these shared experiences; however, a few participants spoke of sometimes overidentifying with their client's body image struggles and eating problems, which then triggered their personal body issues. For instance, Alice shared that there were 'times that I think I have almost surrendered myself to becoming too entangled with it'. Consequently, some participants reported having a lot of negative feelings such as insecurity, inadequacy, and becoming highly critical and punitive towards themselves. This theme echoes findings by Johnston et al. (2005), that some of the disadvantages of recovered therapists working in this field include overinvolvement and enmeshment, therapist vulnerability, and subjectivity. Thus, it is evident that countertransference issues may have personal consequences for recovered therapists by creating a vulnerability for relapse if sensitive material is triggered (Costin, 2009).

V. HEIGHTENED BODY AWARENESS

Some participants noticed feeling more aware of their own bodies when working with this client group, and had a sense that their bodies were being scrutinised. Candice shared that with one client, she felt 'invaded upon with her gaze. My body was being watched and judged'. For the participants this caused discomfort when there were issues of difference in the room, such as perceiving clients as being more/less attractive than themselves; being a higher/lower weight; and having different body shape/size to clients. This echoes feminist literature which suggests it is common for female therapists to experience a heightened awareness of their personal embodied sense of shame with this client population (Ruskay-Rabinor, 1995). For example, some of the participants who had recently been pregnant, spoke about feeling self-conscious about their weight gain and physical changes.

In other instances, some therapists admitted feeling deeply uncomfortable being a size which some of their overweight clients desired to be, while others noticed feeling more self-critical and hypervigilant of their bodies with clients they saw as being thinner, more attractive or in better shape than they were. These concerns of the participants were challenging, as the therapist's physical stature will inevitably have an impact on the subjective experiences of their clients. For instance, Rance, Clarke and Moller's (2014) study suggested that an underweight eating disorder client working with an overweight therapist may have feelings of fear that if they were to change their disordered eating habits, they may end up looking like the therapist. In contrast, an overweight client may experience intense feelings of self-hatred and jealousy if they work with a slim therapist.

Other times that a heightened body awareness arose for the participants included working with body image problems related to physical disabilities, and body dysmorphia from real or imagined imperfections or disfigurement. Bridget had noticed feeling guilty that she was more able-bodied than her disabled client who was in a wheelchair: 'I can walk, and I can go to the toilet, so many of the things he can't do. . . . I feel helpless because I can't change anything for him, I can only listen'. This had helped put her own body concerns into perspective. Another participant who worked with a client suffering from body dysmorphia shared that she had felt a pull in the transference to compare, scrutinise and criticise her client's perceived facial flaws as the client was doing herself. Some of these therapist experiences are indicative of 'projective identification' when the client unconsciously aims to evoke 'the unbearable feeling state' in the therapist which they are unable to contain within themselves (Casement, 2002, p. 137).

VI. FEELINGS OF INEFFECTIVENESS

A shared experience of the participants was a feeling of being ineffective when working with this client population. This included times when the therapists had felt helpless and frustrated with managing their clients' resistance to change and the letting go of self-destructive behaviours, and amongst some of the newly qualified therapists, who perhaps lacked confidence or experience in their clinical work; they had felt deskilled or out of their depth. In Nicola's work with a very underweight client, she shared feeling 'really concerned and wary, and insecure about my ability to help her'. As experienced by the participants in this study, Bloomgarden (2009) suggested that reluctance to change is a relatively common and predictable challenge when treating eating disorders and body image problems.

Consequently, therapists may find themselves in the uncomfortable position of having to take responsibility for helping clients who are strenuously resisting therapy and acting self-destructively, often resulting in the therapist experiencing very negative countertransference reactions such as feelings of sadness, disappointment, fear, panic, shame, incompetence, inadequacy, anger, frustration, disillusionment, hopelessness and impotence. A risk factor for the recovered therapist is that these common countertransference feelings may be exacerbated if their personal insecurities, wounds or current struggles are stirred up by the therapeutic dialogue, or are present independently of the therapeutic interaction. If left unaddressed, this may lead to 'countertransference dominance' if the therapist unconsciously begins to direct the therapeutic work more in line with meeting their own unconscious needs instead of those of the client (Maroda, 2004).

Management of countertransference responses

When working with countertransference, therapists need to monitor their internal mental processes to develop and hone their reflexivity, and continually ask themselves: 'What does this person make me feel like, make me think about, make me want to do?' (O'Brien & Houston, 2007, p. 152). Bloomgarden (2009) proposed that ultimately the therapist's self-awareness is what protects clients from the therapist's thoughtless or unconscious reactions to the influence of their personal issues, or the client's treatment resistance. However this study suggests that this is not easy to do. The findings of the study demonstrate the following ways in which the participants manage their countertransference feelings in the therapy room.

I. CONVEYING EMPATHY

The participants' personal understanding of body image problems seemed to enable a more authentic way of being and relating in the therapy room. When they spoke of conveying empathy to their clients this was by being present in a nonjudgemental way, to 'really hear them' (Alice), with sensitivity and compassion about the personal obstacles which were unique for each client: 'I can really hear what you're saying, and I really do trust that if you can dare to believe, you can form a new relationship with your body' (Sandra). The participants would also share their countertransference feelings with their clients when appropriate. For instance, Leigh stated:

> Countertransferentially, there was a lot of projection coming between us, so I found myself saying to her, just recently, that I do understand that it's very difficult having someone challenge you about your eating, and part of you doesn't want to give it up, and another part that realises that it is a problem.

This may assist in gently challenging clients in a sensitive and caring manner about issues of resistance to recovery, and may deepen the client's understanding about the impact of their eating disorder attitudes and behaviour.

II. EXPLORING DIFFERENCE AND EMBODIED EXPERIENCES

Several writers have discussed and encouraged the intervention of including the therapist's body in the therapeutic dialogue by inviting clients to express how they feel and think about their own body and the therapist's body so they may fully explore the themes emerging between them (Burka, 1996; Costin, 2009; Lowell & Meader, 2005; Orbach, 2004). This was echoed by a number of the participants in the study who spoke about exploring their embodied experiences with their clients. This included talking about the differences or similarities between the therapist's and client's bodies, and any feelings this evoked for the client. For example, Alice had a voluptuous body shape and shared that if clients commented on her appearance she 'would turn that into an interpretation. Not a punitive interpretation, but just wanting to see what it was about, and why the client would think about asking me that, and what the unconscious had provided'. The participants were also aware of body language and embodied countertransference reactions: 'In therapy I use the body quite a lot in that I'm very observant about body language, and I often ask clients what's going on in their bodies. And I do pay attention to what's going on in my body' (Sandra). She felt this provided important insight into the nonverbal communication in the room.

III. SELF-DISCLOSURE

There was a general agreement amongst the participants regarding the potential analytic usefulness of self-disclosure as a therapeutic intervention if used carefully and purposefully. However, the participants strongly emphasised the importance of exercising caution and reflection before using self-disclosure with clients, to carefully determine whether this may assist or impede the work. In this regard, Bunnell (2009) stated that the use of self-disclosure as an intervention should only be done at an appropriate time when one has a sense that the disclosure may enrich the therapeutic process. The participants also suggested that therapists should be mindful that their self-disclosure does not result from overidentifying with a client's issues, thereby making assumptions and losing sight of the client's unique subjective experience: 'It's just working out when is the right time, not to make it about you, but also whether the client's going to be able to receive it, and whether it's gonna be helpful. It may destroy how they see you at that time' (Megan). Therefore, an important consideration is about how much trust and connection has been established in the therapeutic relationship to support the revelation, and whether it will facilitate further analytic exploration (Leibowitz, 1996).

IV. RECOGNISING AND BRACKETING OWN ISSUES

The recovered therapists in the study spoke about the importance of recognising and 'bracketing' their countertransference feelings and personal issues when these come up in the therapy room. Bridget spoke about 'figuring out what's theirs and what's mine in the countertransference. Did I feel like this with that client again, did I come with these feelings or not?'. If Bridget recognised her own issues were being triggered, she was conscious of bracketing her feelings: 'I'm aware that I need to put that back there, and put my professional hat on to give my attention to the client'. This highlights the importance of therapists developing a deep level of self-awareness about their embodied experiences, and their emotional and stress responses, before and during therapy sessions, to assist them in making sense of their countertransference reactions. The process of containing one's countertransference reactions also enables the therapist to develop some clarity about their source and significance (Gabbard & Wilkinson, 1994). This chimes with Bunnell's (2009, p. 91) statement that 'ongoing self-exploration and self-awareness are the most powerful antidote for inappropriate countertransference reactions'. From a relational, Gestalt perspective, an important skill in phenomenological inquiry involves the therapist's capacity to identify and acknowledge any pre-conceptions, judgements and attitudes they may have; and in the moment of 'bracketing' they try to put these to one side, so they may be open and present to experience their unique client in that unique moment (Joyce & Sills, 2014).

Personal and professional self-support strategies

This study found a number of strategies the participants used to support their professional reflective capacity and ethical practice; as well as ways to manage their self-care and maintenance of their own recovery. For instance, in a personal capacity, the participants spoke of becoming more compassionate, respectful and grateful towards their bodies, and were mindful of being less critical and more accepting of their imperfections. This mindset consequently enabled them to adopt a healthier attitude and motivation towards managing their self-care and wellbeing, with more healthy, balanced behaviour around eating and exercise, and regularly creating time for relaxation and reflection which helped the participants to feel more grounded and focused (Verbeek, 2016).

Of great value and importance were the professional self-support strategies used by the recovered therapists, which include personal therapy and clinical supervision.

SUPPORT IN PERSONAL THERAPY

The participants had all experienced being in personal therapy as part of their training requirements. It is essential that all recovered therapists have explored their own embodied experiences and/or eating issues in personal therapy to ensure they feel 'recovered enough' to work safely and ethically with individuals presenting with eating disorders and body image disturbance. Any unresolved issues may have a damaging effect on client work if the therapist has not examined their personal issues in sufficient depth to enable a suitable capacity for self-awareness and reflexivity to develop (Hammersley, 2003).

SUPPORT IN SUPERVISION

The capacity for reflective practice is seen by Evans and Gilbert (2005, p. 133) as being the most important characteristic of any psychotherapist, which requires 'a delicate holding of an awareness of the therapist's own experience and that of the client, while simultaneously standing back and reflecting on the dynamic interaction between the two'. For the participants in the study, it was evident that the use of supervision served to nurture their capacity for reflexivity and self-awareness, which assisted them to be able to continually process countertransference responses, maintain integrity and manage ethical boundaries. The participants all spoke of the importance of finding a trusted supervisor with whom they could disclose their personal history of body image problems, which enabled them to creatively explore their personal process in relation to client work to avoid losing perspective of themselves and the client.

Conclusion

This chapter has explored the relationship between how therapists have worked with personal 'wounds', and how they support their clients in confronting their own struggles and conflicts. If a therapist has had a personal history of problems with body image, weight and food, and they choose to see clients struggling with body image disturbance and eating disorders, it is essential that they have first explored their own body issues in personal therapy so they can be deeply attuned to their personal 'recovery process'. Recovered therapists should be responsible in maintaining their recovery and wellbeing through various self-support strategies (Verbeek 2016); and if personal issues resurface to a significant level when working with this client population, they should consider revisiting personal therapy. Recovered therapists should also focus on nurturing their reflexive capacity by attending regular supervision to continually process and manage their countertransference responses which commonly emerge in the therapy room with this client population. Essentially, this study has highlighted the importance of becoming a reflexive, self-aware therapist: As Jung cautioned,

> the analyst must go on learning endlessly, and never forget that each new case brings new problems to light and thus gives rise to unconscious assumptions that have never before been constellated. We could say, without too much exaggeration, that a good half of every treatment that probes at all deeply consists in the doctor's examining himself, for only what he can put right in himself can he hope to put right in the patient . . . if he feels that the patient is hitting him, or even scoring off him: it is his own hurt that gives the measure of his power to heal. This, and nothing else, is the meaning of the Greek myth of the wounded physician.
>
> (1951, p. 116)

Bibliography

Adams, M. (2014). *The Myth of the Untroubled Therapist: Private Life, Professional Practice*. East Sussex, UK: Routledge.

American Psychiatric Association. (2013). *Diagnostic and Statistical Manual of Mental Disorders* (5th ed.). Washington, DC: Author.

Barbarich, N. C. (2002). Lifetime prevalence of eating disorders among professionals in the field. *Eating Disorders, 10*, 305–312.

Bloomgarden, A. (2009). Working with people who live dangerously: Perspectives on managing negative countertransference during the treatment of eating disorders. In M. Maine, W. N. Davis & J. Shure (Eds.), *Effective Clinical Practice in the Treatment of Eating Disorders: The Heart of the Matter* (pp. 221–234). New York, NY: Routledge.

Bloomgarden, A., Gerstein, F., & Moss, C. (2003). The last word: A 'recovered enough' therapist. *Eating Disorders, 11*, 163–167.

Bowlby, C. G., Anderson, T. L., Hall, M. E. L., & Willingham, M. M. (2012). Recovered professionals exploring eating disorder recovery: A qualitative investigation of meaning. *Clinical Social Work Journal, 43*, 1–10.

Bunnell, D. (2009). Countertransference in the psychotherapy of patients with eating disorders. In M. Maine, W. N. Davis & J. Shure (Eds.), *Effective Clinical Practice in the Treatment of Eating Disorders: The Heart of the Matter* (pp. 79–93). New York, NY: Routledge.

Burka, J. B. (1996). The therapist's body in reality and fantasy: A perspective from an overweight therapist. In B. Gerson (Ed.), *The Therapist as a Person: Life Crises, Life Choices, Life Experiences and Their Effects on Treatment* (pp. 255–275). London, UK: The Analytic Press.

Casement, P. (2002). *Learning from Our Mistakes: Beyond Dogma in Psychoanalysis and Psychotherapy.* East Sussex, UK: Brunner-Routledge.

Costin, C. (2009). The embodied therapist: Perspectives on treatment, personal growth, and supervision related to body image. In M. Maine, W. N. Davis & J. Shure (Eds.), *Effective Clinical Practice in the Treatment of Eating Disorders: The Heart of the Matter* (pp. 221–234). New York, NY: Routledge.

Costin, C., & Johnson, C. L. (2002). Been there, done that: Clinicians' use of personal recovery in the treatment of eating disorders. *Eating Disorders, 10*, 293–303.

Delucia-Waack, J. L. (1999). Supervision for counsellors working with eating disorder groups: Countertransference issues related to body image, food and weight. *Journal of Counselling and Development, 77*, 379–388.

Evans, K. R., & Gilbert, M. C. (2005). *An Introduction to Integrative Psychotherapy.* Hampshire, UK: Palgrave Macmillan.

Gabbard, G. O., & Wilkinson, S. M. (1994). *Management of Countertransference with Borderline Patients.* Lanham, MD: Rowman & Littlefield.

Hammersley, D. (2003). Training and professional development in the context of counselling psychology. In R. Woolfe, W. Dryden & S. Strawbridge (Eds.), *Handbook of Counselling Psychology* (2nd ed., pp. 637–655). London, UK: Sage.

Johnston, C., Smethurst, N., & Gowers, S. (2005). Should people with a history of an eating disorder work as eating disorder therapists? *European Eating Disorders Review, 13*, 301–310.

Joyce, P., & Sills, C. (2014). *Skills in Gestalt Counselling and Psychotherapy* (3rd ed.). London, UK: Sage.

Jung, C. G. (1951). Fundamental questions of psychotherapy (R. F. C. Hull, Trans.). In H. Read, M. Fordham, G. Adler & W. McGuire (Eds.), *The Collected Works of*

C. G. Jung: The Practise of Psychotherapy (Vol. 16, 2nd ed., pp. 111–125). East Sussex, UK: Routledge.

Kearns, A. (2005). *The Seven Deadly Sins: Issues in Clinical Practice and Supervision for Humanistic and Integrative Practitioners.* London, UK: Karnac Books.

Larisey, K. (2012). *The wounded healer: A Jungian perspective* [Online]. Retrieved from www.jungatlanta.com/articles/fall12-wounded-healer.pdf

Leibowitz, L. (1996). Reflections of a childless analyst. In B. Gerson (Ed.), *The Therapist as a Person: Life Crises, Life Choices, Life Experiences and Their Effects on Treatment* (pp. 71–88). London, UK: The Analytic Press.

Levine, M. P., & Smolak, L. (2004). Body image development in adolescence. In T. F. Cash & T. Pruzinsky (Eds.), *Body Image: A Handbook of Theory, Research and Clinical Practice* (pp. 74–82). New York, NY: Guilford Press.

Liebermann, J. (2000). *Body Talk: Looking and Being Looked at in Psychotherapy.* Lanham, MD: Jason Aronson.

Lowell, M. A., & Meader, L. L. (2005). My body, your body: Speaking the unspoken between the thin therapist and the eating-disordered patient. *Clinical Social Work Journal, 33*(3), 241–257.

Maroda, K. (2004). *The Power of Countertransference: Innovations in Analytic Technique* (2nd ed.). Hillsdale, NJ: Atlantic Press.

McKinley, N. M. (2012). Feminist perspectives on body image. In T. F. Cash & L. Smolak (Eds.), *Body Image: A Handbook of Science, Practice and Prevention* (2nd ed., pp. 48–55). New York, NY: Guildford Press.

Murnen, S. K. (2012). Gender and body images. In T. F. Cash & L. Smolak (Eds.), *Body Image: A Handbook of Science, Practice and Prevention* (2nd ed., pp. 173–179). New York, NY: Guildford Press.

Noordenbos, G., & Seubring, A. (2006). Criteria for recovery from eating disorders according to patients and therapists. *Eating Disorders, 14*, 41–54.

O'Brien, M., & Houston, G. (2007). *Integrative Therapy: A Practitioner's Guide.* (2nd ed.). London, UK: Sage.

Orbach, S. (2004). What can we learn from the therapist's body? *Attachment and Human Development, 6*(2), 141–150.

Rance, N. M., Clarke, V., & Moller, N. P. (2014). 'If I see somebody, I'll immediately scope them out': Anorexia nervosa clients' perceptions of their therapists' body. *Eating Disorders, 22*(2), 111–120.

Ruskay-Rabinor, J. (1995). Overcoming body shame: My client, myself. In M. B. Sussman (Ed.), *A Perilous Calling: The Hazards of Psychotherapy Practice* (pp. 89–99). Oxford, UK: John Wiley & Sons.

Sheehy, J. E. (2009). Book review of F. S. Anderson's (Ed.) Bodies in treatment: The unspoken dimension. *Psychoanalytic Psychology, 26*(4), 447–450.

Shure, J., & Weinstock, B. (2009). Shame, compassion and the journey toward health. In M. Maine, W. N. Davis & J. Shure (Eds.), *Effective Clinical Practice in the Treatment of Eating Disorders: The Heart of the Matter* (pp. 163–177). New York, NY: Routledge.

Smith, J. A., Flowers, P., & Larkin, M. (2009). *Interpretative Phenomenological Analysis: Theory, Method and Research.* London, UK: Sage.

Sovak, A. F. (2011). *The experiences of recovered professionals in the eating disorder field* (Doctoral dissertation) [Online]. University of Saint Thomas, St. Paul, MN. Retrieved from http://ir.stthomas.edu/caps_gradpsych_docproj/8

Tiggemann, M. (2004). Media influences on body image development. In T. F. Cash & T. Pruzinsky (Eds.), *Body Image: A Handbook of Theory, Research and Clinical Practice* (pp. 91–98). New York, NY: Guilford Press.

Tiggemann, M. (2012). Sociocultural perspectives on human appearance and body image. In T. F. Cash & L. Smolak (Eds.), *Body Image: A Handbook of Science, Practice and Prevention* (2nd ed., pp. 12–19). New York, NY: Guildford Press.

Verbeek, L. (2016). *Therapists who self-identify as being 'recovered': Experiences working with body image disturbance and eating disorders* (Doctoral dissertation) [Online]. Metanoia Institute and Middlesex University, London, UK. Retrieved from http://eprints.mdx.ac.uk/20831/1/LVerbeekThesis.pdf

Chapter 12

Countertransference and the chance to dream

Paola Valerio

That hour I woke all too suddenly and reluctantly, to the drone of the cat playing the piano – a haunting, eerie sound. I cursed myself for forgetting to close the piano lid. Still, and soon, I accept, sleep is not listening, and another awareness seeps over me; I am flooded by images from that other world; of dreams.

I had been dreaming vividly. *I was in Cyprus, a place of many family holidays. I was surrounded by blue and grey images, the fading morning moon, worn yet despairing faces, young men and children, loud noises banging on the door of our home. There was a boat, an old vessel, bringing many more refugees. The faces of children in particular lingered and I was ashamed to remember that I had not made a decision about opening the door.*

The day of the dream, off the shores of Turkey and Cyprus a refugee boat, like so many, now overcrowded and unfit for purpose, had capsized. This time hundreds of refugees had drowned, mainly men and children. The haunted figures of my dream world now stepped into my morning reality. Was there any connection, had I heard about this tragedy or was this a simple enough coincidence? Either way, the dream exerted a powerful influence upon me. My usual concerns now seemed selfish, shallow, in comparison and the external world was no longer a stranger.

What is the relationship between the dreamer and the dream: the so-called objective world and the interior world of dreams? A therapist's response to a patient's dream or his or her dreaming about the patient? Many of us will be deeply affected by significant dreams.

Freud wrote that dreams are the royal road to the (patient's) unconscious, but this is equally true of the analyst's dreams. Jung became critical of Freud's reductive method of dream analysis, he felt it insufficiently valued the meaning of the unconscious spontaneous production of dream images. Whereas Freud specified that the function of the dream was to act as 'the guardian of sleep', Jung emphasized the purposive and compensatory character of the unconscious and its symbol-making capacity. Jung saw dreams as the royal road to individuation; he distinguished between the personal and archetypal layers of the unconscious in the dream (1934, 1935, 1945). Jung's own dream journal, the Red Book, has now been published (2009). In this book, Jung describes and illustrates, rather beautifully, his own confrontation with the unconscious (along with a measure of humour and irony at times).

In this chapter I focus on countertransference and the dream, primarily from a Jungian perspective. However, this chapter is also about valuing our dreams, and their place, because, in my experience of many years of teaching, I am advised that dream interpretation is not really taught in most trainings, including some of the 'not so classical' Jungian ones. Hence, if analysts don't privilege or encourage dreamwork, that will be the legacy for our patients and clients.

As this chapter includes material written by a trainee and a patient's account of her dreams, the main focus is not an exposition or a critique of theory. For those who prefer a more theoretical journey, I have included suggestions for further reading about dreams and dream interpretation at the end of the chapter.

Introduction to dream material

I was facilitating a dream interpretation workshop for a group of senior and experienced therapists/students when one them brought this dream about her patient, who had come to therapy following his teenage son's suicide.

Trainee's story – the dream

I was preparing the space for my client to arrive. It was a big old Victorian house with big rooms and high ceilings (not my real house). I see my client coming down the sweeping drive in a red sports car/open top, sunny day looking a bit dapper. Meantime, I am panicking as I tidy the hallway, dumping all the coats/shoes in another room. Loads of kids around, family, my parents – getting them all to 'disappear' so I can work. Replace water, clean glasses – I go into the kitchen and my parents are there and I ask my mum to give me a jug of water etc. and she hands me a sherry glass of water which seems ridiculous to me and I am irritated with her. The client arrives and waits on the settee – my sons are in my consulting room watching TV – I am angry with them and ask them to turn it off and go into another room, but the TV won't turn off, I unplug it and cut the cord but it still stays on. I am now running 45 minutes late and the next client has arrived and sits beside the previous client. I race upstairs to see if there is a free room where we can sit. I am tired from all the searching up and down the stairs. All the rooms I look in have someone else in them, one has a huge table prepared for a board room meeting and a butler sorting out the space, pouring water etc. Eventually I find this group in a room and you very quickly work with me on my dream. I am in a foetal position and I am leaning into people for comfort and support. Feels safe, kind and accepting. I race down to check on the clients and they have both left. I wake up from the dream feeling disappointed and sad that they have gone.

Following the dream, the trainee advised us that her client decided that he no longer wished to continue with the therapy. She had two more sessions with him. He thought that the sessions had been helpful, but he felt that was as far as he wanted to go for now at least but that might change. She shared with us how very aware she was of how painful it was to hear his story, because his son had attended her own son's school.

Postdream analysis: Student's associations, recollections

I think the dream felt like me searching within myself for a safe place to really begin to meet him in his grief. We talked about me feeling contained enough to move to a deeper level and I think the dream and the workshop analysis helped me to do that – I wonder if that shift then enabled my client to move deeper but I think that it frightened him and he didn't feel he could cope with the feelings that came up.

In the workshop analysis, we talked about the long, sweeping drive – image – he's well turned out – successful businessman – do I find him attractive – sort of – he's a good-looking man and he's thoughtful and gentle. We thought about the drive as a snake or a penis, the former perhaps more sexual or Freudian, but the snake could also be the ouroboros, a symbol of wholeness in Jungian terms. It felt like the part of him that wanted to move on with his life and not spoil his happiness – 'not let it ruin our lives'. The smart veneer/sports car maintains the façade – the suicide has made his life messy. The TV not turning off – can't block out the noise/images/no control.

In the dream, I remember a feeling of panic and anxiety as I searched for a quiet space (within me). There was a busyness in the house and I remember working hard to find a space of quiet containment, but finding all the rooms to be occupied with people working and my despair at not being able to find somewhere. . . . Meeting my mother, who is anxious and rushing around, but unable to provide me with what I need (sherry glass) and my frustration and disappointment with her. . . . My relief at finding the room and experiencing the warmth and kindness of the group and then being able to go back downstairs. . . . Feeling disappointed that he'd gone.

Paola's recollection

In the workshop, we discussed that there is a message the dreamer is forced to confront through the graphic image of her children in the consulting room – 'she can't turn it off', perhaps reflecting her anxiety and difficulty in thinking about the loss. She feels that she does not have the right nourishment (sherry) to feed him. She is also forced to feel the sadness, to roam the house full of busy but unhelpful characters; the dream forces a bodily experience, not just an intellectual 'knowing', that it is really too much for them as a couple to bear as she also has to confront her own grief and fear.

Student reflections of work with her client after the workshop

Following the dream workshop, in the next session, as usual, we started with him saying that he 'was ok'. Then as he talked about his son he moved into painful and deep feelings of sadness, which he described as very uncomfortable and exposing, but at the same time reassuring, necessary and cathartic. He said that he felt that he was starting to question his own behaviour as a father and feared that he may have been culpable or responsible for his son coming to that decision, and that thought was unbearable. He was beginning to reevaluate and question his 'life' – what he wanted, where he was going, his purpose, relationships, self-worth, etc. We also looked at his anger at having to go through all of this, which quickly moved into sadness – how could he be angry with his son – a frustration, but deep sadness that his son hadn't been able to think of any other way to deal with his problems. We were more able to explore his reluctance to move into feelings of sadness. His priorities were to be there for his family and feeling responsible for looking after their feelings. His desire was to make everything better and try to be the positive influence that could enable everyone to get on with their lives, without living in the shadow of this terrible thing that had happened. I now experienced a deep sadness within me as he talked about not wanting to explore his feelings, for fear of them bubbling over into something unmanageable. Later in the session, I felt his anger as he requested that this be the last session.

Paola's reflections

Following the dream and discussion in the workshop, the trainee seemed more able to use her countertransference to bring the loss into the analytic space, and he enacts this joint loss by leaving her, forcing her to experience a loss also that continues beyond the session.

Group exercise

Jung and Freud had very different views of the unconscious:

For Freud, the unconscious is where we relegate all of our repressed contents. Freud thought we had a sensor that disguised the true meaning of the dream, thus he distinguished between the manifest and latent content of the dream. Many of you will be familiar with Freud's ideas. The manifest content is the distorted substitution, hiding the ego's wishes or desires (latent content). In Freudian analysis, the dreamer is asked to

(continued)

(continued)

free associate to each image in order to get to the latent content which has been repressed.

Can you reinterpret any of the dreams in this chapter using a more Freudian analysis?

Name some similarities and/or differences between Jungian and Freudian approaches in dream interpretation. Are these at all compatible? Discuss.

Dream series (Sofia)

To sleep, perchance to dream – ay, there's the rub.

(Hamlet)

Jung gave special consideration to the initial dream in therapy which he felt often encapsulated a key difficulty or complex that the client was seeking to integrate. He also wrote about the dream series. I have found that the dream series is a common occurrence, by which I mean a theme or particular characters repeat or develop, until there is a resolution of some aspect of the dreamer's unconscious. This development is of course intermingled with work in sessions and hence there is always a relationship with the transference and countertransference constellation.

One of my analysands, Sofia Flores (not her real name but one which she chose), has agreed to share her dream series for this chapter and she has included her recollection of our explorations within sessions but also her own feelings and thoughts between sessions.

Writing about 'cases', let alone with patients, is enormously complicated. I was admittedly very wary about writing this chapter with my patient and quite concerned about professional shaming. In the introduction to this book I have cited Aron's view (in Loewenthal & Samuels, 2017), about co-writing with patients and Kantrowitz (2006), who studied analysts of diverse orientations and demonstrated that relational analysts were more likely to involve their patients in the write up and publication of case reports. Kantrowitz emphasized that there are responsibilities, risks and ramifications that go with professional publication. Of course, the very encounter in which this joint writing project arose was an enactment in itself which also needs to be integrated and understood in terms of the histories of both actors – analyst and patient – both in the unfolding drama of therapy and in my patient's dream series. My feelings and responses to the dreams were discussed in the therapeutic space and she has included what she took from this, which is not entirely my story. The impact of our shared encounter through this chapter will become part of a different story that is not yet known.

Sofia: Initial session

She was in her late 30s, an artist and a photographer. On the day, she arrived for her initial session I was tired but very soon her presence breathed new life into me and the therapeutic space. I was stunned therefore to learn that she had spent her childhood living with the fear of dying, due to an early diagnosis of cancer. I wondered, was there a connection with this history and my countertransference, the space filled so soon with abundant *eros*? She told me she had spent many months in hospital as a girl, accompanied by a watchful mother who slept on the floor, sometimes by her bedside. A special child, she had two older siblings, but later in her dreams (not included here) she met her younger brother who was hiding under her bed, sad and bleeding, and it occurred to her that he had been the abandoned child left with father, whilst her mother performed her vigil with Sofia. She described her mother as a histrionic, narcissistic woman. Her father, whom I felt was invisible and weak, was described by Sofia as a saint. She needed, psychologically, she told me, to leave her mother's house. I wondered, but did not suggest at this point, did she in fact need to leave her father's house? As her story unfolds I consider if her relationships with older men were abusive? At age 14 she had a relationship with Juan, who was 4 years older, and whom she left for an older, married colleague.

Sofia's dream series, which expanded over a 3-month period (told in her own words, all names are fictitious): Initial dream

This dream I have on the second night I spent at my parent's summer house in Florence. The overall feeling is moody and grey and misty. It starts with my older brother and I, standing beside a lake. The lake it's in open nature and it's quiet and grey and the clouds are really low. On the other side of the lake there is a house. More than a house it's a bit like a shack or a hut and we go there. That house I have rented through Airbnb, to spend a few days there with some friends. I just met with my brother Jon to see him beforehand and show him the house. In order to get across the lake until the house, my brother sort of 'flies' like Neo in the Matrix, and then runs across the border of the lake till the house. When we get to the house he looks at me and says, 'Do you know this house?' And I said 'No, I just got it on Airbnb', and he says. 'That is the house where we lived when we were little'. I was only around 4 years old when we moved into this house with the rest of my family. Again, he asks me 'Really, don't you remember?' and I say no, so he tells me that that was where Dad died in an accident while alone with Mum. He implied no one knows what really happened there. After the accident, Ruth, my oldest sister, and he have to wash all of the blood off the walls. The blood belongs to my father and apparently, it was washed off but the walls were never painted. Then he says 'Those years after he came back to the house to properly paint the walls, as the walls asked him for years to be painted'. Then we got inside the house and he points out where the blood would have been in the living room. He gives me a tour of the house. It is dusty, untouched for years. When we get to the main room all of a sudden, the lights go off like electrical cuts a few times. Whenever the lights go off everything becomes black and white, and I see the blood on the walls and a doll sitting on the table. It looks diabolical with fiery eyes, then it becomes the past and it's black and white. Then back to colour, present time: We look to each other and scream and hug. Then again, the lights go off I can see the 'past' again, the doll and the blood, more screaming and hugging, then lights go back to normal.

When this incident happens, I remember everything: all the agony and fear and stuff I experienced as a child – then *I realize* that my present 'witchy' powers and special way of being and what makes me, *me*, comes from that time of my life. *That everything I am and that makes me special comes from there, that's all, it's not supernatural powers I have, but knowledge from childhood experiences* (Sofia's emphasis)*! Then my brother becomes my friend, Fred, but it's still my brother somehow. I tell Fred that house is where I lived when I was little, and that terrible things happened. I ask Peter and Camilla (a friend who had an unhappy childhood) whether they mind leaving the house. I don't want to spend time there. They agree.*

[Initial dream in series ends.]

Sofia's reflections after initial dream

In the first session with Paola, what I got out of it was how my older brother had to deal with my mom's deeds – he and my sister, but my brother more specifically. He had to clean the blood off the walls. He becomes the father; my father was not present.

When Paola asked me about thoughts on blood, I say 'female power' (blood from one's period, blood when we are born, etc.). If blood is female power, then my brother took my mum's away. By sorting out her wrong deeds, he took away her female power and covered up the death, my father's killing.

And who is the doll? What does it represent? Is that me as a child unable to move, stuck in a hospital bed unable to do things, being really hungry but paralyzed as a doll?

What repercussions would all of this have on me?

I am happy because I left the house in the dream, so I am ready to be leaving my parents and their dramas in that house, and I walk away.

Last note: Even though at some points the dream is scary, it is not a nightmare. The general feeling is more like 'Ahhhhhh, I understand now where I came from!'

My mum doesn't represent my external real mum in the dream, but my internalized mum. My real mother needs a man to flourish, as she cannot accept her animus,[1] or, rather, experiences it as negative. My brother is the man who sustained her, her dreams of success and recognition. But in real life, my brother rejected her eventually. My mother projected her needs on him. He was the man she would have liked to marry – not scared of success and very competitive and ambitious. They are a pair – the internal, competitive, envious couple holding me back, mother's animus unfilled turns inwards on her and her husband, becoming angry and bitter as a negative complex, frightening me. They two act as a couple; maybe they represent my animus and my animus in the dream. They are not at peace, but counteract/feed each other through greed, mutual needs/achievements. They are not driven by love. They are not in harmony. I wonder if the paralyzed angry doll (me as a child) decided to look elsewhere to not deal with the pain this couple inflicted on her (myself).

If I think of the six of us, three (father, sister and younger brother) are not ambitious or competitive. The other three (mother, older brother and myself) are. I didn't see that I am ambitious and competitive (or maybe it's better to say I didn't realize and accept it) until after starting therapy and considering this internal animus figure from my dreams.

On the one hand, my 'mother' wanted to succeed through my brother. He did succeed; he became rich and then rejected her. My 'brother' wanted to be an artist, but quit his dream to become materially successful. On the other hand, regarding my brother, I became a successful artist recognized by prestigious institutions and universities. Regarding my mother, I led the life she wishes to have had: freedom, success and independence. I represent for both what they are not, yet do not have and would have liked to be.

So, I see it now: I put all my dreams of succeeding, enjoying my independence and sexual freedom to sleep so I don't hurt them!! I am frozen like the doll, actually up, until recently; I always 'fell in love' with men in order to be approved and recognized by a male figure (as I learned from my mother that that is needed, as well as killing your female power, in order to be validated).

If I look at how this makes me feel, I see how insane the whole thing is. Insane as in no-sane, no-healthy, not-coming-from-love. Maybe that is the inner conflict I always felt: The fight to let go and feel myself free and that 'game' has no room anymore within.

Introduction to Sofia's second dream

The above dream happened the first night I spent at my parents while on summer holidays. Since this dream the way I feel towards 'men' has changed. I don't feel needy anymore, and certainly more independent at all levels.

A few nights ago, I had the following dream, which also evolves inside a house. Although different in context, I wonder whether there is a relationship between them.

Before the dream, I need to contextualize it:

After two weeks of texting and sexting with a man, we decided to spend a weekend together. This experience has been different to others in that this time I decided to stop experiencing myself as a victim or passive (trying to control and stop the male sexual desire, however wanting to go for it), and so I went for what I wanted and we both enjoyed the sexual desire of the other. It was at all times respectful and fun and balanced. The day before he is coming to visit again I learn from a flatmate that no one will be in the house. This made me feel very tense and scared; what if he is a psychopath and I am in danger? I knew instantly this was one of those clever fears, and plausible enough. Then I understood this was part of my sexual trauma from a previous experience 20 years ago, when a male psychologically abused me, not letting me leave a room for more than 10 awful hours, while trying to have intercourse with me. So, I told a few friends, and even though I knew the paranoia grew from an old trauma, I decided to make a safety plan, contacting a friend in case I didn't feel safe.

I went to pick him up, and from the second we met I knew there was nothing to worry about.

That same night, after going for a beer and spending some time engaged in playful safe sex, we went to sleep. I couldn't sleep well . . . I was unsettled inside . . . then I had the following dream.

Sofia's second dream

I am myself in the dream but seem like very innocent and unprotected. Like I have been 'rescued' by an older man who loved me and was taken into a different country so we could be together. I was in love with him; he was very sweet to me until we got into the house. Once in the house (he was like mid 40s or early 50s, dark hair and wore a black leather jacket all the time) he becomes very cold and uncaring, treating me with certain disdain. He tells me what to do: put this here, that there. I am holding a fabric small doll in my hands, in front of my chest. I start realizing there is something wrong. He is not the person I thought he was. I start getting scared. I don't have any other place to go I think . . . we were a bunch of women (girls really) that had been taking into this country to be with the men we loved kind of thing. I realize I have to leave or something bad will happen to me, but how?

So I pretend I am the same innocent girl he thought I was, and play the game until he goes to the toilet. Then I know that's my opportunity. I sneak towards the door to leave. I am very careful closing the door so he doesn't listen.

When I am two levels down, I realize I didn't take my medicine. My heart beats very strongly. I need to go back and get it. I need it! So I go back, open the door very carefully, go inside and take the medicine. I go back to the door and leave on time. I then think 'I don't have the doll' when I leave. I think, I am not a 'young woman' when I leave, but more like myself now. I don't take the doll.

I wake up very altered and nervous.

Sofia's reflections after second dream

I instantly thought that it was a recreation of the abusive experience I had as a young inexperienced woman, in South Africa, which took away part of my female power and self-esteem. But again, as in the previous dream, I leave. I leave a house where there is not love for me. (I leave those negative archetypes behind, having freedom now to revisit them, to 're-do' them from scratch?) In therapy, I explore this animus figure and the doll, which appears again in this dream. Perhaps I think this doll, it's my *persona*,[2] but this time I leave the man behind, I escape.

I wonder whether it means I am a woman now (I regained my female powers) and I am also ready now to leave behind the doll (me), I don't need it.

Authorizing myself to be *really* me and to trust in me, also through the experience with my lover, I freed myself from the trauma of the South African experience. The following day was wonderful (and I slept as a baby for 12 hours in a row). I allowed myself to be loved and celebrated, not for my intellect but for my whole being, without shame or fear. I do not feel dependent on him, and I don't expect anything from him. In fact, I do not wish to have a sentimental relationship with him.

Sofia's third dream: Superhero/fat-cat dream and drawings

I am a male doctor. I work in a lab. I discover by chance something that turns me into a 'superhero'. I only tell my wife, who is a sexy and successful cinema actress. I go to South America or somewhere wild to learn about my superhero powers, how to use it. My alter ego (a famous male comedian), was a fat cat, black and purple/black – a bit like the Cheshire cat. It was a baddy. When I am back from the wild, the cat comes for me. We fight, but hey! I am better than the cat!! He knows I am me and I think my wife told him, since only she knew about my superhero identity. Maybe my wife is jealous for me being a superhero?

The day before the dream I was very happy about all the progress I had had with my artwork. I had broken the meaning of my new artwork. It is deep and it is good art. I was so proud. Then I dreamt this. After this dream, a week of anxiety entered and the critical voice came back, making me feel shit. I was on an online dating rampage, not listening to my instincts in the form of the wise woman. I allowed men to cross lines and I was not respectful with myself.

In the dream, the Wife, my anima – or perhaps my persona – like the doll, betrays my animus, the professor. She is jealous of his success. During the session, my fear to be successful came up again, since that would mean leaving behind my competitive older brother and mother. Separation anxiety seeps in, which is probably a big thing, since I spent so long on my own in hospital as a child!

The successful performing woman betrays the masculine side (I have been working so hard on this side – masculine-success-leadership). The Woman is the inner saboteur in the form of the explosive, sexy woman. She gives way to the Fat Cat. Paola asks what my thoughts/associations/stories about cats are. These are independence, femininity, loneliness, sufficient . . . almost the opposite of the explosive woman. There are many stories about cats, hers and mine. I think now it is my shadow.[3]

I wonder whether Woman and Cat are the same, both sides of my non-balanced femininity . . . man – brown to blue. Blue: communication, calmness, balance/woman = red (angry/sexuality) to green and black (evil, unbalance, unconscious, madness) . . . Doctor: male, intelligent, acting for the good of the world, timid, researcher . . . this is my inner student, superhero: male, powerful, has worked to understand his powers, doer, and good, willing. This is my inner artist, the creator, the Magician in the tarot.

Wife: female, sexy, feminine, imposter, porcelain-doll looking, cruel inside, envious of male success when he becomes a doer, performer (she is an actress), needs social recognition, a pleaser to achieve her own goals, my per-sona, my female side – the fun/flirty/perfect Sofia – who acts and get things done, but not from good, inner peaceful places, but from stress and 'musts', the inner saboteur (she betrays the inner student and brings the Cat out), the one who wants/needs to be successful.

Alter-Ego: cheeky, independent, maleficent, astute, brutal, representation of my envy of people who achieve success maybe (i.e., the comedian)? My shadow, the bridge to somewhere else (i.e., the trickster), my envious side for people who do what I would like to be doing, the Fool in the tarot. So, my inner good student, who wants to liberate the creator or creative force within but is betrayed by my persona, who wants to succeed, but is so afraid of failure that it prefers not to try for real, and is envious of people who are successful. My shadow successfully destroys my creativity. The Wife is totally for me, my mother. My mother is incredibly gifted, but chooses to be on a second plane, and criticizes anyone who tries to succeed, yet believes herself to be part of the monarchy or something like that! The Cat also reminds me of my inner brother who resists seeing me flying high. He used to kick me in the family house, in the corridor when no one saw.

Sofia's drawings and associations on the third dream: In relation to her art/study life, after another session with Paola

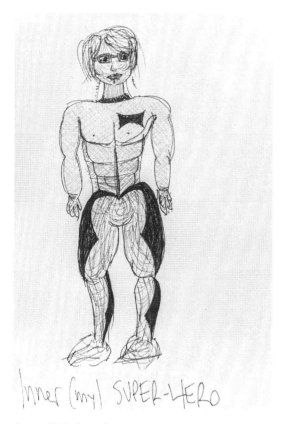

Figure 12.1 Superhero

Sofia's reflections after her session following this third dream

In the first part of the session, Paola suggested, out of the blue, how maybe we had taken for granted superhero being 'positive' and Cat 'negative', perhaps the superhero represented an inflated ego, and therefore the Cat could be a shadow figure asking to be taken into account. She told me about a dream Jung wrote about. I thought it was worth considering, but didn't see her point or think a superhero would be 'negative'. I went on talking about stuff, my mum, and somehow my mind wandered to thinking about Juan (first boyfriend: driven, leader, sexy, strong, confident, successful, etc.). I kept on talking about him, commenting how much my mum liked him, that maybe

Figure 12.2 Wife/actress

she had had a crush on him. How he could contain her, something that my father rarely does.

From there I thought about my 40th birthday party. I started talking about Juan again, who had also been there with his new younger girlfriend, with whom he seems to be really in love, like a teenager. It was the actual day of his birthday, yet he came to my party with his new girlfriend and his two young daughters (3 and 5 years old, maybe). However, I had totally obliterated that memory (the two girls) and didn't mention that to Paola. I just said he came with his new girlfriend. All of a sudden I drifted off and I started talking about my brother being pregnant (note: not my brother and girlfriend, but my brother alone). From then on, I started talking about different subjects, about this and that, random things and then I realized I was totally disengaged and Paola was too. I ask her what had happened? Paola said, 'I drifted away a while ago' and I said 'me too', so we started going backwards to the point where we had both lost contact with each other.

ALTER-EGO

Figure 12.3 Big Fat Cat

I had really lost the plot and then it occurred to me that it was just at the point of talking about my brother being pregnant. I had been talking about Juan when he came to my 40th birthday, and for some reason I then thought about my superhero dream and the Cat in the dream, or the idea that Paola introduced at the beginning of the session, that maybe I could look at the superhero as an inflated side of my ego, and I'm talking about this young girlfriend being very similar to me and he being really in love with her to the point where he could get divorced, and maybe of him losing the girls and all his money, and all of a sudden I realized that he came to my birthday party with his two daughters and yet that I had obliterated them from my memory completely!

I had not looked at the feelings of envy that I had of seeing him with the girls, especially in acknowledging one of them being physically so very similar to me! She was around me all the time, kissing and hugging me. Everyone commented on how similar to me she was. I remember Juan saying that she had a personality very similar to mine. I wonder whether because of that I thought of all the good stuff she was getting that I did not get as a child from my parents. I had wished my parents had divorced when I was young!

I had drifted away when I was talking about my mum fancying Juan and him being a superhero and I just went to talking about something else. I keep on saying I don't mind not being a mother, but maybe I do mind?

Sofia's introduction to the fourth dream

After exploring the dream with Paola and looking into the possibility of the superhero being an inflated ego and thinking I need to look at my dealings with negative emotions, I was thinking of me as Mother Theresa of Calcutta! I have the following dream after this session.

Sofia's dream

> I am in a prairie where all is beautiful and golden, with my friend Eddy. We are both lying down; in between us there are three kittens. They are ginger and white, each resting its head on the next cat's back, forming a circle. The kittens are mine. I caress them. Even though they are mine, I keep on saying I will care for them but don't want to put them down by making them 'mine'. I start cutting my hair, following Jesus' instructions. When I am done, I look at the hair in my hand and it's the same as the kitten's hair. Rose, a classmate in real life whom I find difficult, jealous, insecure, mean and masculine, keeps on telling me I have to name the kittens, having a frenzy about it. I keep calm, not really listening to her. When she is done, I tell her, thanks but they'll be called Thing A, Thing B and Thing C. All in all, everything is golden and calm. Godlike.

Figure 12.4 Cat in hand

——I wake up thinking that Big Fat Cat has become a kitten. The dark beast I kept in the darkroom is out now in the air: in golden air (my negative emotions). I want to take care of them but don't want them as close to me as to name them and make them mine – maybe I am still scared of them (negative emotions, and how to express them). Yet I have become more accepting of them, the Cat it has been tamed, playful and less frightening in this dream.

My anima and animus are gender-crossed. Rose is a rather masculine woman. Eddy is a gay man. Not too sure what to make of that. Neither am I clear about the meaning of Eddy. Guiding me to cut my hair means . . . or that of my hair being the same than the kittens' hair . . . ? I think about inflation again with Paola in the session and the saviour.

Sofia's reflections following fourth dream

This past week I have been feeling sad, all over the place. I have been revisiting moments of my life, which were difficult, and I suffered a lot. I realize I have not had an easy life. I had to do everything on my own, with my own ways. I am very happy to be where I am now, and I am very proud of myself now that I see what I have been able to create for myself. However, seeing the path, I walked with bare eyes. But it hurts.

Last session we talked about my feelings of envy and jealousy. How I always want to be the One – how my older brother and I fought for mum's attention. My way was getting sick.

I said I was Paola's only client, half joking . . . then I SAW it . . . always wanting teachers, tutors, friends' parents . . . anyone in a position of power . . . to love me. I am the One and Only!!!

So, this week I have been integrating the knowledge I am not so special and it has been difficult. At the same time, don't know if it's linked or not, I have let all men go. It's the first time in my life I am not texting/liking/dating/meeting/whatever a guy. And it feels amazing.

Sofia's fifth dream

So, this week I had the following dream about containment. I walk into a room. I am carrying loads of stuff, personal and books/papers. Everything falls over. Somehow people who passed by collected and put things in places around the room. I start looking around the bookshelves, and I finally find my stuff. Bit by bit, I find everything. The feeling is calming; I do everything quite slowly, without stressing. The room has a white light; there are plenty of books, and people come in and out but nicely. I don't feel pressured at any time. I cannot find my handbag, but I know it is there somewhere.

I am expecting a tutor who is coming to help me with my art project; she will help me with video editing. It's the beginning of the academic year. I have recorded something. The video is a blue circle, like the sea. Deep blue: a close up of gentle waves.

I ask my tutor (Paola) to help me editing it so it can be a physical, emotional and psychological container. She looks at me and says: 'You might be on your first year of studying, but you know a lot already!'

I can't find my handbag, but I 'know' that it is in the chair.

Sofia's reflections following fifth dream

On my way home today, after exploring this dream in a session with Paola, I have a realization: The video of the sea equals the image of the three kittens. In the dream, I ask Paola for physical (= kitten A), emotional (= kitten B) and psychological (= kitten C) levels of containment. I feel as if Pandora's Box has opened, and it's time for me to look into the fact that I am not the Only One, the Chosen One. I realize I have endured lots of pain, stress and loneliness and anxiety throughout my 20s and 30s, being single and separated from my family. I have been collecting the broken pieces these days (the kittens, the sea, three as the magical unifying number, like the Musketeers, like God's tiara).

Sofia's sixth dream

This same night I dream of me, looking as I looked today (same clothes, same 'me'), waiting for a lift. It arrives. When doors open, I see myself twice inside. All three of us. Looking exactly the same. I get in. The lift is going down.

It was shocking and surprising. I wake up.

Sofia's reflections following sixth dream

Three cats, three seas, three me . . . all of them derived from the big, fat mean Cat, who was thought to be my inner saboteur first, shadow and then explored as my saviour. I wake up to abstract dreams of the number three, or three objects that repeat themselves endlessly. Paola said something about the holy trinity afterwards, and talked about 'three' or 'third' as a resolution of something of two conflicts/conscious unconscious aspects.

Sofia's seventh dream

I am in a room with my three inner saboteurs. One is small and thin (the scientist from the superhero dream), one is tall, large and fat (the fat mean Cat), and the third one is a smart thin woman (scientist's Wife!).

I turn around (they are like my bodyguards, wearing grey suits and black shades) and tell them, in a kind of matter-of-fact tone, that as much as I love them, I have to turn them in to the police. They understand, and agree. However, the large one says that they will protect me until the police come. We say goodbye and they leave.

Sofia's final eighth dream of this series

The dream is like an old voice whispering in my ear. It says:
   'Old knowledge is good knowledge. You know everything you need. Un-dust
what you already know because you know more that you think. Trust the past.
Bring it on. Integrate everything you have ever learnt'.

Sofia's reflections after final dream

Group exercises

A full interpretation of this dream would have required us to look at all her associations to each image/character in the dream. We would also always consider the dream in terms of the story and plot or resolution in the dream. A common technique is to use amplification; amplifying questions might include. 'What do you think the dream wants to tell you?' 'How do you see the dream now?' and 'How do you feel about the dream?' To further amplify the dream, many analysts would use a fairy tale or anecdote that parallels or explains something related to the dream. Amplification does not involve interpretation as in Freud's model but rather helps to reframe the dream.

From our training, we are very conditioned to look at the dream ego or the 'I' in a dream, but when you do dream interpretations, instead, try asking your client: What is each of the other characters in the dream feeling and trying to communicate with them?

Many of you would agree that, at first glance, the dream above involves transference as the analyst appears in the dream. How might you further think of this relationship to the analyst that could have been missed in our work together?

In my last session before breaking for Christmas, somehow the Big, Fat Cat came around as my relationship with Juan came around too. We were look-ing in therapy at how I might be still upset with my father for allowing that relationship at the time . . . but the Big, Fat Cat took me to someone I never looked at before: Juan's father (my father-in-law). All of the sudden I knew it was him I was angry at. He resembles the Big, Fat Cat quite a lot. He had become my surrogate father for over 7 years. He was a strict, narrow minded, full-of-anger man. He was Juan's God. He, as my parents did, allowed, vali-dated and sustained a 7-years-long sexual relationship while I was still an all too young girl. The session ended with the knowledge that I had to look back into that relationship again. I could trust I was ready to look into the past because of this last dream.

A new chapter has opened for me to explore in my sessions with Paola. Thanks to openly exploring the series of dreams, incorporating at times whatever was occurring in the room, I got to trust both myself and the therapy room as a safe environment. I am ready now to look into all those years of early sexuality when I would sexualize my creative needs, or my real need for connections, and not set personal boundaries in the road to self-acceptance and healing.

Small-Group Exercise

Perhaps try this using your client's dreams (if you have their consent of course)

Think about the dream as theatre – a story or play- and the dreamer is the writer, each character and image in the dream being carefully selected by the dreamer.

What is the story or plot of the dream and what is the resolution or solution?

Don't assume real people: mothers, fathers, husbands (e.g., external figures you always relate to). Sometimes they will do, but also think about these as the subcharacters of the dreamer's own personality.

A useful technique is to avoid always asking the dreamer what she or he, as she or he appears in the dream, is thinking as in the previous exercise. Ask instead about subcharacters, and try to amplify figures and tease out their relationship to the dreamer. This can often reveal more unconscious layers or shadow material than sticking with the dream ego.

Treat the initial dream or dream series with particular care. Jung felt it often revealed a key aspect of the work to be done.

Final thoughts

Sofia's analysis of the dream series is her story and her memories of what we shared; hopefully she has explored and analysed the dream in her own terms without me applying too many theoretical constructs here. Inevitably, there are many other interpretations, and I hope I have resisted my desire to allow

Sofia to present a clever, 'technically' correct version. It was meaningful work for Sofia, and seemed to open up a dialogue with her unconscious and inner figures. I think a turning point was when we both dissociated, as mentioned above, as described by Sofia as 'losing each other'. The evolving relationship with the analyst seemed to assist the dream work, at least in that present moment, of losing, but perhaps more importantly, finding each other again.

Of course, it always a gift for an analyst to have such a creative, motivated patient in therapy, and my countertransference was to bathe in this rich plasma. One day Sofia suddenly asked me if I would be her research supervisor for a project she was undertaking, explaining she had little faith in her current supervisor, a woman who is in fact a well-known academic. Immediately I realized I was also the Fat Cat and/or the inflated superhero analyst. I had wanted to stay in the positive countertransference and avoid her disappointment and anger with me, and therein let her project it elsewhere – her mother, her supervisor. In my countertransference response, there was now an opening for me to deal with her disappointment and anger with me, for making her special and yet not so special. Or indeed was it me who needed to be special, to be, in fact, her saviour, like her mother?

Perhaps having arrived at this place now, we might allow the dream world to breathe fully within the consulting room. Yet in this 'coconstructed' world, a place of neither objective nor subjective certainty, I wonder, indeed worry a little, that despite her enthusiasm for this project, Sofia might one day feel differently about sharing her dreams. We have begun to explore this in therapy and also following Sofia's review of this chapter. Now there's the rub.

Notes

1 In analytical psychology, this archetype finds expression as a feminine inner personality: anima; or as a masculine inner personality: animus. Often in dream interpretation a female figure would be seen as the persona if the dreamer was also a woman.
2 The *persona* is seen as the public face, which we all have and which is an important part of being in the world and adopting different roles, but can become negative if we over-identify with our persona and are not fluid in accepting our various sub-personalities.
3 The shadow, in simple terms, is often paired with the persona; it is usually projected onto others, and importantly it can include positive and negative aspects that are deeply unconscious or unacceptable to the dreamer; it has personal aspects and collective aspects. The 'trickster' is a significant archetypal shadow figure.

Bibliography

Kantrowitz, J. L. (2006). *Writing About Patients*. New York, NY: The Other Press.
Loewenthal, D., & Samuels. A. (Eds.) (2017). *Relational Psychotherapy*. London, UK: Routledge.

Recommended reading

Freud, S. (1900). The interpretation of dreams. *S.E.* IV & V.

Jung, C. G. (1963). *Memories, Dreams, Reflections* (Ed. A. Jaffe). London, UK: Collins and Routledge & Kegan Paul.

Jung, C. G. (1990). *The Red Book: Liber Novus (1915–1930)* (Ed. S. Shamdasani). New York, NY: W. W. Norton.

Jung, C. G. from *The Collected Works:*

——Vol. 4: The analysis of dreams (1909)

——Vol. 8: General aspects of dream psychology (1916/1948)

——On the nature of dreams (1945/1948)

——Vol. 12: Individual dream symbolism in relation to alchemy (1936)

——Vol. 16: The practical use of dream-analysis (1934)

——Vol. 18: Symbols and the interpretation of dreams (1961)

Further reading

Campbell, J. (1968). *The Hero with a Thousand Faces* (Bollingen Series, 2nd ed.). Princeton, NJ: Princeton University Press.

Hall, C. (1966). *The Meaning of Dreams*. New York, NY: McGraw-Hill.

Jung, C. G. (1931). The aims of psychotherapy. In *Collected Works, 16*.

——(1935). The relations between the ego and the unconscious. In *Collected Works, 7*.

Lessing, D. (1971). *Briefing for a Descent into Hell*. London, UK: Cape.

The so-called 'countertransference' and the mystery of the therapeutic encounter

Anastasios Gaitanidis

'Countertransference': how raw and unsophisticated is our psychoanalytic vocabulary. We use this quasiscientific term to order and explain a variety of unconscious processes which lack any consistency or linearity. We employ the prefix 'counter' to signify a reaction to our patient's transference as if we are always capable of identifying our unconscious reactions or we could invent and follow a logical time sequence during which the patient's transference precedes and produces a countertransference in us which we could then gradually modify and give back to the patient through the medium of interpretation. This is all too 'orderly'. There is nothing here about the messiness of the interaction, the moment-to-moment stops and starts, the contemporaneous meeting and losing the other, the unpredictable twists and turns, ups and downs, unexpected curveballs. We need the term *countertransference* to create a false sense of security, to protect us against the inescapable uncertainty of the process. It has the same function as that of a safety bar on a rollercoaster ride: it makes us feel secure but deep down we know that if something goes wrong, no safety device can save us (see Stanton, in preparation).

I learned very quickly that in order to 'make sense' of the unpredictable experiential flow of the therapeutic encounter, I needed to 'bracket' these conceptual safety measures and realise that the tools of my trade are most of the times useless when I am confronted with my patient's experience. How is it possible to use my 'self' as a tool to understand how my patient feels or relates to others when my self is deeply influenced and constituted by the way I relate to my patient? How is it possible to interpret my patient's 'internal' world by looking at his/her impact on my own when both psychic realms are actually externally shaped by this unique encounter and our additional encounters with significant and not-so-significant others? It is tempting to think of myself as someone who could stand back and create a space for reflection and contemplation uninterrupted by the noise of interpersonal interaction, who could maintain the necessary distance from the torrent of emotional emanations so as to be able to utter the ultimate truth about my patient's problems. It is more difficult to accept that often I have only a rough idea of what is going on for me and/or my patient, that the space I am trying to protect and preserve is already colonised by a mixture of my desire to maintain my contemplative stance and my patient's desire to get the answers s/he needs from me, that most of my thoughts, feelings and processes are not immediately (or never) accessible to me.

For this reason, I found some recent relational psychoanalytic perspectives (Mitchell, 1997; Aron, 2002) very useful since they describe countertransference as one of the tools of the psychoanalytic trade which desperately tries to carve out and delimit a complex matrix of unconscious interactions that take place in the space between the therapist and the patient, the space of the 'third'. This is a space that the two participants cannot singularly own, although they are both responsible for its creation. To believe that one of the participants has privileged access to it through the exploration of his or her countertransference is to assert a level of authority and expertise that is artificial and counterproductive. In other words, for the relationals, there is no 'counter' in the therapeutic 'encounter': both participants are equally involved and contributing to it and no one can stand out (or up) and have a view of it from a distance or above.

However, I have come to believe that even this relational postulation of the 'third' is another conceptual tool which attempts to order an experiential process which is ultimately anarchic, wild and inaccessible. The relationals assume that, for therapy to work, the therapist and the patient will have to engage in this 'third', quasi-improvisational 'yes, and . . .' creative play with the occasional impasses, negativities and 'yes, buts . . .' that need to be overcome in order for the play to continue. This overcoming will involve the necessary enactment of relational patterns which need to be repeated so as for the participants to coproduce a different experiential outcome through the very act of repetition. This 'spirally' movement forward (one could imagine it resembling a fractal progression) is a great way of conceptualising therapeutic action and change. Yet, it does not take into account what cannot be contained within the relationship: the ineffable, mysterious quality of the other (both internal and external) whose thoughts and feelings will always be partly enigmatic and who, for this reason, cannot be intersubjectively met (see Laplanche, 1999).

This can be best represented by what a friend of mine, an experienced analyst, once called 'under the counter'-transference (Chris Hauke, personal communication); that is to say, all the feelings and thoughts that would necessarily be hidden from view as they seem to be part of a psychic area that is intimately private and thus incommunicable (Winnicott, 1963), an area which is characterised by a level of obscurity and mystery that needs to be recognised and respected for what it is without trying to make it explicit through the use of conceptual categories. This private, mysterious area is a source of both mischief and creativity and should not be interfered with or exposed/communicated to others; that is to say, it should be kept in the dark. In this respect, there is destructive darkness that needs to be dispelled and illuminated, and there is darkness which contains the most intimate secrets of the soul that needs to be protected and cherished as a potential source of aliveness (Cohen, 2014). In other words, there is a level of obscurity that is enlightening and a level of enlightenment that is obscuring. It is this interplay between obscurity and enlightenment, darkness and light that will be simultaneously revealed and concealed in the following presentation of case material coproduced and co-written by me and my patient:

> *I went into Anastasios' room, told him that I felt about as bad as a person could feel, was suicidal and had no idea why. I had a happy childhood and felt that the depth of my despair must be related to my relationship with my partner but that didn't really ring true. Training to be a psychologist at the Tavistock clinic as a young woman could have offered me some clues that perhaps all was not what it seemed, but it wasn't until my mum became ill, and I was middle aged, that anxiety and its bedfellow depression, struck me like an animal attack from which there was no respite. So extreme that life became an impossible burden, despite being a loving mother to teenage girls.*
>
> *Apart from weekly sessions (which to begin with seemed like a drop in the ocean) and agreed payment, my therapy with Anastasios had no agreed targets or goals, just initially an expectation that I would turn up at the sessions or speak on the phone when I was at my most labile. I liked that; I didn't want to second-guess the toolkit being used, so quickly lacking authenticity in my eyes.*

She was 48. It was autumn 2008. She experienced a crisis, a breakdown. Every aspect of her life was infused with anxiety, nothing made sense anymore. She struggled to make it through the day. She left her home, her partner and two daughters and moved to a scruffy little apartment in the middle of the city. There was no care there, there was no care anywhere. She was the centre of her caring universe and this centre could not hold anymore. Her partner didn't know how to deal with her collapse and her daughters felt abandoned.

She entered the room, sat on the sofa and said, 'I'm looking for a mother. Could you mother me, please?' Bewildering, I thought: She was asking a man she just met to 'mother' her – albeit a therapist. What was going on? A year earlier, her mother started 'losing' her mind – dementia, the silent killer of old people, slowing stripping off her memory, identity and life. This is it then: She was gradually losing her mother and was seeking to replace her. But she had chosen a man as a replacement. This was not going to be easy – but then again nothing that really matters is. Perhaps it was impossible for her to even think to replace her mother with another loving woman. A man who cared (a rare, almost nonexistent, presence in her life) could provide her a more consoling, guilt-free substitute.

Yet, all these speculations seemed to be irrelevant when confronted with the void created by the absence of any satisfactory explanation for the origins and onset of her immense anxiety. She was drowning in an ocean of inexplicable innervations, constantly misfiring and keeping her sleepless and depressed. 'I don't know why this is happening to me. I was never anxious or worried. . . . I was always very cheerful and happy'. Desperate to find anything that made sense, she would walk down various alleys of meaning but only to find a dead end: 'it must be my partner' or 'it must be my job'. She was lost. . . . I was lost with her: I could sense the trauma and the damage done, I could almost touch the pain that tore her apart, but I didn't know what to do, how to help her. But as my supervisor once told me, 'When you feel lost, don't panic! You just need more time. Trust the process!'

> *Anxiety and depression were the symptoms but it soon became apparent that some-how I had undergone a dissolution of the sense of who I was, in Elena Ferrante, the Italian novelist's words, 'smarginatura', a dissolving of the margins. Anastasios asked if I could bring something that was important or represented me in any way. I couldn't, I had no sense of my being, essence or separate self that could be referred to. I had lived and thrived as a competent and mainly happy person to that point, but it seemed that I had been built on sand.*

I hadn't seen anyone in such a state of distress. . . . It was so thickly present in the room, you could cut it with a knife. One day I heard her scream. It was a silent, muffled one. I wanted her to hear it too and express it. She couldn't. I asked her to paint it. What came out resembled Malevich's *Black Square* but without the white frame surrounding it, indicating the presence of an infinite and eternal light. In this square, there were no traces of light, apart from a gap on the upper left-hand corner, a little crack which perhaps one day could allow a ray of hope to get in. The following week she didn't come and didn't call to cancel. I was worried. This was not at all like her. In spite of her utter devastation, she kept her appointments and was always on time. I was very worried. . . . I texted . . . she didn't reply. Another week, another appointment missed – no signs of life. 'Oh darling no, what have you done?' I was about to call her home number with the hope that someone would reply and let me know what transpired. My phone rang, and it was her: 'Anastasios, I had an accident . . . with the car . . . on the motorway.' I wanted to believe it was just an accident. But I knew this wasn't the case. How could I ignore the black square?

'Oh no! What happened? Are you OK?'

'I am OK. Don't worry Anastasios! It was a serious accident but I'm really OK. I won't be able to come to our sessions for a while.'

A huge sigh of relief was quickly succeeded by jolts of internal, silent protest: 'How could you drop your life like this?' 'Why did you not allow me to hold it for you?' And then despair and self-blame followed: 'Have I dropped you too?' 'Was I not enough to sustain you?' 'Have I failed you? Have I?'

But this was not the time to wallow in self-pity. I had to put an end to this litany of self-accusations. This shouldn't be about me. She had to be my priority.

'OK, we need a plan then. You are staying with your sister and you can't drive for the time being. Can you take the train?'

'I am not sure. I feel very frail at the moment. It is better if I don't use any public transport too.'

'OK, I do understand. Will you be able to have telephone sessions every week?'

'Yes, this sounds better! I can do this!'

We carried on with the telephone sessions for a couple of very difficult months as the prospect of a more hopeful future was quickly receding from view and only the dark cloud of hospitalisation seemed to overshadow our exchanges. Yet, when the psychiatrist reassured her this was not going to be the case, our conversations became less gloomy. Her medication also started to work, and I felt a sudden impulse to invite her back to the consulting room.

'It is OK to carry on with the telephone sessions, but I missed you! I missed seeing your face! Do you want to come back now that you are feeling a bit better?'

'Oh Anastasios. I missed you too! I think I can come back next week.'

Some of my more traditional colleagues might criticise me for continuing her therapy via telephone or for being so forthcoming with my desire to see her again. Some might accuse me of being seductive. I don't know. I find my response ordinarily humane. This is the response I would expect from any decent human being when confronted with the intense pain of another. I wasn't going to abandon her at the time of her need. I wasn't going to drop her or leave her only to rely on the care of her psychiatrist (although her help was indispensable). She needed to know that I cared and I was there for her. Having telephone sessions during this difficult, fragile period and saying 'I missed you' made all the difference in the world.

> *Where my heart should be was an empty space. It was ultimately reformed and mended by a process of being truly recognised and appreciated. The therapeutic relationship developed within a frame where Anastasios was able to focus on my needs putting his own into the background. I began to trust that he truly had my best interests at heart; I was not alone. A process began of being able to keep his caring presence in mind (particularly when falling asleep) in symmetry with how he was keeping me in mind during the sessions. This enfolding allowed a growth from the touching of my heart to my also frozen mind, connecting the two, beginning a true and real communication. Once the conversation began to flow, recalling memories and feelings attached to infancy, which had been deeply encased, never wanting to feel again, too, too scary.*

In this new phase of therapy, hope began to creep in. First, she was able to secure early medical retirement which eased her anxiety regarding work and source of income creating thus a sense of material security. Second, our renewed trust in the relationship allowed us to revisit the past more vigorously.

She started bringing memories of her mother having asthma attacks and faint-ing. She recalled feeling scared and helpless – I could imagine her as a little girl witnessing her mother rendered repeatedly unconscious and not knowing what to do to bring her back to her senses (or even back to life as these attacks were quite severe). This was an utterly terrifying experience. We could now find a thread that could connect her present levels of anxiety to these traumatic inci-dents. We also thought it was possible that when she was a baby her mother 'dropped' her – without any warning – during one of these attacks. This is how she almost 'accidentally' dropped her life, and this is why I couldn't allow myself to drop her.

Things started to make sense but this was initially covered by the thin veneer of her 'happy childhood' and the very real love she received from her mother throughout her adolescent and adult life. Her mother was always around to help and support her when she became a mother herself, but not anymore! She was losing her again as she progressively began to 'faint' with no possibility of recovery, or 'coming back to her senses'. And, once again, there was nothing she could do to stop her fainting/fading away.

> *Now in middle age, with the illness and impending loss of my mom, my feelings burst through, but the developing conduit between my heart and unconscious ele-ment of my mind meant that there was an emerging context and story. Memories which have been incomplete and resonant of my family's umwelt could be vocalised and shared, but perhaps as importantly witnessed and believed by Anastasios. No doubt or cynicism, just acceptance and encouragement to further explore. Moving through dark tunnels, impossible to do on my own, much too painful, Anastasios helped me knit together the understanding, the meaning that was percolating up. The memories of my younger me, 6 or 7, how to survive, suffused, I was helped to realise, with guilt and shame, the anger not expressed, better to be a good girl, perhaps there was no other option.*

As the dissociative wall that had been built to protect her from the trau-matic past was gradually demolished, both internal and external instances of violence were examined with a healthy sense of curiosity. I found myself helping her to remove the intense guilt she felt for her mother's medical condition. This was intensified by the emotional absence of her father, the decision of her mother to look after a little boy while she was experienc-ing her asthma attacks ('dropping' my patient again in order to care for a younger child) and the implicit blame her siblings – who were much older than her and perhaps felt displaced by her presence in their mother's life – attributed to her for the mother's illness. She was desperately alone facing an impossible situation and being blamed for something that was not her fault. Perfect recipe for a future disaster! No wonder she found herself taking sole responsibility for everything problematic that was happening in her life.

Anastasios gently questioned my younger self. Was it fair? Was it necessary? Did I deserve it? Wasn't I entitled to have fun and play?

He gave me permission (I needed it) to represent myself, weighing against my default (survival) position of making it better for everyone else. Recognising the injustice, there was an upwelling of anger, now able to be given voice, a novel experience, powerful and ultimately uplifting.

During these times, I found myself standing in the spaces between her disconnected self states so as to build bridges across them (Bromberg, 1996). Recognising the injustice was the first step. Connecting her with her anger about this injustice was the second. But, most importantly, the crucial achievement was questioning her identification with her mother and her mother's legacy. One day she took her mother's wedding ring off her middle finger and gave it to me:

> Could you please hold this for me, Anastasios? It is my mother's wedding ring. It's a gift but it feels too heavy and I can't bear wearing it at the moment. I need someone to hold it for me until I am ready to claim it back again. You are the only person I trust to keep it safe.

I felt honoured by her request but also immensely responsible. Like Frodo in the *Lord of the Rings*, I was trusted to hold this ring of power which nobody else could or even wanted to carry. But unlike Frodo, I wasn't supposed to dispose of it in the hot lava of Mordor; I was meant to keep it safe until the day its rightful owner would feel able to carry it again. I could sense the heaviness of the task, the anxiety it produced. I could understand why she wouldn't stand being permanently wedded to the legacy of this ring. I could see why she couldn't tolerate identifying completely with the past, present and future life of her mother, in spite of the latter's capacity and vivid demonstration of loving care towards her. She needed a respite, a necessary brief distance from this legacy without completely cutting off from it. I soon realised that I was actually performing the role of Sam to her ailing Frodo.

The earlier easy assertion of a happy childhood was not accurate and I found myself both shocked and relieved at having developed an understanding that made sense to me and very importantly believed and validated by Anastasios, just him, as there was no one else in my family who was able to acknowledge or empathise with my position. They had a different story. The power of being helped compassionately to explore my history in this way (including the psychological sequelae of my father's family being dispossessed and persecuted migrants from Ireland and Russia in the mid 1800s) has allowed me to form a robust and cared for sense of self, moving towards a future life that is engendered with promise. As Andrew Solomon says in his wonderful book Far from the Tree: *'Understanding backwards liberated me to live forwards'.*

The ring was safely held and eventually returned. She was ready to receive it. This time though both its material essence and power were transubstantiated. It was melted and mixed with another ring – a gift from her partner's mother – which finally produced three new rings. She kept one for herself and the remaining two she gave to her daughters. The mother had passed away, her absence mourned, her love retained and passed on. The anger was still there but as part of a wider understanding that she didn't need to be either a 'good girl' for the remainder of her life or to make it better for everyone else. She returned home and reunited with her partner and daughters, but she could say 'no' to them when this didn't serve her well. I was very proud of her and I told her so. This was a long, dreary and heavy journey which was made heavier by the fact we had to carry not only her own baggage but also that of her ancestors – histories of forced migration, violence and persecution. I was aware how this corresponded to my own history as an immigrant and son of refugees and acknowledged it to her.

Her therapy continues. She needed to relive the source of her trauma in order to experience a new beginning. Her whole life had to be 'rebooted' so as to start from scratch. I had experienced her gradual transformation from a traumatised toddler to a lonely young girl and angry adolescent. She now sees herself as a woman in her 20s, full of enthusiasm and erotic strivings – some of which are unavoidably transferred onto me. I do not feel the need to imme-diately interpret them away – although she would ultimately (and hopefully) feel the need to transfer them onto someone else or combine them with the feelings she currently has for her partner. I realise they are part of the overall process. In many ways, they represent her gratitude: She wants to take care of me as I took care of her. In her own way, she is also unconsciously helping me regain a sense of optimism and strength after I recently experienced a severe loss in my life. I do not encourage her, but I do not reject her either. To do so will be to deny not only her erotic strivings but also her therapeutic strivings towards me (Searles, 1999) – and I don't want to reject her need to contribute to my wellbeing.

> *Extracting the essence underlying the therapeutic process with Anastasios I turn to another author. In his conclusion to* Being a Beast *Charles Foster says, 'I can't really love X unless X loves me. Now there's a thought!' X in my mind could be a person, animal, life in general? For therapy to be as profoundly successful as it has been for me it behoves the therapist to initially be the person in the relationship who is able to provide love. With this care and attention can come a deep and continuing connection to life and all it has to offer.*

Both my patient and I have attempted to provide a combined summary of what transpired in this therapeutic encounter. We have both checked and agreed the content of this summary. In this respect, I hope that my posi-tion was not 'counter' to that of my patient's, as I wasn't intentionally trying to speak from a position of elevated authority or to articulate anything that wasn't part of our relationship or co-created during its unfolding.

However, I am also aware that this could only be a partial account of this encounter, as any attempt to provide an exhaustive account of it would necessarily falter. Although some aspects of our relationship were brought to light, some others will always remain in the dark. It is crucial to acknowledge that although we tried our best to communicate to each other, and to our audience, the unexpected and uncertain nature of this process, there would be mysterious elements in our encounter that could not be captured and would thus always remain ineffable. It is this mystery that could not be contained in any description of the therapeutic process or any analysis of the patient's or therapist's transferences that fundamentally motivates us to carry on exploring the lives of others as they intimately intermingle and intertwine with ours. And it is in the acknowledgement of our limited capacity to illuminate, explain and coherently narrate our experience of the therapeutic encounter (although this should not – and does not – arrest our desire to narrate it) and our acceptance of its irreducibly obscure and mysterious nature that allows us to surrender our control to the therapeutic process and trust that, by doing this, we'll see each other through.

Bibliography

Aron, L. (2002). *Meeting of Minds: Mutuality in Psychoanalysis* (Relational Perspectives Book Series, Vol. 4). New York, NY: Routledge.

Bromberg, P. M. (1996). Standing in the spaces: The multiplicity of self and the psychoanalytic relationship. *Contemporary Psychoanalysis, 32*, 509–535.

Cohen, J. (2014). *The Private Life: Why We Remain in the Dark*. London, UK: Granta Books.

Laplanche, J. (1999). *Essays on Otherness* (J. Fletcher, Ed., Luke Thurston, Trans.). London, UK: Routledge.

Mitchell, S. (1997). *Influence and Autonomy in Psychoanalysis*. Hillsdale, NJ: The Analytic Press.

Searles, H. F. (1999). *Countertransference and Related Subjects: Selected Papers*. Madison, CT: International Universities Press.

Stanton, M. (In preparation). *Making Sense*. London, UK: Penguin.

Winnicott, D. W. (1963). Communicating and not-communicating leading to a study of certain opposites. In L. Caldwell & H. T. Robinson (Eds.), *The Collected Works of D. W. Winnicott, Vol. 6, 1960–1963*. Oxford, UK: Oxford University Press.

Index

Printed in Great Britain
by Amazon